Agile Software Development with C# and Visual Studio 2026 Fifth Edition

Lynn Smith

ISBN: 979-8-2956-3466-6

ABOUT THE BOOK

This beginner-friendly book introduces the essentials of agile software development using C#. Although many resources cover C# or agile practices separately, few integrate them into a single, cohesive learning path. Each chapter blends both topics so you can understand how agile principles shape real C# development. By the end, you will complete several small projects that apply these ideas in practice. Working with a small group—such as classmates—can further deepen your understanding.

This book is intentionally concise and not meant to serve as a comprehensive reference. It focuses on core concepts suitable for newcomers rather than providing exhaustive detail. To get the most from the material, you are expected to type all code examples yourself; the hands-on experience is essential for building real skill.

Exercises labeled "Programming Challenge" and "Test Your Understanding" appear throughout the chapters, and completing them will greatly reinforce your learning. This fifth edition uses Visual Studio 2026 Community.

Last but not least, we thank Dr. Youlong Zhuang for reviewing this edition and providing valuable suggestions.

CONTENTS

DISCLAIMER

NOTICE OF LIABILITY

Chapter 1: Introduction to C# and Agile

Chapter Learning Outcomes

1.1 Recognize C# as an object-oriented programming language
1.2 Generate a simple program with C# and Visual Studio
1.3 Recall phases in traditional waterfall software development approach
1.4 Recall values in Agile Manifesto
1.5 Recognize the differences between waterfall and agile

1.1 What is C#?

C# is a modern object-oriented programming (OOP) language for developing application software. Applications consist of instructions for the computer, and C# is the language that programmers use to write those instructions. This language is designed to be simple, powerful, and type-safe, making it a popular choice for developing a wide range of applications, including desktop applications, mobile applications, web applications, and games.

C# is often considered easier to learn yet more powerful than other programming languages such as C, C++, or Java. C# code is typically compiled into intermediate language code (IL) that can be executed on any platform with the .NET runtime installed, allowing C# programs to be portable across different operating systems and hardware architectures.

In OOP, applications are developed with reusable classes that can be used to build larger programs. A class is a container with a collection of instructions in it. These instructions can be used in multiple places of a program or even in another program without having to rewrite them. To use the instructions in a class, you create an object of that class. Then all instructions of that class are available with the object.

In the past, learning to code meant memorizing semicolons and obsessing over syntax errors. Today, learning C# in the era of AI means leveraging powerful tools to accelerate your progress while building deeper understanding. You are not just a coder; you are also a Code Reviewer and a Software Architect.

AI tools can generate C# code, suggest completions, refactor patterns, and even help build intelligent features with ML.NET or Azure OpenAI faster than ever. However, they lack intent, full project context, and nuanced judgment. They can produce code that appears flawless but misses requirements, introduces vulnerabilities, or ignores performance best practices.

The Golden Rule of AI Coding: Never accept a line of code from an AI that you cannot explain line-by-line. If you can't explain it, you don't own it.

Before you can start to code in C#, you need to install Visual Studio 2026 Community edition. Search the web for "download visual studio 2026 community edition" and click on the "download" link to download the software. After downloading the file to your local computer, double click to install it.

On the "Visual Studio Installer" window, make sure you check ".NET desktop development" (It is most likely already checked by default.) before clicking on the "install" button.

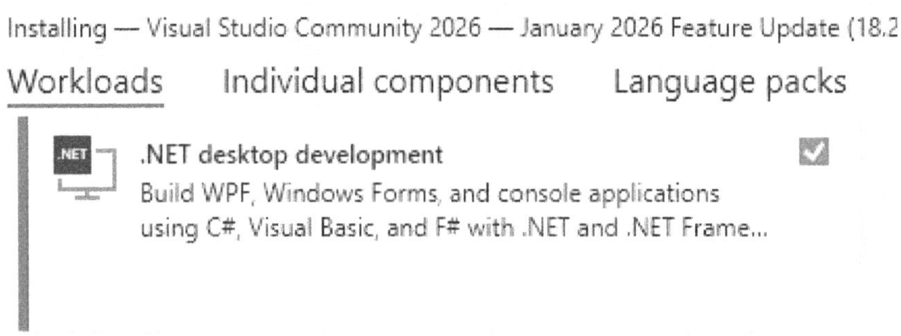

Figure 1.1 .NET desktop development in Installer.

What you have just installed is an Integrated Development Environment (IDE), which includes a text editor to type code into and a debugger to test your code.

After installation is complete, follow the instructions to restart the computer and you are on your way to becoming a C# programmer. Make sure you close all other programs before restarting to avoid losing any unsaved work.

Test Your Understanding 1.1
C# is an OOP ______ that programmers use to write ______ for computers.
A. language, instructions
B. language, manual
C. editor, instructions
D. editor, manual

Test Your Understanding 1.2
An OOP is a way to develop applications such that ________ classes can be used to build larger programs.
A. any
B. useless
C. reusable
D. small

Test Your Understanding 1.3

What is included in Visual Studio IDE?
A. A text editor for typing in code
B. A text editor for typing in code and turning in homework
C. A text editor for typing in code and a debugger to test the code
D. A visually appealing text editor liked by many programmers

Test Your Understanding 1.4
What is C#?
A. A mobile application
B. An object-oriented programming language
C. A type of computer hardware
D. A website development tool

Test Your Understanding 1.5
What are applications in C#?
A. A collection of classes
B. A container for instructions
C. A type of computer hardware
D. A type of operating system

Test Your Understanding 1.6
What makes C# a popular choice for developing applications?
A. It costs less if you want to buy
B. It runs natively on any operating system without additional runtimes
C. It allows direct memory manipulation without restrictions, like C or C++
D. It is simple, powerful, and type-safe

Test Your Understanding 1.7
What is a class in object-oriented programming?
A. A type of operating system
B. A container with a collection of instructions in it
C. A collection of applications
D. A type of computer hardware

1.2 Your First C# Program

On your PC's desktop, create a new folder named 'Agile'. You will save all project files in this folder for organization purposes. Launch Visual Studio. The first time you start Visual Studio, it will prompt if you want to sign in by creating an account. I suggest that you create an account now even though it has the option, "Not now, maybe later". If you don't create an account, it will prompt you again after 30 days without the 'not now' option. Creating an account only requires an email address.

When prompted with 'Sign up for Copilot Free,' click to sign up or sign in. The startup process may take several minutes. Please be patient.

Start a new project by clicking "Create a new project" on the "Get started" page.

In the "Create a new project" window, type "C# console app core" into the "Search for project templates" search box. Select the one similar to the following. Click "Next".

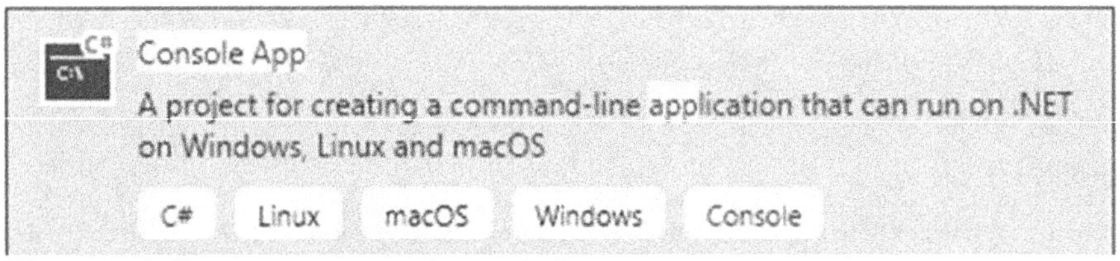

Figure 1.2 Create a new project window.

A new window, "Configure your new project", will pop up. Give a name to the project, e.g. Chapter1Example1. Browse for the location you want to save the project to by clicking on the "…" symbol on the right. Check the "Place solution and project in the same location" box. Click the "Next" button to continue.

On the "Additional Information" window, select the default framework ".NET 10.0 (Long-Term Support)" and click the "Create" button to start a new project.

A default program with default code will be displayed. Delete all lines of code. Add one line of instruction:

```
Console.WriteLine("Welcome to Agile");
```

Finally, click on the little green triangle "Play" button (Chapter1Example1) on the top to run the program. The result is shown below:

```
Welcome to Agile
```

You have just used Visual Studio IDE to write your first application in C# and to run the program. You can now press the enter key to close the program.

1.3 Explanation for Your First Program

There is only one line of code for the computer to follow. The instruction tells the computer to display the text "Welcome to Agile!" on the console screen. It uses a pre-developed class called Console. The Console class has a method called WriteLine() that will display the message on the console. "Welcome to Agile" is a C# string literal and must be inside a pair of quotation marks.

A class in C# is a container that often has many methods in it. A method is a group of instructions for a common objective. The Console class has many methods. In the code window, after typing the class name "Console" and a dot, you can see a popup menu for all available methods and properties.

You created a program with a line of C# by using a premade class (Console) and its method (WriteLine())!

Test Your Understanding 1.8
A class is a container that groups things, such as _____, together.
A. methods
B. namespaces
C. instructions
D. statements

Test Your Understanding 1.9
A(n) _____ is a logical group of C# statements for a common objective.
A. namespace
B. class
C. method
D. instruction

Test Your Understanding 1.10
In the following statement, what is "Console"? Console.WriteLine("Welcome to Agile!");
A. a namespace
B. a class
C. a method
D. a computer monitor

Test Your Understanding 1.11
In the following statement, what is "WriteLine"? Console.WriteLine("Welcome to Agile!");
A. a namespace
B. a class
C. a method
D. a computer monitor command

Programming Challenge 1.1
Chapter1Example1 has one line of instruction. You can add more. Pay attention to the sequence of the instructions and how they affect the result. With Chapter1Example1 open, ask GitHub Copilot to generate more code. Specifically, in Visual Studio, locate the "GitHub Copilot Chat" panel on the right side. In the "Ask Copilot" text box, type: "Write a C# console application that prints Welcome to Agile from Copilot and play the tone of Mary had a little lamb." (Copy the prompt without quotation marks.)
Once Copilot generates the code, copy and paste it directly below your existing code in the editor. Then, click the "Play" button to run the program -- this should display two lines of output in the console and play the melody of "Mary Had a Little Lamb." Finally, rewrite the code with sequential statements only.

1.4 What Is Software Development?

There are several philosophies on software development. We will examine two major approaches. Let's use an example to explain the concepts.

Mr. Lincoln has been the owner of a small toy retailer since 1994. He worked in toy manufacturing for many years before being laid off when the company moved the whole manufacturing operation to China. He decided to use his experience with the toy industry and became a retailer that sold toys made in China. He was told that computers can increase his business's efficiency and effectiveness. One difficulty he has with his business is keeping track of inventory and the price of each product. He decided to buy a laptop and recently started using it. After a few days using the laptop, though, he decided that computers saved paper, but made little difference otherwise. Can you develop an efficient application to help Mr. Lincoln?

Mr. Lincoln's computer needs application software that can help him keep track of inventory and prices.

A small group of students from a local university taking a systems analysis and design course volunteered to help Mr. Lincoln.

They start by interviewing Mr. Lincoln about his business mission and strategy, business operations, budget, timeline, and scope for the software development. Following the Systems Development Life Cycle (SDLC) from their textbook, they are beginning the planning phase. In a couple of days, they turn in a business plan which includes all they can find out about the business and a feasibility study on the project. The students plan to develop an application with C# to handle the inventory with little cost to Mr. Lincoln.

The professor of the class and Mr. Lincoln approve the business plan based on the benefits and costs of the project, the manageable scope, and the timeline. The group then starts the analysis phase: determining the software requirements from Mr. Lincoln.

Mr. Lincoln wants something simple and easy to use. He wants to be able to update or enter new inventory whenever a new shipment from a supplier arrives. The application needs to be able to automatically update the inventory whenever a sale is made. He also wants to have the ability to quickly check the price for a certain toy. Finally, Mr. Lincoln wants to be able to have a print of his inventory on paper and a print of the receipt for customers. During the interview, the students ask many questions, such as the product return policy, issues regarding inventory loss or damage, and data about suppliers, products, and sales. They also want to know if Mr. Lincoln keeps a price update history. The students then write the analysis report outlining the detailed requirements from Mr. Lincoln and submit copies to the professor and Mr. Lincoln. This is the analysis phase of SDLC.

After the professor and Mr. Lincoln approve the requirements, the group begins the design phase. They draw a use case diagram to show the interaction between the users and the system. It clearly defines what features the system will have and the boundary of the system. They have mock up screens for Mr. Lincoln to see if that is the user interface he wants. The specifications for all input and output forms are completed. Entity Relationship Diagrams for the business data are reviewed by the professor.

After the professor and Mr. Lincoln approve the design, the team starts to actually code. They use C# and make sure all code runs as expected. They also ask Mr. Lincoln to complete a user acceptance test to make sure he really likes the application. This is called the development phase of SDLC.

Both the team and Mr. Lincoln fully test the system and feel it is a good replacement for Mr. Lincoln's spreadsheet-based system. The team then publishes the application in Mr. Lincoln's working computer. The team also leaves a simple user manual, just in case Mr. Lincoln gets lost while using the new system. This is called the deploy phase of SDLC.

A few days later, the team meets with Mr. Lincoln and asks about his experience with the new system. Mr. Lincoln made a long list of things he wants to change. The team politely says they will discuss it with the professor and come back to Mr. Lincoln. Unfortunately, it's close to the end of the semester, and nobody wants to continue with Mr. Lincoln's change request, since the whole application may need to start all over again. They wish Mr. Lincoln told them earlier. This stage is often called maintenance, which can lead to a new round of SDLC.

Test Your Understanding 1.12
With SDLC, a feasibility study of the project is typically included in the _______ phase.
A. planning
B. analysis
C. design
D. development

Test Your Understanding 1.13
With SDLC, determining software requirements from the user(s) is typically included in the _______ phase.
A. planning
B. analysis
C. design
D. development

Test Your Understanding 1.14
With SDLC, actual coding and testing of a software project is typically done in the _______ phase.

A. planning
B. analysis
C. design
D. development

Test Your Understanding 1.15
With SDLC, drawing mockup screens for clients and developers is typically done in the _______ phase.
A. planning
B. analysis
C. design
D. development

Test Your Understanding 1.16
With SDLC, publishing the completed software project to the customer's computers is typically done in the _______ phase.
A. deploy
B. maintenance
C. design
D. development

Test Your Understanding 1.17
With SDLC, updating a currently used application is typically done in the _______ phase.
A. deploy
B. maintenance
C. design
D. development

Test Your Understanding 1.18
With SDLC, business plan is typically done in the _______ phase.
A. planning
B. analysis
C. design
D. development

Test Your Understanding 1.19
A ______ diagram shows the interaction between the users and the system.

A. use case
B. user
C. system
D. user-system

Test Your Understanding 1.20
A ______ diagram clearly defines what features the system will have and the boundary of the system.
A. use case
B. feature
C. boundary
D. user-system

1.5 Waterfall Approach

The team's work for the toy retailer is an example of the waterfall approach. This approach establishes well-structured phases that the developers can follow. At the end of each phase, the team produces one or more deliverables, such as the business plan at the end of the planning phase and the system analysis report at the end of analysis phase. There are also milestones to mark the end of each phase (usually the approval from the stakeholders). At the end of the deploy phase, the application is delivered to the customer as a whole, and the project can be closed (Pargaonkar, 2023). Figure 1.3 shows the sequence of phases in a typical waterfall approach.

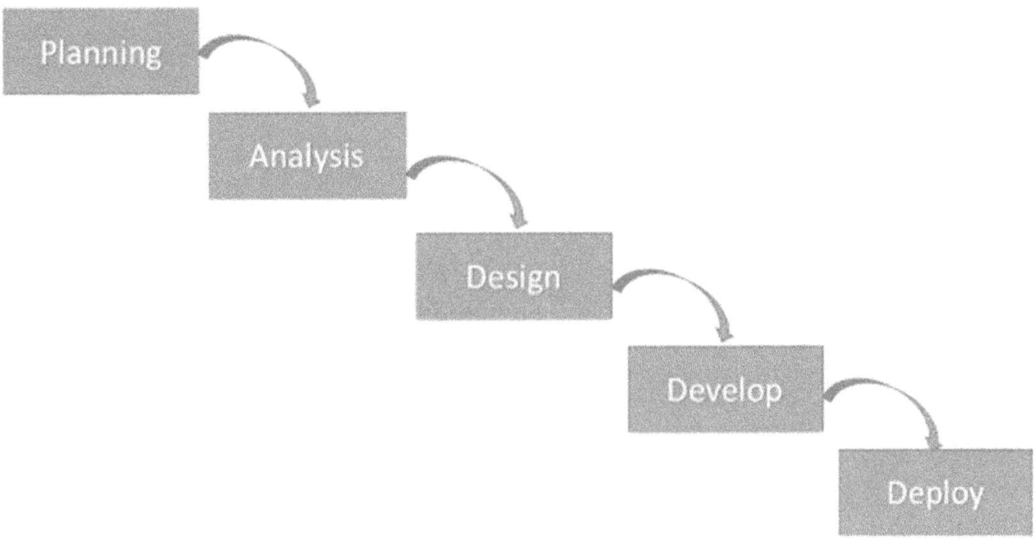

Figure 1.3 Traditional waterfall approach for software development.

Advantage	Explanation
Well-Defined Phases	It simplifies managing and planning the development process.
Clear Deliverables	It is easy to measure progress and ensure that the project is on track.
Predictability	It can be used to estimate the time and cost required for each phase.
Easy to Understand	It can be clearly and easily communicated to stakeholders and team members.

Table 1.1 Advantages of the Waterfall Approach:

Test Your Understanding 1.21
Stakeholders approving the business plan is an example of a project ______.
A. beginning point
B. closing point
C. milestone
D. deliverable

Test Your Understanding 1.22
In the waterfall approach, the approval from the stakeholders is often called _______.
A. green light
B. approved
C. start your engine
D. milestone

Test Your Understanding 1.23
Which of the following is NOT an advantage of the waterfall approach?
A. It has well-defined phases
B. It is easy to understand
C. It is predictable
D. It fits small projects

Test Your Understanding 1.24
What is the benefit of clear deliverables in the waterfall approach?
A. It makes it easy to manage and plan
B. It makes it easy to estimate the time and cost required
C. It makes it easy to measure progress
D. It makes it easy to understand

Test Your Understanding 1.25
What is the advantage of the waterfall approach for estimating time and cost?
A. It is predictable
B. It has well-defined phases
C. It is easy to understand
D. It has clear deliverables

Test Your Understanding 1.26
What is the advantage of the waterfall approach for communication?
A. It is predictable
B. It has well-defined phases
C. It is easy to understand
D. It has clear deliverables

Test Your Understanding 1.27
What is the benefit of well-defined phases in the waterfall approach?
A. It makes it easy to measure progress
B. It makes it easy to ensure the project is on track
C. It makes it easy to manage and plan the development process
D. It makes it easy to estimate the time and cost required

1.6 What's Wrong with the Waterfall?

The waterfall approach for systems development has been used for a long time and is still used by many businesses. However, over the years, professionals noted several problems.

The first major problem with the waterfall is the requirement for customers to know up-front what they want (Mikoluk, 2013). Customers usually have a general sense of what they want, but never a complete, detailed picture. As seen with Mr. Lincoln, many customers may know what they want at the beginning, but change their minds after seeing and running the application. By then, it is often too late for the development team to make any changes. In other words, customers won't see the finished application until it is done, which makes adjustments difficult. The Waterfall approach also assumes that all requirements have been specified in advance, which is unrealistic. That assumption, coupled with limited user involvement, reinforces the tendency of the waterfall model to lock in requirements too early, even after business conditions have changed.

The second problem has to do with the clear lines between roles in this approach (Bastos et al., 2025). In other words, the waterfall method relies on specialists working together, which can be inefficient. System analysts do not know much about coding, and programmers may not care much about testing. A designer might plan something without knowing how difficult it is to code. As a result, it is neither realistic nor efficient to have such a team working on the same objectives. The best the team can do is cooperation. In cooperation, the role of customers was also narrowly defined. Users were often only involved in the requirements determination or analysis phases of the project. Quality assurance people also get paid according to how many bugs are found, so they are inclined towards more bugs in the product. What the team needs is collaboration, not cooperation.

The third problem is that the waterfall makes it hard to backtrack. Once the next phase starts, the previous phase cannot be changed since project managers need to freeze the design at a particular point so programmers can begin to code. This becomes problematic when customers want to change with business conditions during the development process. Additionally, the amount of effort spent on implementing a specific design makes it difficult to change once it is developed (Valacich and George, 2017).

Test Your Understanding 1.28
Which of the following is a major problem with the waterfall?
A. The customers should know how to program in at least one language.
B. There exists a clear line between roles such as analyst, designer, and programmer.
C. The team cannot plan for the next phase.
D. The project managers have too much power.

Test Your Understanding 1.29

Which of the following is NOT a major problem of the waterfall approach for software development?
A. Locking in requirements too early.
B. Too much repeating work.
C. Clear lines between roles.
D. Once the next phase starts, the previous phase(s) cannot be changed

1.7 What Is Agile Methodology?

The agile methodology is a different way to achieve the same goals as the waterfall methodology. The Agile approach breaks the project into smaller pieces, each of which is developed in a sequence similar to the Waterfall phases, and then integrates these pieces incrementally. However, since the project is now divided into smaller pieces, phases are no longer clearly segregated, and can instead be completed concurrently as feasible. How does this simple change dramatically affect the success of software development?

As stated previously, there are three major problems with the traditional waterfall approach. The first problem is that customers cannot predict everything they need before development starts. Agile, on the other hand, develops a small part of the software based on the known requirements in less time. Then the software is shown to the customers, who can give feedback and more requirements. By completing the software in small increments, customers are better able to visualize the final product and provide a more thorough list of requirements. With small pieces, there's also less documentation to work on.

The second problem concerns the clear lines between team roles, which make collaboration difficult. In waterfall, teams consist of specialists who focus solely on their own role. With agile, team members are expected to be familiar with the entire process, on top of having their own expertise. You can think of the team as a small business, where even the owner has multiple roles, such as procurement manager, customer service, and marketing manager. When necessary, an agile team can seek help from a subject-matter expert (SME).

Finally, as stated in the third problem, it is difficult to go back and make adjustments in the waterfall. Since the agile approach works in small pieces, fine tuning is incorporated along the way, and there is less of a need to "go back". Any changes that are needed will be reflected in the next 'pieces'.

Figure 1.4 shows such an approach. You should compare Figure 1.3 and 1.4 and see the differences between the two approaches.

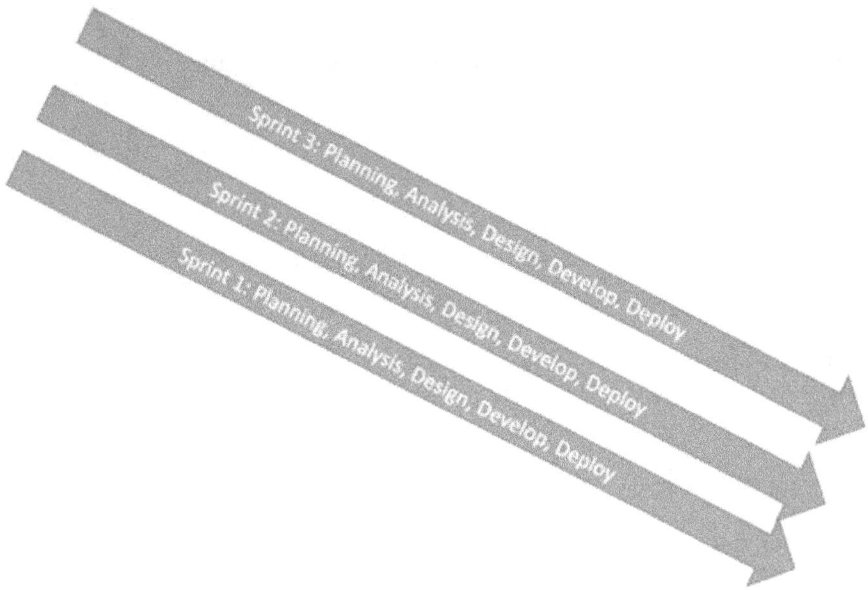

Figure 1.4 Agile approach to software development.

A sprint in agile is defined as the whole process of building one or more small "pieces" of the application. Every sprint has a deliverable. A deliverable can be any piece of functional software. Each sprint includes all planning, analysis, design, coding/testing, and deploying steps, but in a very different way than waterfall. You will see the differences throughout the book when you learn more about agile.

Test Your Understanding 1.30
How does agile solve the problem of locking in requirements too early in the waterfall approach?
A. Requirements are not necessary in agile.
B. Requirements are only needed at the end of each sprint.
C. Requirements can be added after the customers see how some features work.
D. Requirements are created by the development team.

Test Your Understanding 1.31
How does agile solve the problem of too clear lines between team roles in the waterall approach?
A. Each member plays multiple roles.
B. Take away the lines.
C. Developing small pieces does not require more than one person.
D. All roles are played by subject matter experts (SME).

Test Your Understanding 1.32
How does agile solve the problem of "going back" in waterfall approach?
A. In agile, each piece is so small that there is no need to go back.
B. Agile makes it impossible to go back.
C. Agile only allows one team member to go back if necessary.

D. Agile members can go back at any time.

Test Your Understanding 1.33
In agile, the process of working on each smaller increments of an application is called a ________.
A. method
B. sprint
C. development
D. task

1.8 Agile Is an Umbrella Term

Throughout the years, different companies and developers have created their own methodologies to avoid the problems of the traditional waterfall, as you've learned in section 1.6. Eventually, these developers decided to have a meeting to exchange their ideas and philosophies. In 2001, seventeen of them held a meeting at Snowbird, Utah. They formed the Agile Alliance group, whose mission was to promote the agile software development approach. They summarized the common characteristics of their approach and came up with four values and twelve principles (http://agilemanifesto.org/), which they called the Agile Manifesto.

The methodologies the practitioners used before the meeting (some are still in use today) include Scrum, extreme programming, Kanban, lean software development, crystal methodology, Dynamic Systems Development Methodology (DSDM), and Feature-Driven Development (FDD). This book will focus on Scrum, the most popular of all, and also briefly mention extreme programming and Kanban along the way.

Test Your Understanding 1.34
Which of the following is NOT one of the agile methodologies?
A. Scrum
B. eXtreme Programming
C. Kanban
D. C#

1.9 What Are the Four Values of Agile?

The four values actually involve eight values. The purpose of the other four values is to show the importance of the four on the left in Figure 1.5

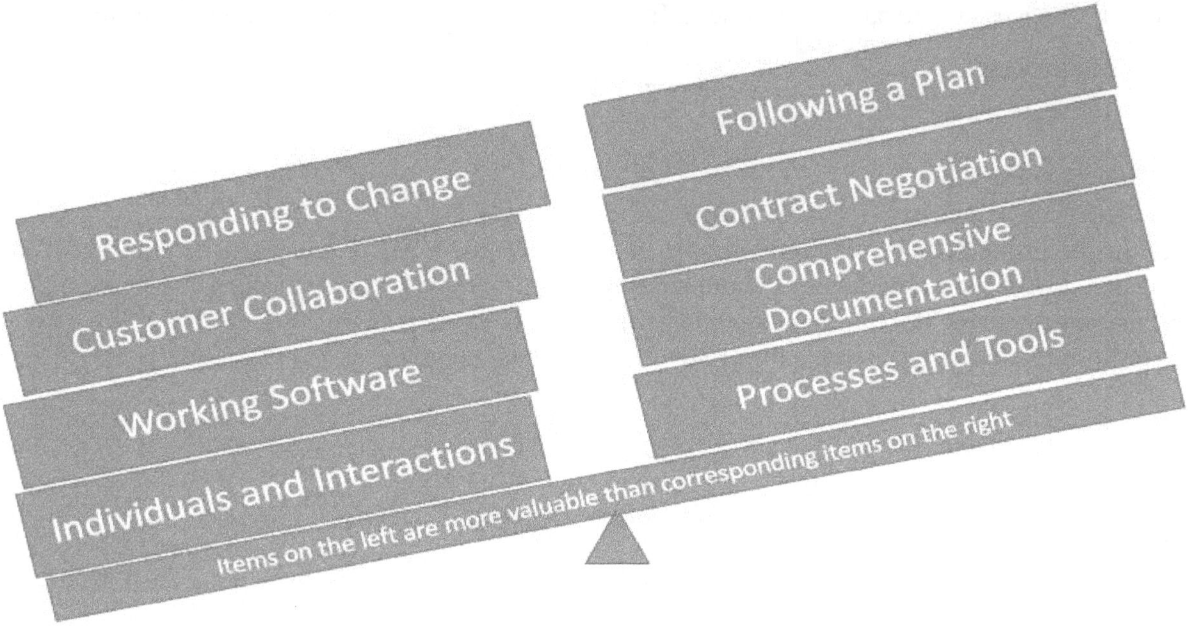

Figure 1.5 Four values of the Agile Manifesto

The first value, 'Individuals and Interactions', emphasizes the importance of the people, not the processes or the tools, that develop the software. It is equally important that the team work together through interaction and communication to reach their goal. This value suggests that people can choose their own way to develop software instead of following certain work procedures.

The second value, 'Working Software', stresses that the end product of the development is the software, not the documentation. Documentation is a helper, not the end result.

The third value, 'Customer Collaboration', highlights that customers and the development team have the same goal. The only way to achieve the goal is through collaboration. In the traditional approach, the customer requirements are usually documented in the contract and the team often wastes time negotiating the scope of the project.

The fourth value, 'Responding to Change', underlines the fact that change is not avoidable. While a plan is good, a plan is still based on a prediction of the future, which is often not accurate. In such a case, the plan needs to be updated. Continuous planning improves the chances of success. Change should be part of the plan. This allows the team to check the changes, get feedback and make revisions. Such practice delivers more valuable software for the customers. As shown in Figure 1.3, the traditional plan is made early in the project and can thus be a nightmare to follow. However, even though changes are unavoidable, agile does not support daily changes in software development. In agile, change is typically made between sprints, not while a sprint is in progress.

Test Your Understanding 1.35
Which of the following is a correct statement about agile?
A. In agile, how things are done is more important than who does the things.
B. In agile, teams do not need to write any documentation so time can be saved for coding.
C. In agile, customers and the development team cooperate for the same goal.
D. In agile, responding to change is more important than following the plan.

1.10 What Are the Twelve Principles in Agile?

The complete list of the twelve principles is available at http://agilemanifesto.org/principles.html. In this section, we will summarize them in five points:

1. Working software should be delivered frequently instead of as one big software delivered at the end of the project. Using our C# example in this chapter, instead of completing the whole application at once, you would write the code that can display "Welcome to Agile" first. After you make this message display correctly, you add code to display "Welcome to Agile from Copilot.". After you display the second message, you add code to make the melody. With this approach, if anything goes wrong, it is easy to identify and fix it. Also, if the customers want something different, it is easy to accommodate.

2. The purpose of software development is to meet customer requirements. We should allow customers room to change their mind. For example, when they see the background color is green, they may want to make the font text color to be red for better contrast. The development team should have no difficulty adding that, even though the customer did not mention font color at the beginning. On the other hand, you should also work closely with the customer to cut costly changes that can be avoided.

3. The quality of the software depends on the development team. The team should be "self-organizing", meaning that they can work toward the common goal with great autonomy. The lines between the roles are blurred. Team members learn from each other. They work as a team, not as a sum of the individuals.

4. Continuous improvement is critical to the success of the team. They learn from their own experiences. What worked well? What didn't work? They also learn from innovations in the field, and challenge themselves for better performance.

5. Simplicity can help one avoid many problems in software development and save money. Just make the software solve the business problems without the extra bells and whistles that the customers did not request.

Test Your Understanding 1.36
Frequent delivery of software allows better _______.
A. communication
B. rest for the team
C. customers
D. contract to be settled

Test Your Understanding 1.37
Which of the following statements is NOT correct about agile?
A. In agile, change requests from the customer are welcome.
B. The agile team should be "self-organizing", meaning that they can work toward the common goal with great autonomy.
C. The agile team should not be affected by the innovations in the field.
D. In agile, working software should be delivered frequently in order to get timely customer feedback.

1.11 Chapter Summary

In this chapter, you learned that computers execute instructions written in a programming language. In C#, individual statements are organized into methods, methods are grouped into classes, and classes are contained within namespaces. You also explored how to use built-in classes and their methods to write your own code—including leveraging AI to generate a simple C# program. Additionally, you examined the phases of the traditional Waterfall software development approach and compared them with the modern Agile methodology. The chapter concluded with a brief overview of the Agile Manifesto and its core values.

1.12 References

Bastos, R. A., Pierott, R. M. R., Navarro, L. L. L., Tam, V. W., Najjar, M. K., & Haddad, A. N. (2025). Comparative analysis of communication in project management approaches: waterfall, agile, and hybrid. *International Journal of Construction Management*, 1-29.
Mikoluk, K. (2013), Agile Vs. Waterfall: Evaluating The Pros And Cons, Available at https://blog.udemy.com/agile-vs-waterfall/ accessed November 15, 2016.
Pargaonkar, S. (2023). A comprehensive research analysis of software development life cycle (SDLC) agile & waterfall model advantages, disadvantages, and application suitability in software quality engineering. *International Journal of Scientific and Research Publications*, *13*(8), 120-124.

Valacich, J. and George, J. (2017), Modern Systems Analysis and Design 8th Edition, Pearson, Boston.

1.13 Solutions to Test Your Understanding

1.1 A; 1.2 C; 1.3 C; 1.4 B; 1.5 B; 1.6 D; 1.7 B; 1.8 A; 1.9 C; 1.10 B; 1.11 C; 1.12 A; 1.13 B; 1.14 D; 1.15 C; 1.16 A; 1.17 B; 1.18 A; 1.19 A; 1.20 A; 1.21 C; 1.22 D; 1.23 D; 1.24 C; 1.25 A; 1.26 C; 1.27 C; 1.28 B; 1.29 B; 1.30 C; 1.31 A; 1.32 A; 1.33 B; 1.34 D; 1.35 D; 1.36 A; 1.37 C;.

Chapter 2: C# Statements and Agile Characteristics

Chapter Learning Outcomes

2.1 Recognize variables and their corresponding data type
2.2 Use operators to solve problems
2.3 Recall characteristics of agile
2.4 Recognize different types of agile

2.1 What Is a Variable?

As you learned in Chapter 1, to program is to write instructions by following C# syntax. Sometimes, a value you need in the instruction may not be known at the time of programming or has changed over time. You can use a variable to be a placeholder for an unknown value or change the value stored in a variable.

Instructions in a program can reference and manipulate a variable. Additionally, variables make instructions more readable to programmers. A variable is a reserved space in computer memory that is used to store things like values. It is a named memory location to temporarily store data.

For example, in the last chapter, you displayed "Welcome to Agile" on the screen. What if you want to display "Welcome to C#"? You can use a variable to store the value you want to welcome and let the user decide what value to put in that variable. You can reference the value stored in the variable in many instructions.

Another example, if you want to calculate the square of a number that the user enters, you can use a variable, say x. Then you can calculate the square of x as x*x before the user enters a number. The result value will depend on what value the user enters for x. This way your program is more powerful and flexible.

Test Your Understanding 2.1
In programming, a ______ can be used to store some value for later use.
A. variable
B. C#
C. storage
D. container

Test Your Understanding 2.2
You use a ______ to be a placeholder for an unknown value or change the value stored in a variable.
A. variable
B. C#
C. storage
D. container

Test Your Understanding 2.3
The variables in a program can make program instructions ______.
A. more readable to programmers
B. run faster
C. more readable to computers
D. more readable to both programmers and computers

Test Your Understanding 2.4
A variable is a ______ in computer memory that is used to store things like values.
A. reserved space
B. fixed-length space
C. named space
D. reserved space with a programmer defined name

Test Your Understanding 2.5
If you want to write code to calculate the square of a number that the user enters when the program is running, ______.
A. you can use a variable to represent the number entered by a user
B. you cannot do it because a computer is dumb
C. you cannot do it because you don't know what number the user may enter
D. you can do it as long as the user does not enter any unexpected number

Example 2.1

Problem:

Write a program that asks the user for the name, and then displays the "Welcome to Agile, your name" message on the console screen. "Your name" will be replaced by the name user entered.

Solution:

Start a new console app in Visual Studio called Chapter2Example1. Save it to the Agile folder on your desktop (you followed the instructions and created the Agile folder in Chapter 1). With the default Program.cs open in the window, replace the default code with the following lines:

```
// prompt user for a name
Console.WriteLine("Enter your name: ");
// store the user entered value in a variable
string name = Console.ReadLine();
// compose and display a message
Console.WriteLine("Welcome to Agile, " + name);
```

Explanation:

The double slashes // indicate that this line is a comment. The C# compiler will ignore such lines. But, it helps programmers understand the code.

Ignore any green underline for now. The ReadLine() method of Console class will read the value the user enters from the keyboard. The method waits for the user to input a response. Once the user enters the text and presses the "Enter" key, the entered text is returned as a string value and the program continues to execute. The left side of the equal sign declares a variable named "name" of string data type (explained in the next section). The equal sign assigns the value to the variable. The user must press the "Enter" key for the end of the value.

The "+" operator concatenates the string "Welcome to Agile, " and the value stored in the variable "name".

Click on the green start button to run it. Type in your name when prompted and you should see "Welcome to Agile, your name". Push the enter key to close the program.

```
Enter your name:
Lynn Smith
Welcome to Agile, Lynn Smith
```

C# Variable naming rules:

A variable in C# can contain letters, numbers, and underscores only, and the first character cannot be a number. No spacing is allowed, and you cannot use the C# reserved keywords, such as class, virtual, or abstract. Additionally, a variable name is case sensitive, e.g. 'name' and 'Name' are different.

Test Your Understanding 2.6
Which of the following is NOT a legal variable name for C#?
A. studentName
B. student name
C. studentName1
D. nameOfStudent

Test Your Understanding 2.7
Which of the following is a legal variable name for C#?
A. abstract
B. class
C. Class
D. virtual

Test Your Understanding 2.8
In C#, how do you concatenate the string "Welcome to Agile, " and the string "Lynn" to make a new string "Welcome to Agile, Lynn"?
A. "Welcome to Agile, " + "Lynn"
B. "Welcome to Agile, " concatenate "Lynn"
C. "Wlecome to Agile, " append "Lynn"
D. "Lynn" append "Welcome to Agile, "

Test Your Understanding 2.9
Which of the following is NOT a legal variable name for C#?
A. studentName
B. student_name
C. studentName1
D. 2studentName

Test Your Understanding 2.10
Variable names are case ______ in C#, which means 'student' and 'Student' are treated differently.
A. sensitive
B. dependent
C. specific
D. based

Test Your Understanding 2.11
In C#, how do you get the user input from the console?
A. Console.Reader()
B. Console.ReaderInput()
C. Console.ReadLine()
D. Console.Input()

Test Your Understanding 2.12
In C#, what will the following line of code do? Console.WriteLine("Enter your name: ");
A. Do nothing unless the user enters a name.
B. Display the text "Enter your name: " on the console screen.
C. Display the text "Enter your name: " on the console screen and store user name in a variable.
D. Wait for the user to enter a name

Test Your Understanding 2.13
In C#, what will the following line of code do? // Console.WriteLine("Enter your name: ");
A. Do nothing unless the user enters a name.
B. Display the text "Enter your name: " on the console screen.
C. Write a name for the user
D. Do nothing because it is commented out

2.2 What Is Data Type?

Please note that in the code example above (Example 2.1), '*string*' is a data type in C# that was added before the variable 'name'. Specifying a data type helps the compiler allocate the correct amount of memory space for the variable's value. This means if you create a variable for a number, you cannot put text inside it This is similar to selecting a room type when booking a vacation rental, where you need to specify the size and type of room that meets your needs.

Other commonly used simple data types include *int* (for storing whole numbers, such as 5 or 12), *double* (for storing floating point numbers, such as 3.14), and *decimal* (for storing floating point numbers with higher accuracy; you will use this type for money values). The data type *char* is used for single characters, and the data type *bool* is used to store a Boolean value, such as true or false.

A literal value, such as 3.14, will be treated as a double data type. To make it as a decimal data type, use 3.14m. The suffix indicates a decimal data type. See Programming Challenge 2.2 solution for an example.

One important thing to know about data type is its value range. For example, for *int*, the valid range of values is from -2,147,483,648 to 2,147,483,647. If you try to store a value out of that range, an error will occur. For a complete list of built-in data types, visit https://msdn.microsoft.com/en-us/library/ya5y69ds.aspx. Just click on the type name on the page to view more details.

Test Your Understanding 2.14
In C#, you _____ to store any whole number.
A. can declare an int data type variable
B. can declare a double data type variable
C. can declare a decimal data type variable
D. cannot declare a variable

Test Your Understanding 2.15
In C#, if you want to store the value of a student's letter grade (one of 'A', 'B', 'C', 'D', 'F', 'I', 'P'), what is the most appropriate data type?
A. int
B. double
C. char
D. string

Test Your Understanding 2.16
What is the difference between a double and a decimal data type in C#?
A. double works for integers.
B. decimal works for integers.
C. double has higher accuracy.
D. decimal has higher accuracy.

Test Your Understanding 2.17
If students take a course that can only receive the grade of pass or fail, what data type would be most appropriate for storing the grade?
A. double
B. decimal
C. char
D. bool

Test Your Understanding 2.18
If you need to store the number of students who registered for a class, what data type would be most appropriate for storing the number?
A. int
B. decimal
C. char
D. bool

Test Your Understanding 2.19
If you need to store a student's GPA for a university, what data type would be most appropriate for storing the GPA?
A. int
B. decimal
C. char
D. double

Test Your Understanding 2.20
If you need to store a student's full name for a university, what data type would be most appropriate for storing the name?
A. string
B. decimal
C. char
D. double

2.3 What Is an Operator?

Computers are good at calculations, so you can use operators to add, subtract, multiply, and divide, etc., on numbers and variables. Let's see an example.

Example 2.2

Problem:

A bag holds 50 candies. The calorie information on the bag indicates that there are 25 servings in each bag and that a serving equals 100 calories. Write a program that lets the user enter the number of candies they ate and then displays the number of total calories consumed.

Solution:

Start a console app in Visual Studio called Chapter2Example2. Save it to the Agile folder on your desktop.

With the default Program.cs open in the window, replace the default code with the following:

```
// use constant variables to hold values
const int NUMBER_OF_CANDIES_IN_BAG = 50;
const int SERVINGS_PER_BAG = 25;
const int CALORIES_PER_SERVING = 100;
// first, compute how many candies per serving
double numberOfCandiesPerServing = NUMBER_OF_CANDIES_IN_BAG / SERVINGS_PER_BAG;
// next, compute how many calories per candy
double caloriesPerCandy = CALORIES_PER_SERVING / numberOfCandiesPerServing;
// prompt user for number of candies consumed
Console.WriteLine("How many candies did you eat?");
// get the number from the user and store it in a variable
int candiesAte = int.Parse(Console.ReadLine());
// compute how many calories consumed
double caloriesConsumed = candiesAte * caloriesPerCandy;
// display the result on console screen
Console.WriteLine($"You have consumed {caloriesConsumed} calories.");
```

Output:

```
How many candies did you eat?
3
You have consumed 150 calories.
```

Explanation:

The first three lines declare and initialize three constant variables. Unlike a regular variable, the value stored in a constant variable cannot be changed by statements later on. It is a better practice to use constants when you don't want the value to be changed in the program. The benefits include preventing accidental modification, clarity and readability, and avoiding magic numbers (i.e., unexplained literal values that make code harder to understand and maintain).

The "/" symbol is a division operator used in C#. The "*" is a multiplication operator.

The following line:

```
int candiesAte = int.Parse(Console.ReadLine());
```

converts a string value to an int value so that we can apply multiplication on it. Most data types have a Parse() method that allows you to convert a string value to a desired type. Note that only a number like "2" can be converted to an integer. You cannot convert "Two" to an integer by the Parse() method. Also note that Console.ReadLine() always returns a string type even if you typed in 2 on keyboard.

The "$" sign in front of a string indicates that this is an interpolated string which you can insert a variable in the string within a pair of curly braces. You can also format the variable, e.g. {caloriesConsumed:N2} will make the value displayed in two decimal places. or{somevariable:C} will make the value displayed as currency.

Test Your Understanding 2.21
What is the difference between the following two statements?
Statement1: int numberOfCandiesInBag = 50;
Statement2: const int numberOfCandiesInBag = 50;
A. Statement1 is a simpler statement without the keyword const and is thus recommended.
B. Statement2 will not allow later statements in the program to accidentally change the value and is thus recommended.
C) Statement1 and Statement2 are the same.
D) Only one of the statements is correct.

Test Your Understanding 2.22
Which of the following is NOT a benefit of using constant variables in C#?
A. Clarity and readability
B. Preventing accidental modification of the variable's value
C. Avoiding magic numbers
D. Reduce the learning curve for beginners

Test Your Understanding 2.23
What data type is used in C# to represent a value entered via keyboard input by a user?
A. string
B. default
C. char
D. It depends on what value the user enters

Test Your Understanding 2.24
Most data type in C# has a Parse() method that allows you to convert a ______ value to a desired type.
A. string
B. default
C. char
D. decimal

Test Your Understanding 2.25
In C#, put a "$" sign in front of a string to indicate this is a(n)______ string which you can insert a variable in the string within a pair of curly braces.
A. special
B. dollar
C. interpolated
D. currency

Test Your Understanding 2.26
Suppose x is a decimal variable in C#, what will the following code do? {x:N2}
A. Make the value displayed as a whole number

B. Make the value displayed in two decimal places
C. Make the value displayed with no decimal places
D. Make the value displayed with no decimal places twice

Test Your Understanding 2.27
Suppose x is a decimal variable in C#, what will the following code do? {x:C}
A. Make the value displayed as currency
B. Make the value displayed as code
C. Make the value displayed as a C# value
D. A compiler-time error. C should be C#

Programming Challenge 2.1
Lynn's Pizza Restaurant needs an application to calculate the number of slices a pizza can be divided into. Your application should let the user enter the radius of the pizza in inches, then display how many slices this pizza can be cut assuming one slice is no less than 15 square inches. (Hint, the area of a whole pizza is calculated by Area = πr^2, where π is 3.14 and r is the radius. You may also use Math.PI for 3.14 where Math is a prebuilt class and PI is one of its properties. A method of Math called Floor can remove the decimal portion of a number.)

Example 2.3

Problem:

Write a program that prints the minimum number of quarters, dimes, nickels, and pennies that a customer should get back as change. Ask the user for a change amount, such as 1.23, or 0.54. Then the program should display the number of each type of coin needed.

Solution:

Start a console app in Visual Studio called Chapter2Example3. Save it to the Agile folder on your desktop.

With the default Program.cs open in the window, replace the default code with the following code:

```
// prompt the user for the amount of change
Console.WriteLine("Enter change amount:");
// store the amount in a variable
decimal changeAmount = decimal.Parse(Console.ReadLine());
// convert the amount to a whole number of cents
int changeInCents = (int)(changeAmount * 100);
// compute number of quarters (25 cents) needed
int numberOfQuarters = changeInCents / 25;
// compute the remainder
int remainderAfterQuarters = changeInCents % 25;
// compute number of dimes (10 cents) needed
int numberOfDimes = remainderAfterQuarters / 10;
// compute the remainder
int remainderAfterDimes = remainderAfterQuarters % 10;
// compute number of nickels (5 cents) needed
int numberOfNickels = remainderAfterDimes / 5;
```

```
// compute the remainder, this is the number of pennies needed
int remainderAfterNickels = remainderAfterDimes % 5;
int numberOfPennies = remainderAfterNickels;
// display result
Console.WriteLine($"Number of Quarters: {numberOfQuarters}");
Console.WriteLine($"Number of Dimes: {numberOfDimes}");
Console.WriteLine($"Number of Nickels: {numberOfNickels}");
Console.WriteLine($"Number of Pennies: {numberOfPennies}");
```

Output:

```
Enter change amount:
1.23
Number of Quarters: 4
Number of Dimes: 2
Number of Nickels: 0
Number of Pennies: 3
```

Explanation:

The (int) operator explicitly casts a decimal type variable to an int type. It will remove any decimal places. See what happens if you remove the second pair of parentheses (`int changeInCents = (int)changeAmount * 100;`). It will remove the decimal in change amount before multiplication.

The "/" operator is an arithmetic division operator. Be careful when you divide two integers because in that case, only the quotient will be returned. For example, if you divide 4 by 3 using the "/" operator, the result will be 1 instead of 1.3333. This is because the "/" operator performs integer division when both operands are integers, and it rounds down to the nearest integer. The % operator is a useful arithmetic operator called module, which is a way to calculate the remainder of an integer division.

Test Your Understanding 2.28
What will be the result of the following statement? Console.WriteLine ((int)5.67);
A. 5
B. 6
C. 7
D. An error

Test Your Understanding 2.29
What will be the result of the following statement? Console.WriteLine ((int) 5.9 * 2);
A. 5
B. 10
C. 11
D. 12

Test Your Understanding 2.30
What will be the result of the following statement? Console.WriteLine ((int) (5.9 * 2));
A. 5
B. 10
C. 11
D. 12

Test Your Understanding 2.31
What will be the result of the following statement? Console.WriteLine (5%3);
A. 5
B. 3
C. 2
D. 1

Programming Challenge 2.2
Lynn's Pizza Restaurant also sells cookies. One cookie costs 12 cents. A dozen cookies cost $1.20. Any number of cookies less than a dozen costs 12 cents each. For example, 10 cookies would cost $1.20, 11 cookies would cost $1.32, 12 cookies would cost $1.20, 13 cookies would cost $1.32, and 30 cookies would cost $3.12. Write a program to ask the user for the number of cookies, then display the total cost. The output should look like this:

```
How many cookies do you buy:
30
Total cost for 30 cookies is $3.12
```

Programming Challenge 2.3
Smith's Fast Food sells burgers, fries, and drinks only. The price of a burger is $1.50. The price of a serving of French fries is $1.20. A cup of drink is $1.00. Write a program that asks the user for the number of items for each food, then displays the total cost (Assuming no sales tax.). Remember to use const for the unit price of each food. The output should look like this:

```
How many burgers would you like?
3
How many servings of fries would you like?
2
How many cups of drink would you like?
1
The total Cost is $7.90
```

Programming Challenge 2.4
Lynn's Pizza Restaurant needs a tip calculator for customers to calculate tips. The program will prompt the user to enter a purchase amount. Then, the program will calculate and display tips at 15%, 18%, and 20%, as well as display the total cost of the meal including the tip. You should use const for those tip percentages instead of literal values. We will assume there is no state sales tax. The output should look like this:

```
How much do you spend?
20
At 15% Tip Rate:
Tip Amount: $3.00
Total Amount: $23.00
At 18% Tip Rate:
Tip Amount: $3.60
Total Amount: $23.60
At 20% Tip Rate:
Tip Amount: $4.00
Total Amount: $24.00
```

2.4 Core Agile Characteristics

Agile practice is very different from traditional practices. There are five characteristics that differentiate agile from traditional development approaches (Ashmore and Runyan, 2014):

1. Self-Organizing Teams

In agile software development, a self-organizing team is a cross-functional group that collectively determines how best to accomplish their work without external direction. These teams are responsible for planning their work during sprint planning sessions, organizing tasks, and allocating responsibilities among team members based on their skills and capacity. Unlike traditional hierarchical teams with project managers assigning tasks, self-organizing teams operate with collective autonomy to decide how they will work together and who will take ownership of different processes or decisions along the development lifecycle.

Self-organizing teams thrive on collaboration, trust, and collective responsibility for delivering working software. To facilitate effective communication and coordination, these teams establish regular self-organized events such as daily stand-ups to synchronize work and plan the next 24 hours toward the Sprint Goal, and sprint planning sessions to determine upcoming work. The team composition typically includes diverse skills necessary to deliver complete functionality -- developers, testers, designers, and product owners -- working collaboratively in shared spaces or through effective remote collaboration tools.

Practical implementation requires clear boundaries: while the team has autonomy over how to accomplish their work, they remain accountable for delivering committed user stories and meeting sprint goals. Team members select tasks based on their expertise and development goals rather than having work assigned to them, fostering greater ownership and motivation. This approach enables teams to adapt quickly to changing requirements and continuously improve their processes through regular retrospectives, ultimately leading to higher quality software delivered more efficiently.

2. Continuous Improvement (solving your own problems)

In agile, each team member is responsible for ensuring that problems from a past or current iteration are not carried into the next. This creates a higher level of engagement from employees, because they will be responsible for any problems that arise.

In the past, team members relied on the project manager to resolve issues. In agile, the team is empowered and encouraged to seek out answers and improvements on its own.

3. Quick customer feedback

In a non-agile environment, the team won't deliver the software to the customer until the whole application is finished. This makes customer feedback difficult, considering the relatively long process. Furthermore, the final delivered application might be very different from what the customers envisioned at the start. Customers may also have changed their minds during the process.

In an agile environment, the team will demo the completed part of the software to the customer at the end of each sprint. A sprint only delivers an increment instead of the whole application. Agile utilizes small increments and more frequent feedback. As a result, when all pieces are put together, the software is more likely to meet the customer's vision.

4. Blurring the lines between roles in a team

Before agile, a software development team would have needed to hire specialists, such as analysts, programmers, and testers. In the agile setting, there are no C# programmers or testers; everyone is a team member. That is one reason why this book merges agile and C#: so by the end of this book, you will be able to practice agile with actual software development as an agile team member.

For instance, in a conventional setting, a tester would wait for the programmer to finish the code before starting the testing, and the programmer would consider the work complete once the tester started. This often led to low-quality results and blaming each other. In an agile setting, where programmers and testers collaborate to develop high-quality software, the only thing that matters is the end result. The entire team is responsible for completing the software.

Agile teams usually include members with a broad skill set, such as analyzing, designing, programming, and testing. However, members are expected to participate in any role the team needs them to fill (Highsmith, 2002). This situation differs from the traditional waterfall structured environments, where teams often specialize according to function (e.g., analyst, designer, developer, tester) (Nerur et al, 2005).
In agile, systems analysts might perform programming and design responsibilities in their job even though it is not required of them. A developer might also perform programming, testing, and configuration management tasks that would be fragmented in a traditional setting.

5. Physical Workspace

In agile, the physical workspace differs from traditional setups in that cubicles are removed, and team members work in close proximity to each other. This facilitates easy and quick communication, leading to increased efficiency and potentially better software quality. However, some employees may feel a lack of privacy due to the open workspace.

Test Your Understanding 2.32
Which of the following statements about agile is true?
Statement1: In an agile team, members get to pick any task they want, even their own project from another company.
Statement2: In an agile team, there is no project manager role.
A. Statement1 only
B. Statement2 only
C. both Statement1 and Statement2
D. neither Statement1 nor Statement2

Test Your Understanding 2.33
Which of the following statements about agile is true?
Statement1: In an agile team, compared to a traditional team, members get more frequent feedback.
Statement2: In an agile team, every member is equally capable at analyzing, designing, programming, and testing.
A. Statement1 only
B. Statement2 only
C. both Statement1 and Statement2
D. neither Statement1 nor Statement2

Test Your Understanding 2.34
What is a self-organizing team in agile software development?
A. A team with a formal hierarchy and structure.
B. A group of individuals who work together with an individual's own goal.
C. A team responsible for planning, executing, and delivering software products with the autonomy to make decisions and solve problems.
D. A team that follows traditional project management practices.

Test Your Understanding 2.35
What is the composition of self-organizing teams in agile software development?
A. Teams composed primarily of senior developers who can handle architecture, coding, and deployment independently
B. Groups of like-minded specialists (e.g., all backend developers or all frontend developers) who coordinate across teams
C. Teams that include only technical roles (developers, architects, DevOps engineers) with no business or product representation
D. Cross-functional teams with members possessing diverse skills and expertise needed to deliver complete, valuable increments of working software

2.5 Agile Success Factors

Agile methodologies have increased software development success rates, improved software quality, and shortened the time it takes to reach the market. It also enhances the motivation and productivity of the development team (Ghani et al., 2015, Rigby et al., 2016). What makes agile so successful?

Research on agile success (Sammon et al., 2009) started with ten factors and narrowed it down to four. These factors make the difference between success and failure (Dhir et al, 2019).

1. Organizational and Reporting Structure

In agile, work cannot be done alone. Whether success is achieved can be determined by organizational structure. An example of a successful structure is organic organization (Bennis, 1969), which is identified as having little job specialization, few layers of management, decentralized decision making, and little direct supervision. These attributes allow flexibility and adaptability. An organization with organic structure is more likely to succeed with an agile approach.

2. Organizational Process

The organizational process can impact agile success similarly to the organizational structure. Organizational processes are a standardized and systematic set of procedures, policies, and practices used to achieve organizational goals and objectives. Processes that promote the sharing of best practices across the organization to facilitate organizational learning and process improvement are better suited for agile (CMMI Product Team, 2007). However, certain processes like the Capability Maturity Model, which refines an organization's software development process, may not be compatible with agile methodologies due to differing mindsets.

3. Documentation Requirements

Even though agile methodologies do not prohibit documentation, the more time the team spend on documentation, the less time they have to work on the software. Thus, the documentation requirements affect the success of an agile approach. The documentation should be kept at a minimum.

4. Layout of Workspace

Similar to item 5 of the core agile characteristics discussed earlier in this chapter, layout of workspace is an important factor for the success of agile. While both an open plan office and a clustered cubicle approach are popular among IT companies, experts in agile suggest some kind of isolated room for a single team. This allows members to chat freely and promotes communication and teamwork. Furthermore, this layout facilitates bonding without the interference of other teams (Muldoon, 2014).

Test Your Understanding 2.36
Which of the following is NOT a success factor for agile approach discussed in the book?
A. Team cellphone usage policy
B. Organizational and reporting structure
C. Organizational process
D. Documentation requirement

Test Your Understanding 2.37
An organization with ______ structure is more likely to succeed with an agile approach.
A. hierarchical
B. functional
C. matrix
D. organic

Test Your Understanding 2.38
Which of the following processes may not be compatible with agile methodologies?
A. Six Sigma
B. Capability Maturity Model
C. Lean manufacturing
D. Total Quality Management

Test Your Understanding 2.39
What is the recommended workspace layout for agile teams by the author?
A. An open-plan office
B. A clustered cubicle approach
C. An isolated room for a single team
D. A shared workspace for multiple teams

For organizations that are new to agile software development, Cooke (2011) suggested five steps to success.

1. Choosing the right kick-off point. Many developers switched to agile because they were struggling with their current project. That may not be the right time. They should take a step back and try to understand agile better, get prepared, and then start. The best time to start agile is when the team is well prepared and ready for the agile approach.

2. Choosing the right project(s). For example, a project that is not burdened by any legacy systems or pre-existing management techniques might be a good 'first' agile project. The success of the first project is often critical for persuading management to adopt the agile approach.

3. Choosing the right methodologies and practices. As you will learn in the next section, there is more than one flavor of agile approach. The organization culture, team member backgrounds, and the project can all affect the appropriate methodologies and practices. You can combine different types of agile or even create one for yourself as long as you follow the agile principles.

4. Choosing the right method of introduction. Like many other practices, agile can be introduced top down or bottom up. With top down, you have the organizational mandate on using agile. This approach is usually easier for the team because the champions are often the top management. With bottom up, you might be the champion.

5. Avoiding common traps which include undermining agile principles, insufficient communication and training, and using agile as a doctrine instead of a tool.

Test Your Understanding 2.40
For organizations that are new to agile software development, Cooke (2011) suggested five steps to success. Which of the following is NOT a step?
A. Choosing the right kick-off point
B. Choosing the right project(s)
C. Choosing the right project manager(s)
D. Choosing the right methodologies and practices

Test Your Understanding 2.41
Can organizations create their own agile methodologies?
A. Yes, as long as they follow the agile principles
B. No, agile methodologies are standardized and cannot be modified
C. Yes, but only if they have a large development team
D. No, creating new methodologies is prohibited in agile

2.6 Types of Agile.

As you have learned in chapter one, agile is an umbrella term. In this section, you will discover a few major types of agile methodologies, namely scrum, extreme programming (XP), and Kanban. In the rest of the book, we may not always differentiate which type of agile is used.

2.6.1 Scrum

Scrum is a lightweight framework. It is simple to understand, but difficult to master. Unlike the traditional waterfall project management methodology that requires comprehensive documentation and heavyweight processes, scrum is lightweight and focuses on working software and team collaborations. Its organization, roles, events, and artifacts are easy to understand, but applying it to the field can be difficult. Teams are free to develop different processes and techniques as long as they follow the rules, roles, and events of the scrum framework. As a result, there are many flavors of scrum.

The term 'scrum' was introduced by Takeuchi and Nonaka (1986) regarding business operations. They explained that projects using small cross-functional teams historically produced the best results. They compared these high-performance teams to "scrum" formations in Rugby.

Scrum for software development was introduced in 1993 by Jeff Sutherland at Easel Corporation, using the study by Takeuchi and Nonaka (1986) as the basis for adopting their analogy as the name of the process for software development.

Scrum is based on the empirical process control theory (Viscardi, 2013). According to this theory, knowledge comes from experience, and decisions should be made according to what is known. It has three foundations (Crisan et al., 2015): transparency, inspection, and adaptation.

The transparency foundation indicates that the software developed should be visible to all stakeholders. Inspection specifies that experienced inspectors should check the scrum artifacts against the team goals on a regular basis. Adaptation suggests that if any differences are found in the inspection, the team should adjust the related processes or materials.

Scrum includes three roles, five events, and three artifacts. These will be covered in more detail in later chapters. Scrum is the most popular agile practice. This book mostly follows scrum practice.

Test Your Understanding 2.42
The ______ foundation of scrum indicates that the software developed should be visible to all stakeholders.
A. Transparency
B. Collaboration
C. Inspection
D. Adaptation

Test Your Understanding 2.43
Scrum is ________ and focuses on working software and team _______.
A. lightweight, collaborations
B. heavyweight, collaborations
C. lightweight, corporations
D. heavyweight, corporations

Test Your Understanding 2.44
Which of the following is NOT a scrum foundation?
A. Transparency
B. Collaboration
C. Inspection
D. Adaptation

Test Your Understanding 2.45
According to the author, Scrum framework includes ___ roles, ___ events, and ___ artifacts.
A. 1, 2, 3
B. 3, 4, 5
C. 3, 2, 5
D. 3, 5, 3

2.6.2 Extreme Programming (XP)

XP is another popular agile methodology (Amir et al, 2013). It requires that customers be part of the team. It uses a process similar to sprint called 'iterations'. It has the following four characteristics: continuous integration, user story, team velocity, and pair programming.

1. Continuous Integration: XP requires frequent releases and very short development cycles. A cycle can be as short as one day. The idea of small iterations is the same as scrum's sprints, save for the length, which is one day compared to a sprint's two weeks.

2. User story: These are software requirements written in a specific format. It is short and can fit on an index card. The story serves as a conversation between the customer and the development team, not a

specification from the customer for the team. An example of a user story is "As the owner of the company, I want to be able to check the up-to-date inventory data so that I can better manage my business". Based on this user story, the development team may ask if the owner wants to see one inventory item at a time by searching or displaying all inventory at once. This starts the conversation and helps both customers and the team understand the requirements better. The size of a user story is measured by story points. Every user story has story points estimated by the development team to reflect how much effort is needed to complete the story.

3. Team Velocity: This is a way to measure how much work can be done in a certain amount of time by the team. This velocity is measured by the number of story points. For example, a team doesn't usually say how many stories they can complete in one iteration, but rather how many story points they can complete. It is done this way because not all user stories require the same amount of effort.

4. Pair Programming: This is used to help produce high quality software. In this technique, two team members take turns controlling the keyboard. While one member types, the other one watches and brainstorms. This technique works well when a programmer and a tester form a team. Code does not need to be completed then inspected. The code is checked as it is typed into the program.

Test Your Understanding 2.46
Frequent releases and very short development cycles describe which characteristic of extreme programming?
A. continuous integration
B. pair programming
C. user story
D. team velocity

Test Your Understanding 2.47
Which characteristic of extreme programming (XP) is kind of similar to a scrum sprint?
A. continuous integration
B. pair programming
C. user story
D. team velocity

Test Your Understanding 2.48
Which of the following is NOT a characteristic of extreme programming (XP)?
A. continuous integration
B. transparency
C. user story
D. team velocity

Test Your Understanding 2.49

Two team members working on the same task to increase product quality is which characteristic of extreme programming (XP)?
A. continuous integration
B. user story
C. team velocity
D. pair programming

2.6.3 Kanban

The Kanban methodology has three characteristics (Ashmore and Runyan, 2014).

1. Visualizing the workflow: A Kanban board is used to map the workflow in columns based on the status of a task. The task to be done is written on sticky notes and placed on a board. The board has columns that represent different stages of work, like ready, develop, test, and done. As work progresses, the sticky notes move across the board from one column to another.

2. Limits on works in progress (WIP): A Kanban team only works on a few tasks at a time. By doing this, they can focus on solving problems and completing tasks without getting overwhelmed. It's easy to see how many tasks are in each stage (a stage is a column on the Kanban board), so the team can identify any bottlenecks or problems and fix them quickly. For example, if too many bugs start to pile up, the whole team can stop working on new features and focus on fixing the bugs. This helps ensure that the work is of high quality.

3. Measure the lead time: The team tracks how long it takes to finish a task. By doing this, they can see how long it takes to complete a task from start to finish and work on ways to improve the process.

Test Your Understanding 2.50
Which of the following is NOT a characteristic of Kanban methodology?
A. continuous integration
B. visualizing the workflow
C. limiting works in progress
D. measuring the lead time

Test Your Understanding 2.51
In Kanban methodology, it is easy to identify the ______ because the number of tasks in progress is limited.
A. shortest
B. longest
C. bottleneck

D. winner task

2.7 Chapter Summary

In this chapter, you learned how to write C# statements by using variables and operators. You should follow rules for naming variables and select the appropriate data type for each variable. There are many more data types and operators used in C# that can be looked up online. You also learned the characteristics of agile and the success factors. You should know there is more than just one type of agile. In fact, there are many hybrid types, such as scrumban, which combines both scrum and Kanban.

2.8 References

Amir, M., Khan, K., Khan, A., and Khan, M. (2013), An Appraisal of Agile Software Development Process, International Journal of Advanced Science & Technology 58, pp. 57-86.
Ashmore, S. and Runyan, K. (2014), Introduction to Agile Methods 1st Edition, Boston, Addison-Wesley Professional.
Bennis, W. (1969). The Mature of Organizational Development. Reading, Mass,: Addison-Wesley.
CMMI Product Team, (2007), CMMI® for Acquisition, Version 1.2, Carnegie Mellon University, Software Engineering Institute, http://chrguibert.free.fr/cmmi12/cmmi-acq/text/index.php, Visited Nov. 18, 2016.
Crisan, E., Belieiu, I. and Ilies, . (2015), The Place of Agile in Management Science - A Literature Review, Managerial Challenges of the Contemporary Society, 8: 1, pp. 62-65.
Dhir, S., Kumar, D., & Singh, V. B. (2019). Success and failure factors that impact on project implementation using agile software development methodology. In Software Engineering (pp. 647-654). Springer, Singapore.
Ghani, I., Bello, M., and Bagiwa, I. (2015) Survey-based Analysis of Agile adoption on performance of IT organization, Journal of Korean Society for Internet Information, October, 16(5), 87-92.
Highsmith, J. (2002). Agile software development ecosystems. Boston: Addison Wesley.
Muldoon, N. (2014), Building an Ideal Agile Team Workspace, http://www.velocitycounts.com/2014/01/building-best-agile-team-workspace/, Visited November 18, 2016Nerur, S., Mahapatra, R. K., & Mangalaraj, G. (2005). Challenges of migrating to agile methodologies. Communications of the ACM, 48(5), 72-78.
Rigby, D. K., Sutherland, J., and Takeuchi, H. (2016), Embracing Agile, Harvard Business Review 94(5), 40-50.
Sammon, D, McAvoy, J, and Owens, I. (2009), Agile Teams: Reflective Debate and Shared Understanding, Proceedings of the European Conference on Information Management & Evaluation, p535-543.
Sutherland, Jeff. (1995) Business Object Design and Implementation. 10th Annual Conference on Object-Oriented Programming Systems, Languages, and Applications Addendum to the Proceedings. *OOPS Messenger 6:4*:170-175. ACM/SIGPLAN October.
Takeuchi, H.; Nonaka, I. (1986), The new new product development game, Harvard Business Review. Jan/Feb, Vol. 64 Issue 1, p137-146
Viscardi, S. (2013), The Professional ScrumMaster's Handbook: A Collection of Tips, Tricks, and War Stories to Help THE Professional ScrumMaster Break the Chains of Traditional Organizatin and

Management, Packt Publishing, Birmingham, U.K.

2.9 Solutions to Programming Challenges

Programming Challenge 2.1

```
// define slice size (each slice is 15 square inches)
const int SLICE_SIZE = 15;
// prompt user for the radius of the pizza
Console.WriteLine("Enter radius of the pizza (inches):");
// store the value in a variable
double radius = double.Parse(Console.ReadLine());
// compute the area of the pizza
double area = Math.PI * radius * radius;
// compute the number of slices
double numberOfSlice = area / SLICE_SIZE;
// display the result to the user
Console.WriteLine($"The pizza can be cut into {Math.Floor(numberOfSlice)} slices");
```

Programming Challenge 2.2

```
// set const values
const int DOZEN_COOKIES = 12;
const decimal DOZEN_COST = 1.2m;
const decimal SINGLE_COOKIE_COST = 0.12m;
// prompt user for number of cookies bought
Console.WriteLine("How many cookies do you buy?");
// store the value in a variable
int numberOfCookies = int.Parse(Console.ReadLine());
// divide the number by DOZEN_COOKIES to find how many dozens
int dozens = numberOfCookies / DOZEN_COOKIES;
// module to find the remainder
int dozenRemainder = numberOfCookies % DOZEN_COOKIES;
// calculate the cost, m converts a double value to a decimal value
decimal totalCost = dozens * DOZEN_COST + dozenRemainder * SINGLE_COOKIE_COST;
// display the total cost in currency format
Console.WriteLine($"The total cost for {numberOfCookies} cookies is {totalCost:C}");
```

2.10 Solutions to Test Your Understanding

2.1 A; 2.2 A; 2.3 A; 2.4 D; 2.5 A; 2.6 B; 2.7 C; 2.8 A; 2.9 D; 2.10 A; 2.11 C; 2.12 B; 2.13 D; 2.14 D; 2.15 C; 2.16 D; 2.17 D; 2.18 A; 2.19 D; 2.20 A; 2.21 B; 2.22 D; 2.23 A; 2.24 A; 2.25 C; 2.26 B; 2.27 A; 2.28 A; 2.29 B; 2.30 C; 2.31 C; 2.32 B; 2.33 A; 2.34 C; 2.35 D; 2.36 A; 2.37 D; 2.38 B; 2.39 C; 2.40 C; 2.41 A; 2.42 A; 2.43 A; 2.44 B; 2.45 D; 2.46 A; 2.47 A; 2.48 B; 2.49 D; 2.50 A; 2.51 C; .

Chapter 3: C# Flow Control and Agile Roles

Chapter Learning Outcomes

3.1 Recognize syntax for conditional statements
3.2 Recognize syntax for repeating statements
3.3 Recall types of roles in agile
3.4 Describe major responsibilities for each role in agile

3.1 Conditional Statements

Computers follow instructions. So far, you've seen the instructions are sequential; one statement is executed after the other in the order they are presented. This limits the use of the programs, since they cannot change the execution sequence. The real world often requires different statements to be executed when certain conditions are true. For example, an online store may waive the shipping and handling fees if an order is $25 or more. In other words, the calculation for an order costs $30 is different from that for an order costs $24.

3.1.1 If Statements

C# has conditional statements, including an 'if' statement. If a condition is true, a block of statements will be executed. If not, a different block of statements will be executed. The if statement allows you to check more than one condition with "else if" statements.

Example 3.1

Problem:

Write an application that asks the user for a numeric score of a student's test. If the score is 90 or higher, display the message "Congratulations". Otherwise, display "Thank you for using the system."

Solution:

Start a console app in Visual Studio called Chapter3Example1. With the default Program.cs open in the code view, replace the default code with the following:

```
// prompt user for a score
Console.WriteLine("Enter a student score:");
// store the score in a variable
double score = double.Parse(Console.ReadLine());
```

```
// check to see if the score is 90 or higher
if (score >= 90)
{
    Console.WriteLine("Congratulations!");
}
else
{
    Console.WriteLine("Thanks for using the system.");
}
```

Output:

Click the green start button to run it. Type in a number less than 90 and press the enter to see "Thanks for using the system" on the console screen. Push enter to end the program.

```
Enter a student score:
89
Thanks for using the system.
```

Click the green start button again. This time, type in a number greater than or equal to 90 and push enter to see "Congratulations!" on the console screen. Push enter to end the program.

```
Enter a student score:
90
Congratulations!
```

Explanation:

An if statement includes a condition `(score >= 90)`. If the condition is evaluated to be true, the statements inside the braces block (only `Console.WriteLine("Congratulations!");` in this case) are executed. Otherwise, the statements inside the else block will be executed (in this case, `Console.WriteLine("Thanks for using the system.");`). The 'else' part of an if statement is optional.

You can also add an "else if" statement to the if statement. For example, if you wanted to display "Good job!" for students who scored between 80 and 90, you can add the following instructions right before the "else" line:

```
else if (score >= 80)
{
    Console.WriteLine("Good job!");
}
```

An if statement usually includes all statements you want to execute under certain conditions in a pair of braces as shown above code. However, some people prefer no braces when there is only one line of statement in the block. You are encouraged to use braces so that the code is more readable.

A comparison operator, such as < (less than), <= (less than or equal to), > (more than), >= (more than or equal to), == (equal to), !=(not equal), is often used to compare two values and evaluate to a true or false value.

Example 3.2

Problem:

An online store sells books only. Each book costs $3.25. Shipping and handling fees are $5.00. Shipping and handling fees are waived for orders with total cost (before tax or any fees) of $30 or more. Write a program to prompt the user for number of books in the shopping cart. Then, display the total cost (book cost plus shipping and handling fees) assuming no sales tax.

Solution:

Start a console app in Visual Studio called Chapter3Example2. With the default Program.cs open in the code view, replace the default code with the following:

```
// Define constant
const double BOOK_COST = 3.25;
const double SHIPPING_COST = 5.00;
const double SHIPPING_THRESHOLD = 30.00;
// Prompt the user to enter the number of books in the shopping cart
Console.Write("Enter the number of books in your shopping cart: ");
// Store the user number in a variable called numBooks
int numBooks = int.Parse(Console.ReadLine());
// Calculate the bookTotal before shipping and handling fees
double bookTotal = numBooks * BOOK_COST;
// Declare a variable to store shipping total
double shippingTotal = 0.0;
// Determine the shipping total
if (bookTotal < SHIPPING_THRESHOLD)
{
    shippingTotal = SHIPPING_COST;
}
// Calculate the grand total
double grandTotal = bookTotal + shippingTotal;
// Display the grand total with currency format
Console.WriteLine($"Total cost:{grandTotal:C}");
```

Output 1:

```
Enter the number of books in your shopping cart: 9
Total cost:$34.25
```

Output 2:

```
Enter the number of books in your shopping cart: 10
Total cost:$32.50
```

Explanation:

In this solution, we first define some constants to represent the cost of a single book, the shipping cost, and the shipping threshold (the total cost at which shipping is waived). We then prompt the user to enter the number of books in their shopping cart, and calculate the total cost of the books and the total cost of shipping.

If the total cost of the books is less than the shipping threshold, we add the shipping cost to the total. Finally, we calculate the grand total (the cost of the books plus the cost of shipping), and display it to the user with two decimal places using string formatting (currency format).

The Write() method is different from the WriteLine() method. The former does not include a line break so that all values are displayed in a row.

Test Your Understanding 3.1
C# allows your program to execute a block of statements only when certain ______ are true.
A. numbers
B. conditions
C. WriteLines
D. Consoles

Test Your Understanding 3.2
When a condition is true, an if statement can execute a block of statements inside a pair of ______. If there is only one statement in the block, the pair of ______.
A. parentheses, parentheses is optional
B. parentheses, parentheses is still required
C. curly braces, curly braces is optional
D. curly braces, curly braces is still required

Test Your Understanding 3.3
When executing the following if statement:

```
if(score >= 90)
{
    Console.Write("Congratulations!");
}
if (score >= 80)
{
       Console.Write(“Good job!”);
}
else
{
    Console.WriteLine("Thanks for using the system.");
}
```

For a score of 95, what is on the console screen?
A. Congratulations!
B. Good job!
C. Congratulations!Good job!
D. Thanks for using the system.

Test Your Understanding 3.4
When executing the following if statement:

```
if(score >= 90)
{
    Console.Write("Congratulations!");
}
else if (score >= 80)
{
        Console.Write("Good job!");
}
else
{
    Console.Write("Thanks for using the system.");
}
```

For a score of 95, what is on the console screen?
A. Congratulations!
B. Good job!
C. Congratulations!
   Good job!
D. Thanks for using the system.

Test Your Understanding 3.5
When executing the following if statement:

```
if(score >= 90)
{
    Console.Write("Congratulations!");
}
    Console.Write("Thanks for using the system.");
```

For a score of 95, what is on the console screen?
A. Congratulations!
B. Thanks for using the system.
C. Compiler-time error. The last line must be inside an else statement.
D. Congratulations!Thanks for using the system.

Programming Challenge 3.1
Write an application that prompts the user to enter two integers. Then displays a menu like this:
Enter 1, 2, or 3
1. Addition
2. Multiplication
3. Exit

After the user enters the selection (1, 2, or 3), the application will display the result based on user inputs and the menu selection. Here are two sample outputs:

```
Enter the first integer: 2
Enter the second integer: 3

Enter 1, 2, or 3
1. Addition
2. Multiplication
3. Exit
Your choice: 1
2 + 3 = 5
```

```
Enter the first integer: 2
Enter the second integer: 3

Enter 1, 2, or 3
1. Addition
2. Multiplication
3. Exit
Your choice: 2
2 * 3 = 6
```

Programming Challenge 3.2
An online store sells cookies only. Each cookie costs 75 cents. Shipping and handling fees are $7.00. Shipping and handling fees are waived for orders with total cost (before tax or any fees) of $25 or more. Write a program to prompt the user for number of cookies in the shopping cart. Then, display the total cost (cookie cost plus shipping and handling fees) assuming no sales tax. Here are two sample outputs:

```
Enter the number of
cookies: 33

Cookie cost: $24.75
Shipping: $7.00
Total cost: $31.75
```

```
Enter the number of
cookies: 34

Cookie cost: $25.50
Shipping: $0.00
Total cost: $25.50
```

3.1.2 Switch Statements

The switch statement is similar to the if statement in that it executes a block of code based on certain conditions. However, there are two major differences: 1) switch can test for multiple values of a test variable in one go, and thus executes faster than an if statement. For example, if you want to display the month in letters when given a number (ex. - February in response to '2'), a switch statement is faster than an if statement. 2) a switch statement is often more readable for more complex comparisons.

Example 3.3

Problem:

Write an application that prompts the user for an integer between 1 and 12. The application will display the corresponding name of the month in letters.

Solution:

Start a console app in Visual Studio called Chapter3Example3. With the default Program.cs open in the code view, replace the default lines with the following:

```
// prompt user for an integer between 1 and 12
Console.WriteLine("Enter a whole number between 1 and 12:");
// store the number
int numericMonth = int.Parse(Console.ReadLine());
// declare a variable to store month in word
string monthInWord;
switch (numericMonth)
{
    case 1:
        monthInWord = "January";
        break;
    case 2:
        monthInWord = "February";
        break;
    case 3:
        monthInWord = "March";
        break;
    case 4:
        monthInWord = "April";
        break;
    case 5:
        monthInWord = "May";
        break;
    case 6:
        monthInWord = "June";
        break;
    case 7:
        monthInWord = "July";
        break;
    case 8:
        monthInWord = "August";
        break;
    case 9:
        monthInWord = "September";
        break;
    case 10:
        monthInWord = "October";
        break;
    case 11:
        monthInWord = "November";
        break;
    case 12:
        monthInWord = "December";
        break;
    default:
        monthInWord = "That is not a whole number between 1 and 12";
        break;
}
Console.WriteLine(monthInWord);
```

Explanation:

A switch statement begins with a match expression (numericMonth in the example), followed by a series of case keywords. The case line indicates the match pattern, which can be a constant pattern (as in the example) or a relational pattern. If a match is found, the block of statements is executed. If no match is found, the execution will go to the "default" block. Remember to include the "break" keyword that indicates the end of a block. If you skip a "break", there will be a compiler error. However, you may combine multiple case pattern into one, like this:

```
case 10:
case 11:
case 12:
    monthInWord = "October/November/December";
    break;
```

Example 3.4

Problem:

An online store sells books only. Each book costs $3.25. Shipping and handling fees are based on the shipping options. Available shipping options re: 1) same day; 2) overnight; 3) 2-4 days; and 4) 5-7 days.

Options	Same day	Overnight	2-4 days	5-7 days
Fees	$10.00	$8.00	$5.00	$3.00

Write a program to prompt the user for the number of books in the shopping cart. Then, display the total cost (book cost plus shipping and handling fees) assuming no sales tax.

Solution:

Start a console app in Visual Studio called Chapter3Example4. With the default Program.cs open in the code view, replace the default lines with the following:

```
const double BOOK_PRICE = 3.25;
double shippingFee = 0.0;

Console.Write("Enter the number of books in your shopping cart: ");
int numOfBooks = int.Parse(Console.ReadLine());

Console.WriteLine("Choose a shipping option:");
Console.WriteLine("1 - Same day ($10.00)");
Console.WriteLine("2 - Overnight ($8.00)");
Console.WriteLine("3 - 2-4 days ($5.00)");
Console.WriteLine("4 - 5-7 days ($3.00)");

Console.Write("Enter an option number: ");
int optionNum = int.Parse(Console.ReadLine());

switch (optionNum)
{
    case 1:
        shippingFee = 10.00;
        break;
    case 2:
        shippingFee = 8.00;
        break;
    case 3:
        shippingFee = 5.00;
        break;
    case 4:
```

```
        shippingFee = 3.00;
        break;
    default:
        Console.WriteLine("Invalid option number!");
        break;
}

double totalCost = BOOK_PRICE * numOfBooks + shippingFee;
Console.WriteLine($"Total cost: {totalCost:C}");
```

Explanation:

The constant variable BOOK_PRICE is set to 3.25, the price of each book.
The variable shippingFee is initialized to 0.0 to make sure it will not be null.
The user is prompted to enter the number of books in their shopping cart using Console.ReadLine().
The available shipping options and their fees are displayed using Console.WriteLine().
The user is prompted to enter an option number using Console.ReadLine().
The switch statement determines the shipping fee based on the option number entered by the user.
The total cost is calculated by multiplying the number of books by the book price and adding the shipping fee.
The total cost is displayed using Console.WriteLine(). The :C format specifier is used to display the cost with currency format.

Test Your Understanding 3.6
A switch statement begins with a ______, followed by a series of ______ keywords.
A. match expression, switch
B. match expression, case
C. int value, switch
D. int value, case

Test Your Understanding 3.7
The if statement and switch statement are similar. Which of the following is a factor when you prefer to use a switch statement?
A. Performance and security
B. Performance and readability
C. Conciseness and security
D. Conciseness and readability

Test Your Understanding 3.8
What will be displayed on console screen after the following code?

```
int numericMonth = 3;
string monthInWord;
switch (numericMonth)
{
    case 1:
        monthInWord = "January";
        break;
    case 2:
        monthInWord = "February";
        break;
```

```
    default:
        monthInWord = "That is unexpected";
        break;
}
Console.WriteLine(monthInWord);
```

A. January
B. February
C. That is unexpected
D. A compiler-time error

Test Your Understanding 3.9
What will be displayed on console screen after the following code?

```
int numericMonth = 1;
string monthInWord;
switch (numericMonth)
{
    case 1:
        monthInWord = "January";
    case 2:
        monthInWord = "February";
        break;
    default:
        monthInWord = "That is unexpected";
        break;
}
Console.WriteLine(monthInWord);
```

A. January
B. February
C. That is unexpected
D. A compiler-time error

Test Your Understanding 3.10
What will be displayed on console screen after the following code?

```
int numericMonth = 1;
string monthInWord;
switch (numericMonth)
{
    case 1:
    case 2:
        monthInWord = "February";
        break;
    default:
        monthInWord = "That is unexpected";
        break;
}
Console.WriteLine(monthInWord);
```

A. January
B. February
C. That is unexpected

D. A compiler-time error

Programming Challenge 3.3
Write an application to prompt the user to enter an integer between 1 and 7, and have the application display the English word for that number. For example, if the user enters 5, the application will display 'five'.

Programming Challenge 3.4
An online store sells cookies only. Each cookie costs 75 cents. Shipping and handling fees are based on the shipping options. Available shipping options are: 1) same day; 2) overnight; 3) 2-4 days; and 4) 5-7 days.

Options	Same day	Overnight	2-4 days	5-7 days
Fees	$10.00	$8.00	$5.00	$3.00

Write a program to prompt the user for the number of cookies in the shopping cart. Then display the total cost (cookie cost plus shipping and handling) assuming no sales tax.

3.2 Repeating Statements

In the last chapter, you learned how to tell computers what to do in sequential order. In the last section, you learned how to tell computers to execute only certain instructions when a condition is true. With conditional statements, you can branch the route of execution in more than one way. In many situations, sequential and conditional statements may not be enough. In Example 3.1, you might have noticed that it is inconvenient to run the program only once. How about modifying the code so that the program can run until the user wants to quit?

3.2.1 The 'while' Loop

A while loop will check a condition. If the condition is true, it will execute the statements in the block. If the condition is false, it will quit the loop. This is similar to the if statement. The difference is that an if statement only checks the condition once and executes the statement block once. The while loop will check the condition repeatedly and thus may execute the block of statements multiple times until the condition is false. It is very important that you are able to change the condition inside the execution block. Otherwise, the loop may go on infinitely.

Example 3.5

Problem:

Modify Example 3.1 so that it will prompt the user for a score and display the message based on the score. The application can repeat the prompt and display the message until the user enters a negative score.

Solution:

Start a console app in Visual Studio called Chapter3Example5. With the default Program.cs open in the code view, replace the default code with the following:

```
// prompt user for a score
Console.WriteLine("Enter a student score (-1 to terminate):");
// store the score in a variable
double score = double.Parse(Console.ReadLine());
// start a loop
while (score >= 0)
{
    // check to see if the score is 90 or higher
    if (score >= 90)
    {
        Console.WriteLine("Congratulations!");
    }
    else
    {
        Console.WriteLine("Thanks for using the system.");
    }
    // prompt user for another score
    Console.WriteLine("Enter a student score (-1 to terminate):");
    // store the score in the same variable, replacing the old one value
    score = double.Parse(Console.ReadLine());
}
```

Execute the code. Type in a score less than 90 and see the message "Thanks for using the system." on the console screen. Next, type in a score greater than 90 and see the message "Congratulations!" on the console screen. You can repeat this as many times as you want. To end the program, enter any negative number. Press enter to end the program.

Explanation:

The `while` keyword starts a while loop, which repeatedly executes a block of code as long as a specified Boolean condition remains true. The structure is similar to an `if` statement in that it evaluates a condition -- but unlike an `if`, the `while` loop continues to re-evaluate the condition after each iteration.

Here's how it works:

1. The condition following the `while` keyword is evaluated.
2. If the condition is `true`, the statements inside the curly braces `{ }` are executed.
3. After the last statement in the block runs, control returns to the top of the loop, and the condition is checked again.
4. If the condition is `false`, the loop exits, and execution continues with the next statement after the closing brace.

Be careful to ensure that something inside the loop eventually changes the condition so it can become `false`. If you accidentally comment out (using `//`) the lines that read new input, the condition will never change. As a result, the loop will run forever (infinite loop) and print "Congratulations!" endlessly.

To prevent this, always include logic within the loop body that can modify the variables used in the loop condition. In the example, allowing the user to enter a new value (such as a negative number) ensures the loop can eventually terminate.

Test Your Understanding 3.11
C# allows your program to ______ running a block of statements as long as certain conditions are true by using _____ loop.
A. selective, while
B. selective, if
C. repeat, while
D. repeat, if

Test Your Understanding 3.12
When programming, you ______ statements inside a loop that can change the ______ of the loop.
A. avoid writing, switches
B. avoid writing, conditions
C. usually write, switches
D. usually write, conditions

Programming Challenge 3.5
Update Programming Challenge 3.1 so that a user can repeat the practice until exit.

3.2.2 The 'for' Loop

Before learning the 'for' loop, you need to know a type of variable called 'array' that often works with loops. In the last chapter, you learned how to use variables to hold values for calculation or display. One variable can hold only one value at a time. This can be inconvenient. For example, if a class had 10 students, and you wanted to order the scores from high to low, you would need to declare 10 variables, one for each student. An array could make this process much more efficient.

An array is a variable that can hold many values of the same type. Each is differentiated by its index. Let's see an example that uses an array.

Example 3.6

Problem:

A class has 5 students. The school needs an application that can ask the user to enter each student's numeric score for a test, and then display the average, highest score, lowest score, and all five scores from high to low in a row.

Solution:

Start a console app in Visual Studio called Chapter3Example6. With the default Program.cs open in the code view, replace the default code with the following:

```
int[] scores = new int[5];

for (int i = 0; i < scores.Length; i++)
{
    Console.WriteLine("Enter a score:");
    scores[i] = int.Parse(Console.ReadLine());
}

Console.WriteLine($"Average: {scores.Average():N2}");
Console.WriteLine($"Highest: {scores.Max()}");
Console.WriteLine($"Lowest: {scores.Min()}");

foreach (int s in scores.OrderByDescending(x => x))
{
    Console.Write(s + " ");
}
```

Execute the program. Type in 5 whole numbers, each between 0 and 100. Press the enter after each number. After all 5 scores are entered, you should see the statistics on the console screen. Press enter to end the program.

Explanation:

The first line declares an array that can hold 5 int values. Note the difference between declare and initialize a simple type variable and an array:

```
int score = 90;
int[] scores = new int[5];
```

The array variable *scores* holds 5 integers, which are all 0s by default. The "new" keyword indicates that this is a reference type. The reference type means that the actual 5 integers are not stored in the array variable 'scores'. Only the memory address of the 5 integers are stored in the variable 'scores'. You will learn more about reference type in Chapter 5 when you learn classes and object-oriented programming. If you want to initialize an array other than the default values, you can do it like this:

```
int[] scores = new int[4]{3, 5, 8, 10};
```

The number "4" in the square bracket is optional.

To access a value in an array, use the index. For example, you can print the first value in the above array (which is 3) to the console screen:

```
Console.WriteLine(scores[0]);
```

Note the array index starts counting from zero, not one.

Similarly, if you want to change the value of the second score in the array, use the following statement:

```
scores[1] = 12;
```

This will change the second value from 5 to 12.

Be very careful of the index value, since they start counting from zero. In the above example, if you use scores[4], you will receive an array out of bound error because there is no element with the index of 4.

A 'for' loop starts with the 'for' keyword. It repeats the statements inside the pair of curly braces. An int variable "i" is used to control the number of repetitions. Here are the steps for the loop:

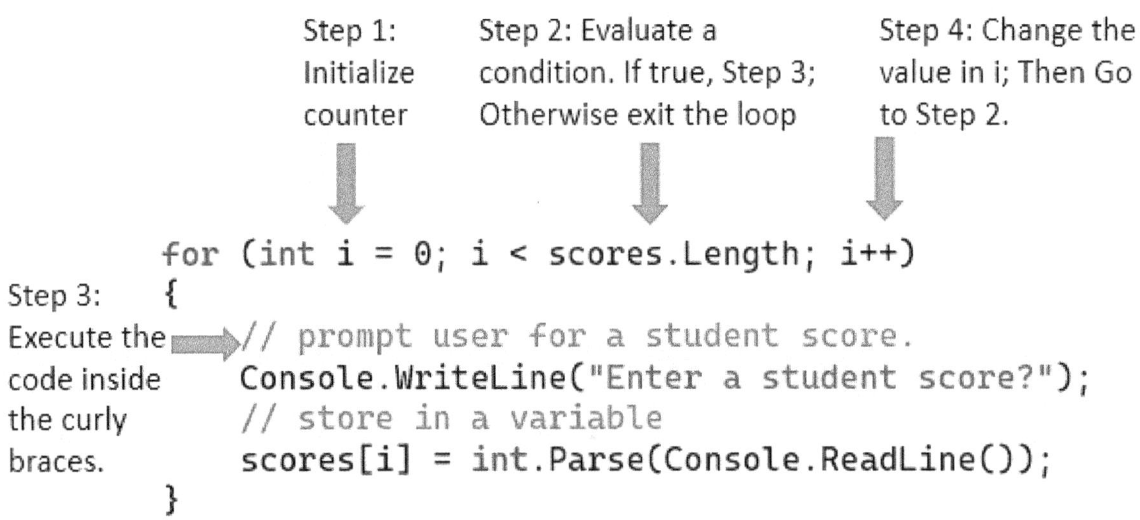

Step 1. i = 0

Step 2. Check to see if this is true: i < scores.Length; if true, continue to Step 3. If false, exit the loop. The Length property of an array holds the number of elements in the array.

Step 3. Execute the statements in the block enclosed with braces.

Step 4. The i++ statement increases the value in i by 1.

Step 5. Go back to Step 2 above.

This process will continue until the condition in Step 2 is no longer true.

The program utilizes the built-in methods of arrays (Average(), Max(), Min()) to print the statistics.

The program applies the foreach loop. It is sometimes called shorthand for loop. The foreach loop gives out one element at a time from an array without using additional code to arrange the index. An array has a built-in OrderByDescending() method which requires a lambda expression (x=>x) as input. We will discuss more about lambda expression later in this book and our advanced agile book. The code also adds a blank space after each value.

Test Your Understanding 3.13
Which of the following statements is true?
Statement1: When you know how many repeating loops you need in the code, the 'for' loop is a good choice.
Statement2: When you don't know how many repeating loops you need in the code, the 'while' loop is a good choice.
A. Only Statement1 is true.
B. Only Statement2 is true.
C. Both Statement1 and Statement2 are true.
D. Neither Statement1 nor Statement2 is true.

Test Your Understanding 3.14
A(n) ______ is a variable that can hold many values of the same type. Each is differentiated by its index.
A. super variable
B. multi-value variable
C. global variable
D. array

Test Your Understanding 3.15
What can be stored in the following variable "scores"?
int[] scores;
A. the memory address of an int array.
B. the memory address of an array.
C. a group of 5 int values.
D. an int array.

Test Your Understanding 3.16
What does a reference type of variable do?
A. hold an integer value only
B. hold a floating-point value only
C. hold a string value only
D. hold memory address only

Test Your Understanding 3.17

Given the following statement about a C# array:
int[] scores = new int[4]{3, 5, 8, 10};
What will be printed on the console screen with the following statement?
Console.WriteLine(scores[3]);
A. 3
B. 5
C. 8
D. 10

Test Your Understanding 3.18
Given the following statement about a C# array:
int[] scores = new int[4]{3, 5, 8, 10};
What will be printed on the console screen with the following statement?
Console.WriteLine(scores[4]);
A. 3
B. 4
C. 5
D. Out of bound error.

Programming Challenge 3.6
Write an application that can ask the user for the inches of rainfall for each month in a year. Then the application will display the average, highest, and lowest inches of rainfall for the year. It should also display all 12 rainfall from high to low in a row.
If you want to display the name of the month, use the following (assuming "i" is the counter variable):
CultureInfo.CurrentCulture.DateTimeFormat.GetMonthName(i+1)

Example 3.7

Problem:

A class has 6 students. The school needs an application that can ask the user to enter each student's numeric test score and then display the number of As (score between 90 and 100 inclusive), number of Bs (score between 80 and 89), number of Cs (score between 70 and 79), number of Ds (score between 60 and 69), and number of Fs (score under 60). The app then displays the average, highest, and lowest numeric scores. It should also display all numeric scores from low to high in a row.

Solution:

Start a console app project in Visual Studio called Chapter3Example7. With the default Program.cs open in the code view window, replace the default code with the following:

```
// create an int array that can hold 6 student scores
int[] scores = new int[6];
// using a loop to prompt user for scores, one at a time
for (int count = 0; count < scores.Length; count++)
{
    Console.WriteLine("Enter a score:");
```

```
    scores[count] = int.Parse(Console.ReadLine()!);
}
// variables to hold number of As, Bs, Cs, Ds, and Fs
int numberOfA = 0;
int numberOfB = 0;
int numberOfC = 0;
int numberOfD = 0;
int numberOfF = 0;
// using a loop to check each score to find letter grade
for (int count = 0; count < scores.Length; count++)
{
    if (scores[count] >= 90)
        numberOfA++;
    else if (scores[count] >= 80)
        numberOfB++;
    else if (scores[count] >= 70)
        numberOfC++;
    else if (scores[count] >= 60)
        numberOfD++;
    else
        numberOfF++;
}
// Display the result
Console.WriteLine($"Number of As: {numberOfA}");
Console.WriteLine($"Number of Bs: {numberOfB}");
Console.WriteLine($"Number of Cs: {numberOfC}");
Console.WriteLine($"Number of Ds: {numberOfD}");
Console.WriteLine($"Number of Fs: {numberOfF}");
Console.WriteLine($"Average: {scores.Average():N2}");
Console.WriteLine($"Highest: {scores.Max()}");
Console.WriteLine($"Lowest: {scores.Min()}");
// display all scores from low to high in a row
foreach (int s in scores.OrderBy(x => x))
{
    Console.Write(s + " ");
}
```

Programming Challenge 3.7

Body Mass Index (BMI) is used to determine weight status.

BMI value	Weight Status
Below 18.5 (<18.5)	Underweight
Between 18.5 and 25 (>=18.5 and < 25)	Normal Weight
Between 25 and 30 (>=25 and < 30)	Overweight
30 or more (>=30)	Obese

A class has 6 students. The school needs an application that can let the user enter each student's BMI and display the number of students in each weight status, class average BMI value, highest, and lowest BMIs. The app should also display all BMIs from low to high in a row.

3.3 Logical Operators

Logical operators evaluate two Boolean expressions (except for the NOT operator) and return with true or false. In this section, you will learn these operators: AND, OR, and NOT.

The AND operator, represented by &&, only returns true when both operands are true. The OR operator, represented by | |, returns true when at least one of the operands is true. Unlike the AND and OR operators, which work on two operands, the NOT operator has a single operand. The NOT operator, represented by !, returns true when the operand is false and returns false when the operand is true.

Example 3.8

Problem:

Modify Example 3.5 so that it will prompt the user for a score and display the message based on the score. The application can repeat the prompt and display the message until the user enters a negative score or a score above 100. The difference from Example 3.5 is that, in this problem, the message is only displayed when the score is in the range of 0 to 100.

Solution:

Open Chapter3Example5 in Visual Studio. Change the below line:

```
while(score >= 0)
```

to

```
while(score >= 0 && score <= 100 )
```

&& is a logical AND operator, which requires both the (score >= 0) and (score <= 100) operands to be true to execute the statements in the block.

Test Your Understanding 3.19
Which of the following statements about logical operators is correct?
Statement1: Logical operators such as &&, | |, and ! can only be used in the conditional expression in the repeating statement, such as 'while'.
Statement2: Logical operators allow the application to handle more complex conditional statements.
A. Statement1 only.
B. Statement2 only
C. Both Statement1 and Statement2
D. Neither Statement1 nor Statement2

Test Your Understanding 3.20
What is the value of the following logical expression?
(5>3) && (3>5)
A. True
B. False
C. 2
D. -2

Test Your Understanding 3.21
What is the value of the following logical expression?
(5>3) || (3>5)
A. True
B. False
C. 2
D. -2

Test Your Understanding 3.22
What is the value of the following logical expression? !(5>3)
A. True.
B. False.
C. 2
D. -2

Test Your Understanding 3.23
What is the correct way to test if x is 3 or 4?
A. x = 3 || 4
B. x == 3 || 4
C. x = 3 || x = 4
D. x == 3 || x == 4

Programming Challenge 3.8
Write an application that can display a horizontal bar chart.
The application should prompt the user to enter a whole number between 1 and 50. Then the application will display that number of asterisks on the console screen. For example, if the user enters 9, it will display *********.
The application should continue to prompt the user for a whole number and display that number of asterisks, only terminating when a zero, negative number, or a number larger than 50 is entered.
Hint: If you want seven asterisks, just repeat the following line 7 times, Console.Write("*");

Programing Challenge 3.9
Write an application that will display whole numbers from 1 to 30 consecutively in 30 lines. If a number is divisible by 2, display "TT" instead of the number. If a number is divisible by 3, display "TTT" instead of the number. If a number is divisible by both 2 and 3, display "TTTTTT" instead of the number. The first 11 lines will look like this:
1
TT
TTT
TT
5
TTTTTT
7
TT
TTT
TT
11

Programming Challenge 3.10
Smith's Fast Food sells burgers, fries, and drinks only. The price of a burger is $1.50. The price of a serving of French fries is $1.20. A cup of drink is $1.00. A combo (one item of each) will receive a $.70 discount. There is a limit of one discount per order. Write a program that asks the user for the number of items for each food, then displays the total cost, discount if any, and total cost after discount (Assuming no sales tax.). Remember to use const for the unit price of each food.
Hint: the discount limit makes the coding easier. Customers receive a $.70 discount as long as they have at least one burger, one serving of fries, and one cup of drink.
Here is a sample output with no discount:

```
How many burgers would you like?
0
How many servings of fries would you like?
1
How many cups of drink would you like?
2
The total cost: #3.20
```

Here is a sample output with one combo discount:

```
How many burgers would you like?
1
How many servings of fries would you like?
1
How many cups of drink would you like?
2
The total cost: #4.70
Discount: $0.70
Total cost after discount: $4.00
```

Here is a sample output with the limit of one combo discount:

```
How many burgers would you like?
2
How many servings of fries would you like?
2
How many cups of drink would you like?
2
The total cost: #7.40
Discount: $0.70
Total cost after discount: $6.70
```

3.4 Agile Roles

You learned in Chapter One that the Agile Manifesto values individuals and interaction more than the process and tools. You also learned that agile blurs the lines between different roles in the traditional development team (ex. - programmers can also be involved in design, analysis, and testing). However, agile does have three distinct roles. This section will describe these three roles: product owner, scrum master, and team members.

Test Your Understanding 3.24
Which of the following does agile value more in the Agile Manifesto?
A. Individuals
B. Interaction
C. Individuals and interaction
D. Process and tools

Test Your Understanding 3.25
Agile blurs the lines between different ______ in the traditional development team.
A. tasks
B. roles
C. processes
D. project

Test Your Understanding 3.26
Which of the following is NOT an agile role?
A. Product Owner
B. Scrum Master
C. Team Members
D. Designer

3.4.1 Product Owner

As you learned in Chapter One, one major issue of the Waterfall approach was the lack of user involvement. The product owner fills part of this gap. A product owner is typically a business manager who works on the development team. The product owner may not know much about programming or testing, but they play the critical role of gathering business requirements for the development team.

The product owner owns the software and can represent the customers who are paying for the project. The product owner must work with the scrum team on a daily basis. When a team member has a question about the requirements, they can just ask the product owner without having to leave the room. This enhances communication between the developer and the business.

The product owner's primary responsibilities include writing user stories (discussed in Chapter 5) in collaboration with the Scrum Master (discussed later in this chapter) and prioritizing those stories with other business managers based on the business value they deliver (Gottesdiener & Gorman, 2013). They also work closely with the development team to ensure requirements are clear, concise, and well understood (Larman & Vodde, 2010).

Additionally, the product owner is also responsible for communicating with stakeholders, including customers, users, and management. They ensure that stakeholders have a clear understanding of the product vision and the progress of the development team (Larman & Vodde, 2010).

Product owners are responsible for making decisions about the product. They must be able to make decisions quickly and effectively to ensure that the development team can move forward with the project (Cohn, 2009).

Product owners are responsible for accepting or rejecting work done by the development team. They ensure that the work meets the requirements and is of high quality (Schwaber, 2011).

Product owners are responsible for managing the product backlog. They ensure that the backlog is up-to-date and that the development team has a clear understanding of what needs to be done next (Cohn, 2009).

Product owners are responsible for providing feedback to the development team. They must be able to provide constructive feedback that helps the team to improve the product (Schwaber, 2011).

It is important to note that the product owner is not just a business user. The product owner is the champion or sponsor of the project and has the authority to make decisions for the project, particularly decisions regarding whether a feature is done and can be released (Pichler, 2010).

The product owner is usually a single person, not a committee, so the time it takes to reach an agreement is reduced. They play a critical role in the success of the project. They direct the product vision and goals and decide what the business values are. There are six characteristics of a good product owner (Pham and Pham. 2012; the authors listed seven, but we think the last characteristic belongs to the scrum master):

1. Deep knowledge of the product being developed.
2. Good at meeting stakeholder's expectations, even with conflicting priorities.
3. Able to gather requirements that achieve the product vision and goals.
4. Be fully available to actively engage with the team at all times.
5. A good organizer who can handle issues on both business and technological sides.
6. A good communicator who can express the requirements from the business to the development team effectively and send frequent feedback to the development team.

Test Your Understanding 3.27

What is the primary job of a product owner in Agile software development?
A. Communicating with stakeholders
B. Writing up and prioritizing the requirements
C. Making decisions about the product
D. Managing the product backlog

Test Your Understanding 3.28
Who are the stakeholders that the product owner communicates with?
A. Development team
B. Management
C. Development team and management
D. Project managers

Test Your Understanding 3.29
Which of the following is NOT a responsibility of a product owner?
A. Making quick and effective decisions
B. Providing requirements for the development team
C. Evaluating the work of the team
D. Providing feedback to the development team

Test Your Understanding 3.30
Which of the following is NOT a responsibility of a product owner in providing requirements to the development team?
A. Ensuring that the team has a clear understanding of the requirements
B. Writing up the requirements alone
C. Prioritizing the requirements based on business values
D. Ensure that the work meets the requirements

Test Your Understanding 3.31
Which of the following statements about the responsibility of a product owner regarding the work done by the development team is correct?
Statement 1: Accepting or rejecting work done by the team.
Statement 2: Providing constructive feedback to the team.
A. Statement 1 only
B. Statement 2 only
C. Both Statement 1 and Statement 2
D. Neither Statement 1 nor Statement 2

Test Your Understanding 3.32
Which of the following is NOT a responsibility of a product owner in managing the product backlog?
A. Ensuring the development team has a clear understanding of what needs to be done next
B. Prioritizing the requirements based on business values
C. Updating the backlog
D. Estimating story points

Test Your Understanding 3.33
According to the text, how many product owners are in a typical agile team?
A. 1
B. 2
C. 3

D. 1 or 2

Test Your Understanding 3.34
Which of the following statements about the product owner is correct?
Statement1: The product owner must be a good programmer.
Statement2: The product owner is critical to the success of the development team, but does not write a single line of code.
A. Statement1 only.
B. Statement2 only.
C. Both Statement1 and Statement2.
D. Neither Statement1 nor Statement2.

Test Your Understanding 3.35
Which of the following is a characteristic of a good product owner?
A. Leadership skills
B. A skilled programmer
C. Deep knowledge of the product being developed
D. Be available to actively engage with the team at least once a day

Test Your Understanding 3.36
Which of the following is a characteristic of a good product owner?
A. Good project manager
B. Deep knowledge of programming language being used
C. Good organizer who can handle business issues
D. Good communicator between the business and the team

3.4.2 Scrum Master

The scrum master has two major responsibilities. One is to ensure team productivity and the other is to monitor project progress by facilitating all scrum meetings and communicating between the team and the business (Resnick et al., 2011, Viscardi, 2013).

To ensure team productivity, the scrum master works as a facilitator and motivator of the development team (Jongerius, et al., 2014). They ensure that the team functions as smoothly as possible, whether that is making sure meetings are on time, or that a sick team member is accounted for. Scrum masters should try their best to keep team morale high and remove any obstacles. If the music from next door is too loud, or too many external meetings are requested from the company, the scrum master will be responsible for talking to the people next door, or communicating with the company manager. Because the scrum master manages the team by servicing them, they are often referred to as the “servant leader” (Liden et al., 2014).

To oversee the progress of the project, the scrum master is responsible for coordinating all meetings, including the daily scrum meetings, which serve to identify any problems and make necessary adjustments to overcome them. The scrum master ensures that every team member understands the project's objectives, stays informed about the project's status, and works collaboratively to achieve the goals. Moreover, the scrum master may determine the size of the team, preferring fewer members if they deem that additional members would not enhance productivity.

The scrum master also acts as a liaison between the team and the clients. Even though the product owner can communicate directly with the development team, the scrum master is usually the first to learn of any major changes from the business side (ex. - major feature changes, budget cuts).

The scrum master also educates and coaches the team on agile (Measey and Radtac, 2015). This includes visualizing team goals and championing the implementation of new technical practices. The team buy-in to the agile approach is critical to success.

Finally, the scrum master makes sure that the team follows agile principles effectively (Cooke, 2010). This includes, but is not limited to, accounting for meeting attendance and ensuring that only the high priority items from the product backlog are selected for the sprint backlog.

Test Your Understanding 3.37
The scrum master is like a project ______ for the team.
A. leader
B. manager
C. facilitator
D. partner

Test Your Understanding 3.38
Servant leader is a term used to describe the ______.
A. product owner
B. scrum master
C. team members
D. none of the choices

Test Your Understanding 3.39
What are the two major responsibilities of a scrum master?
A. to ensure team productivity and manage the project
B. to ensure team productivity and monitor project progress
C. to monitor project progress and manage the project
D. to manage the project and help the team in any technical problems

Test Your Understanding 3.40
In an agile team, who serves as a communicator between the business and the development team?

A. scrum master
B. product owner
C. both scrum master and product owner
D. neither scrum master nor product owner

3.4.3 Team Members

Team members are people who actually develop software. How they work determines the quality, scope, budget and schedule of the project. The first step towards teamwork is ensuring trust and transparency between members. This is typically stated in the team working agreement (Payton, 2015).

The agreement should be created via a discussion between team members and the scrum master. The objective is to have a positive and productive experience. The agreement should be written and posted in an easy to see place. It will serve as reference throughout the project.

Team size is typically around five to nine people. This magic range may have originated from a classic publication by Miller (1956) describing limits to how much information human beings can keep in working memory. This range was accepted by the Scrum Guide (2016). Too many members may make collaboration difficult, while too few members can create gaps in skill sets necessary to deliver the software. Do note that there have been cases where three- or four-member teams are successful.

There are five characteristics that an agile team member should have (Cooke, 2012):

1. Multi-skilled: An agile team blurs the lines between traditional roles. Every member needs to be comfortable working in roles they are not used to.

2. Open-minded and flexible: This characteristic ensures that members are not only able to do work outside their expertise, but are willing to do it.

3. Highly communicative: Interactivity is one of the four values stated in the Agile Manifesto. Idea sharing, pair programming, and collaboration all require excellent communication skills.

4. Self-motivated: A self-motivated person can work both as a team player as well as an individual. Agile encourages individual members to decide how they want to work, and what to work on beyond what is assigned by the manager.

5. Holistic thinker: A member in an agile team should be able to appreciate both the technical and business

contexts of the product.

In an agile software development team, members have several responsibilities that contribute to the team's success. These responsibilities include:

Participating in Sprint events: Team members are responsible for attending all sprint events (a Chapter 4 topic) such as sprint planning meetings, where they will work with the product owner to define the sprint goal and select items from the product backlog that the team will work on during the sprint. Members must attend daily stand-up meetings, where they will share progress updates, identify any obstacles or challenges, and collaborate with other team members to resolve issues. At the conclusion of each sprint, team members are required to attend two meetings: the sprint review and retrospective meetings. The sprint review meeting involves showcasing the finished software (known as the increment) to clients and obtaining feedback. In the retrospective meeting, the team will analyze the outcomes of the sprint and pinpoint areas for improvement to enhance the next sprint's performance.

Collaborating with the product owner and other team members: Team members must work closely with the product owner to understand the requirements for each item in the product backlog. This includes asking questions, seeking clarification, and providing feedback to ensure that the team is building the right product. Within the team, members collaborate continuously as a cross-functional unit -- regardless of individual expertise -- to design, build, test, and integrate work throughout the sprint. Rather than operating in role-based silos, the entire team shares collective responsibility for delivering a high-quality, potentially shippable increment that meets customer requirements.

Completing Sprint Tasks: During each sprint, team members are responsible for completing their assigned or self-picked tasks on time and to the best of their abilities. This includes coding, testing, and other development activities.

Agile methodology favors a set up where all team members are physically located in the same place, as explained in Chapter 2. Then, is it possible for a virtual team to succeed? The answer is yes, as long as team dynamic and collaboration can be established (Crowder and Friess, 2015). Ideally, the team will meet at the beginning of the project and regularly during the project as budget permits.

Test Your Understanding 3.41

Which of the following is NOT a responsibility of team members in an agile team?
A. Work closely with the product owner
B. Complete assigned tasks on time
C. Attend all sprint events
D. Manage the product backlog

Test Your Understanding 3.42
What is the responsibility of team members while collaborating with the product owner and other team members?
A. Completing assigned tasks on time
B. Working closely with other team members
C. Understanding requirements for each item in the product backlog
D. Serving as a liaison between the team and the clients

Test Your Understanding 3.43
What is the purpose of the daily stand-up meeting?
A. To review the sprint's results
B. To identify areas for improvement for the next sprint
C. To share progress updates and identify obstacles
D. To receive user feedback

Test Your Understanding 3.44
What is the purpose of the sprint review meeting?
A. To showcase increment and obtain feedback
B. To identify areas for improvement for the next sprint
C. To define the sprint goal
D. None of the options listed

Test Your Understanding 3.45
What is the responsibility of team members during sprint planning meetings?
A. Work closely with the product owner
B. Attend all sprint events
C. Select items from the product backlog
D. Manage product backlog

Test Your Understanding 3.46
For a virtual agile team to succeed, the team must establish _______.
A. team dynamic
B. collaboration
C. both team dynamic and collaboration
D neither team dynamic nor collaboration

Test Your Understanding 3.47
Agile team members have ______, e.g. analysis, coding.
A. different working hours
B. different responsibilities
C. different goals
D. same responsibilities

Test Your Understanding 3.48

Which of the following is NOT a characteristic of an agile team member?
A. Multi-skilled
B. Highly communicative
C. Self-motivated
D. Atomistic thinker

Test Your Understanding 3.49
Which of the following is NOT an agile role?
A. Project manager
B. Product owner
C. Scrum master
D. Team members

Test Your Understanding 3.50
The normal size for an agile team is ____ people.
A. three to five
B. five to nine
C. nine to eleven
D. more than eleven

Test Your Understanding 3.51
The _____ is(are) the person(s) who make(s) sure that the team follows the agile principles effectively.
A. product owner
B. scrum master
C. team member
D. product owner and scrum master

3.5 Chapter Summary

In the C# sections of this chapter, you learned how to selectively execute a block of statements based on certain conditions. You also learned how to repeat a block of statements either a pre-defined number of times or as long as certain conditions are true. You can solve most problems with just these three constructions: sequence, conditional, and repetition. You will use these constructions for the rest of the book. In the agile sections of this chapter, you learned the three roles of agile: product owner, scrum master, and team members. These distinct roles work in collaboration toward the project objectives.

3.6 References

Cohn, M. (2009). Succeeding with agile: Software development using scrum. Addison-Wesley Professional.
Cooke, J. L. (2010). Agile Principles Unleashed : Proven Approaches for Achieving Real Productivity in Any Organisation. Ely: IT Governance Publishing. Cambridgeshire, UK
Cooke, J. L. , 2012, Everything You Want to Know About Agile: How to Get Agile Results in a Less-Than-Agile Organization. Ely: IT Governance Publishing. Cambridgeshire, UK

Crowder, J. A and Friess, S. 2015, Agile Project Management: Managing for Success, Springer.
Gottesdiener, E., & Gorman, M. (2013). Discover to deliver: Agile product planning and analysis. EBG Consulting, Inc.
Jongerius, P., Offermans, A., Vanhouche, A. Sanwikarja, P., and Geel, J.V. 2014, Get Agile: Scrum for UX, design and development, BIS Publishers, Amsterdam.
Larman, C., & Vodde, B. (2010). Scaling lean & agile development: Thinking and organizational tools for large-scale scrum. Addison-Wesley Professional.
Liden, R. C., Wayne, S. J., Liao, C., and Meuser, J. D. 2014, Servant Leadership and Serving Culture: Influence on Individual and Unit Performance, Academy of Management Journal, Oct, 57:5, p 1434-1452.
Measey, P. and Radtac, 2015, Agile Foundations -- Principles, Practices and Frameworks, BCS, Swindon, UK.
Miller, G. A. 1956, The Magic Number Seven, Plus or Minus Two: Some Limits on Our Capacity for Processing Information, Psychological Review, 63, p. 81-97.
Payton, T. 2015, How to create agile team working agreement, Visited November 19, 2016, https://www.scrumalliance.org/community/articles/2015/march/how-to-create-agile-team-working-agreements
Pham, A. and Pham, P. 2012, Scrum in Action: Agile Software Project Management and Development, Course PTR, Boston, MA.
Pichler, Roman. 2010. Agile product management with Scrum: Creating products that customers love. Boston: Addison-Wesley.
Resnick, S., De la Maza, M., Bjork, A., 2011, Professional Scrum with Team Foundation Server 2010, Wrong Guides Series, Wrox, Indianapolis, IN.
Schwaber, K. (2011). Agile project management with Scrum. Microsoft Press.
Schwaber, K. and Sutherland, J. 2016, The Scrum Guide, available at www.scrumguides.org Visited November 19, 2016.
Viscardi, S. 2013, The Professional ScrumMaster's Handbook: A Collection of Tips, Tricks, and War Stories to Help THE Professional ScrumMaster Break the Chains of Traditional Organization and Management, Packt Publishing, Birmingham, U.K.

3.7 Solutions to Test Your Understanding

3.1 B; 3.2 C; 3.3 C; 3.4 A; 3.5 D; 3.6 B; 3.7 B; 3.8 C; 3.9 D; 3.10 B; 3.11 C; 3.12 D; 3.13 C; 3.14 D; 3.15 A; 3.16 D; 3.17 D; 3.18 D; 3.19 B; 3.20 B; 3.21 A; 3.22 B; 3.23 D; 3.24 C; 3.25 B; 3.26 D; 3.27 B; 3.28 C; 3.29 C; 3.30 B; 3.31 C; 3.32 D; 3.33 A; 3.34 B; 3.35 C; 3.36 D; 3.37 C; 3.38 B; 3.39 B; 3.40 C; 3.41 D; 3.42 C; 3.43 C; 3.44 A; 3.45 C; 3.46 C; 3.47 D; 3.48 D; 3.49 A; 3.50 B; 3.51 B;.

Chapter 4: C# Methods and Agile Events

Chapter Learning Outcomes

4.1 Recognize a method in C# as a logical group of statements
4.2 Exemplify method usage with method call
4.3 Implement methods with parameters and return
4.4 Recall types of events in agile

4.1 A Method Is a Logical Group of Statements

When you give instructions to computers, you write statements by following C# syntax. Applications often have thousands of lines of statements, if not millions. You need a better way to organize these statements. One way is by grouping them into methods.

Statements that accomplish the same task can be grouped into a method. Suppose you would like every line of message displayed in the console to have a blank line before and after the text, with a line of asterisks to separate the messages. You can code this with or without utilizing a method, as we will demonstrate in the next two examples.

Example 4.1

Problem:

Write an application to display the line of text: "C# is fun." Insert a blank line before and after the text and add a line of asterisks after the second blank line. The output looks like this:

```

C# is fun.

**********
```

Solution:

Create a console app project called Chapter4Example1. Replace the default code with the following:

```
Console.WriteLine();
Console.WriteLine("C# is fun.");
Console.WriteLine();
Console.WriteLine("**********");
```

Example 4.2

Problem:

Write an application to display the line of text: "C# is fun." Insert a blank line before and after the text and add a line of asterisks after the second blank line. This time, use a method.

Solution:

Create a console app called Chapter4Example2. Replace the default code with the following:

```
DisplayText();

static void DisplayText()
{
    Console.WriteLine();
    Console.WriteLine("C# is fun.");
    Console.WriteLine();
    Console.WriteLine("**********");
}
```

Explanation:

The first line calls the DisplayText() method, which displays the message. One common error for beginners is having a method but never calling the method. The statements inside a method will not be executed automatically except in the invisible Main() method. The method call triggers the statements in the method to be executed. As a result, the sequence of the methods in a class does not matter.

The rest of the code defines a method named DisplayText(). The keyword, static, is a modifier. It makes the DisplayText method static. Not all methods have to be static; this method has to be static because it will be used in the invisible Main method, which is static. The rule is that a static method, such as the Main method, can only call other static methods, such as the DisplayText method.

The 'void' is a keyword for the return type. In this example, the methods do not return anything, so 'void' is used.

DisplayText is the method name. You can name your own method anything you'd like. Just follow the same rules as for naming variables. Conventionally, the first letter of every word in a method name is capitalized (ex. - DisplayStudentName()).This style of function name is called Pascal case.

You cannot skip the ( ) after the method name. It is called the parameter list. A parameter list is used to input any values to be used in the method. In this example, the method does not need anything, so the parameter list is blank. However, the pair of parentheses must still be there.

All statements inside the pair of curly braces {} are part of the method body. These statements are executed to accomplish the goal of the method.

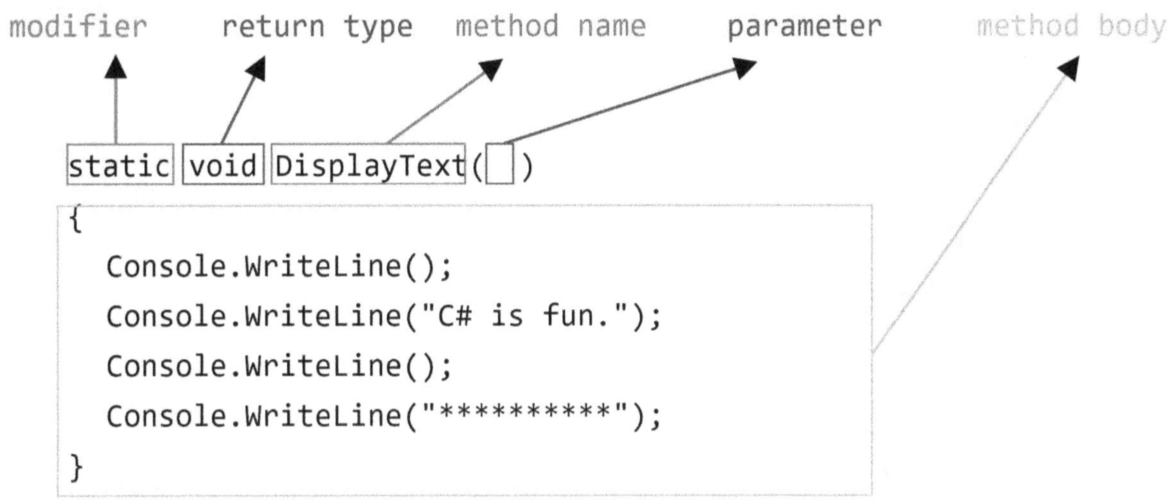

Figure 4.1 Components of a method

Test Your Understanding 4.1
In C#, a ______is a logical group of statements with a common goal.
A. method
B. container
C. logical operator
D. logical object

Test Your Understanding 4.2
In C#, which of the following is NOT a component of a method?
A. method variable
B. method modifier
C. method return type
D. method name

Test Your Understanding 4.3
In C#, which of the following is NOT a component of a method?
A. method modifier
B. method return type
C. method goal
D. parameter list

Test Your Understanding 4.4
In C#, what is the parameter in a method?

A. a pair of parentheses
B. value(s) to be used in the method from outside of the method
C. the border of the method
D. an optional value of the method

Test Your Understanding 4.5
In C#, what happens if you write a method and do not call it?
A. an error
B. a compiler error
C. statements inside the method will not execute
D. statements inside the method can only execute once

Test Your Understanding 4.6
The following code shows a method.
```
static void MyMethod()
{
    Console.WriteLine("Agile is fun!");
}
```
What is "MyMethod"?
A. return type
B. method name
C. parameter
D. method body

Test Your Understanding 4.7
The following code shows a method.
```
static void MyMethod()
{
    Console.WriteLine("Agile is fun!");
}
```
What is "void"?
A. return type
B. method name
C. parameter
D. method body

Test Your Understanding 4.8
The following code shows a method.
```
static void MyMethod()
{
    Console.WriteLine("Agile is fun!");
}
```
What is "()" on the first line of the code?
A. return type
B. method name
C. parameter
D. method body

Test Your Understanding 4.9
The following code shows a method.

```
static void MyMethod()
{
    Console.WriteLine("Agile is fun!");
}
```

What is "Console.WriteLine("Agile is fun!");?

A. return type
B. method name
C. parameter
D. method body

Programming Challenge 4.1

Create a console app with a method: DisplayMenu. Copy all code from Programming Challenge 3.1. Next cut the four consecutive lines of Console.WriteLine and paste them inside the DisplayMenu method. In their original location, add a method call.

4.2 A Method Can Have Parameters

In the previous section, you learned that a method is a logical grouping of statements designed to perform a specific task. To carry out that task, a method may require one or more values from outside its definition -- these are called parameters.

Example 4.3

Problem:

Modify Example 4.2 DisplayText() method so that it can display different messages (not just "C# is fun") according to the parameter value passed in from outside. Then, call the methods by passing different values.

Analysis:

The original method DisplayText() in Example 4.2 did not get any input (parameter is blank), so it can only display what is written in it. If you allow the method to receive some inputs (arguments), then it will be able to display the inputs. For example, if the user wants to display "Agile is more fun", you don't need to change the method. Just pass the message when calling the method.

Solution:

Update Example 4.2 so that the Program class looks like this.

```
DisplayText("C# is fun!");
DisplayText("Agile is more fun!");

static void DisplayText(string message)
{
```

```
        Console.WriteLine();
        Console.WriteLine(message);
        Console.WriteLine();
        Console.WriteLine("**********");
}
```

Explanation:

This time, the parameter of 'DisplayText' is no longer blank. It has a string variable called "message". This means if you want to use/call this method, you have to provide a string value as an argument.

In the method body, Instead of displaying "C# is fun." on the console screen, it will display any string value passed in by the caller.

Note that the method call is different from the method call in the earlier example where you didn't pass an argument to the method. This time, you have to provide a string value, e.g. "C# is fun!"

The second line is calling the DisplayText method again with a different argument ("Agile is more fun!"). One benefit of having a method is that you can write it once and call it many times. The value(s) a method expects are often called the parameter(s), and the value(s) passed into the method are often called argument(s). In the example, "message" is a parameter and "Agile is more fun" is an argument.

Test Your Understanding 4.10
Which of the following statements accurately describes a primary benefit of defining a method?
A. You typically result in fewer lines of code when you use a method only once.
B. Methods automatically prevent bugs that would otherwise occur from copy-pasting nearly identical code.
C. You can write a method once and call it multiple times.
D. Changing the behavior of a method in one place automatically updates every location where that method is used.

Test Your Understanding 4.11
Suppose a method body has only one line of statement: Console.WriteLine($"The sum is {a+b}");
Which of the following is a correct method header?
A. static void MyMethod()
B. static void MyMethod(a, b)
C. static void MyMethod(int a, int b)
D. static void MyMethod(int a+b)

Test Your Understanding 4.12
Suppose a method header is: static void MyMethod(string a).
Which of the following is a correct way to call the method?

A. MyMethod;
B. MyMethod();
C. MyMethod("hello");
D. MyMethod(7);

Test Your Understanding 4.13
The variable(s) that show(s) in the method header is often called a(n) ________.
A. parameter
B. argument
C. agile
D. C#

Test Your Understanding 4.14
The value(s) that is(are) passed to a method is often called a(n) _________.
A. parameter
B. argument
C. agile
D. C#

Test Your Understanding 4.15
A method may accept ______ value(s) to work on.
A. up to one
B. up to two
C. up to three
D. zero or more

Programming Challenge 4.2
Smith's Fast Food sells burgers, fries, and drinks only. The price of a burger is $1.50. The price of a serving of French fries is $1.20. A cup of drink is $1.00. Write a console app with one method: DisplayPrice. The DisplayPrice method accepts a name of the food (burgers, fries, or drinks) and displays the corresponding price as shown in the sample output. Outside the method includes the following four lines:

```
DisplayPrice("hamburgers");
DisplayPrice("fries");
DisplayPrice("drinks");
DisplayPrice("lobsters");
```

The output looks like:

```
$1.50
$1.20
$1.00
We don't sell that.
```

4.3 A Method can Return a Value

So far, your methods do not return anything, as represented by the "void" keyword in the method header.

A method often returns a value after the method's work.

Example 4.4

Problem:

Write a method named Plus() that will accept two whole numbers and return the sum of the two values. Demonstrate the Plus() method by calling it from outside the method.

Solution:

Create a console app called Chapter4Example4. Replace the default code with the following:

```
int a = 3;
int b = 5;
int total = Plus(a, b);
Console.WriteLine($"{a} + {b} = {total}");

static int Plus(int a, int b)
{
    int sum;
    sum = a + b;
    return sum;
}
```

Explanation:

The return type for the Plus() method is not void; it is int. This indicates that the Plus() method will return an int value. The parameter list for this line contains two variables. This means the Plus() method will accept two int values. As a result, this method will accept two input values of int type and return one value of int type.

The keyword "return" inside a method returns a value that matches the return type declared in the Plus() method header.

Note that the method call passes two int values because the method's parameter list specifies exactly two int parameters. The arguments must match the parameters in number, type (int), and order. Additionally, when a method returns a value, you typically assign that returned value to a variable for later use.

Test Your Understanding 4.16
Which of the following statements accurately describes the invoking of the Plus method given below?
static int Plus(int a, int b){return 3; }
A. The Plus method accepts two int values that can be of different types and in any order.
B. The Plus method accepts two int values that must be of the same type, but the order doesn't matter.
C. The Plus method accepts two int values that must be of the same type and in the same order.
D. The Plus method accepts two int values that sum up to 3.

Test Your Understanding 4.17

Suppose a method header is: static int MyMethod()
Which of the following is the correct method body?
A. Console.WriteLine("Agile is fun!");
B. return int;
C. return 4;
D. return 4.15;

Test Your Understanding 4.18
Suppose a method header is: static void MyMethod()
Which of the following is the correct method body?
A. Console.WriteLine("Agile is fun!");
B. return int;
C. return 4;
D. return 4.15;

Test Your Understanding 4.19
Suppose a method header is: static double MyMethod()
Which of the following is the correct method body?
A. Console.WriteLine("Agile is fun!");
B. return double;
C. return 4;
D. return 4.15;

Test Your Understanding 4.20
Which of the following statements about methods is true?
Statement1: A method must have a "return" keyword inside the method body.
Statement2: A method returned value inside the method body must match the return type in the method header.
A. Statement1 only.
B. Statement2 only.
C. Both Statement1 and Statement2.
D. Neither Statement1 nor Statement2.

Test Your Understanding 4.21
Which of the following statements about methods is true?
Statement1: A method may return one or many values or references by using multiple return statements.
Statement2: If a method header includes a void keyword, the method should still have a return statement.
A. Statement1 only.
B. Statement2 only.
C. Both Statement1 and Statement2.
D. Neither Statement1 nor Statement2.

Programming Challenge 4.3
Write a method named Multiply() that will accept two whole numbers and return the multiplication product of the two values. Demonstrate the Multiply() method by calling it from outside the method.

4.4 A Method Can Return More Than One Value

A method can only return one value by using the return statement. If you want a method to return two or more values, you can use the "out" parameter modifier.

Example 4.5

Problem:

Write a method named Divide() that will accept two whole numbers and return the quotient and the remainder of these two values. Demonstrate the Divide() method by calling it from outside the method.

Solution:

Start a new project called Chapter4Example5. Type the code as shown below:

```
int a = 14;
int b = 5;
int quotient = Divide(a, b, out int remainder);
Console.WriteLine($"{a} / {b} = {quotient}R{remainder}");

static int Divide(int x, int y, out int r)
{
    int quotient;
    quotient = x / y;
    r = x % y;
    return quotient;
}
```

Explanation:

To call a method that returns more than one value, such as the `Divide` method in the example, you write the method call as usual, but you also include an `out` parameter to receive the additional value. In the statement: `int quotient = Divide(a, b, out int remainder);` the method returns the quotient as its standard return value, while the remainder is returned through the `out` parameter. The `out int remainder` syntax declares a new variable named `remainder` inline and passes it by reference to the method, allowing the method to assign a value to it. Note that the `out` keyword appears before the type (`int`) in the parameter list, indicating that this parameter is used to return data from the method rather than pass data into it.

The `Divide()` method definition includes a parameter named `r` of type `int`, prefixed with the `out` modifier. Inside the method body, a value -- the remainder -- is assigned to this `r` parameter before the method returns.

The `out` modifier allows a method to modify the value of a variable passed from the calling code. To see the difference between using `out` and not using it, add the line `x = x * x;` just before the `return` statement in the above code. You'll notice that this change does not affect the original variable (e.g., `a`) passed into the method, because without the `out` keyword, the parameter is passed by value, meaning the method works with a copy of the original data. Only parameters marked with `out` (or `ref`) can modify the caller's original variable.

Here is a complete example to demonstrate the difference between "out" and no "out":

```
int x = 2;
int y = 12;
Console.WriteLine($"Before method call: x={x}, y={y}");
Fun(x, out y);
Console.WriteLine($"After method call: x={x}, y={y}");

static void Fun(int x, out int y)
{
    x = 4;
    y = 24;
}
```

You may notice that the value in x is not changed while the value in y is changed.

Using the "out" parameter modifier allows you to return more than one value back from a method.

Test Your Understanding 4.22

What is the outcome of the following C# code execution?

```
int x = 2;
Console.Write($"Before method call: x={x}");
Fun(x);
Console.Write($" After method call: x={x}");
static void Fun(int x)
{
    x = 4;
}
```

A. Before method call: x=2 After method call: x=4
B. Before method call: x=2 After method call: x=2
C. Before method call: x=4 After method call: x=2
D. A compiler error because the value in x cannot be changed with a method

Test Your Understanding 4.23

What is the outcome of the following C# code execution?

```
int x = 2;
Console.Write($"Before method call: x={x}");
Fun(out x);
Console.Write($" After method call: x={x}");
static void Fun(out int x)
{
    x = 4;
}
```

A. Before method call: x=2 After method call: x=4
B. Before method call: x=2 After method call: x=2
C. Before method call: x=4 After method call: x=2
D. A compiler error because the value in x cannot be changed with a method

Test Your Understanding 4.24
Which of the following statements about methods is correct?
Statement1: The 'out' parameter modifier makes it possible for a method to return more than one value.
Statement2: The 'out' parameter modifier is required only when declaring a method.
A. Statement1 only.
B. Statement2 only.
C. Both Statement1 and Statement2.
D. Neither Statement1 nor Statement2.

Programming Challenge 4.4
Write a method called SumAndDifference() that will accept two whole numbers and return the sum and the difference of the two values (ex. - if the two input whole numbers were 5 and 2, the sum would be 7 and the difference would be 3). Demonstrate the method by calling it from outside the method.

Programming Challenge 4.5
Write a method called Square() that will accept a whole number between 1 and 20. The method will print a solid square of asterisks with that number of asterisks on each side. Outside the method, prompt the user to enter a whole number between 1 and 20. Then call the method to display a solid square of asterisks. For example, if a user entered 3, the output would look like:

```
* * *
* * *
* * *
```

Example 4.6

Problem: Rock Paper Scissors

Develop a console application in C# to allow a user to play Rock-Paper-Scissors against the computer. On the console screen, a player can type Rock, Paper, or Scissors. At the same time, the computer will display one of the three words at random. Then the application will display who is the winner. Additionally, the application will prompt the user if he or she wants to play again.

Solution:

This example has the most lines of code so far. Divide the code into methods for better organization and comprehension. Build one part at a time. Save and test each part before moving on to the next step.

Step 1: Computer always wins

Start a new project called Chapter4Example6. Type in the code as shown below:

```
static string UserShape()
{
    string str;
    str = "ROCK";
    return str;
}

static string ComputerShape()
{
    string str;
    str = "PAPER";
    return str;
}

static string Winner(string user, string computer)
{
    string winner = "Nobody";
    if (user == "ROCK" && computer == "PAPER")
        winner = "computer";
    return winner;
}
```

Explanation:

The UserShape() method always returns "ROCK" for testing purposes. The full method will be in Step 2.

The ComputerShape() method always returns "PAPER" for testing purposes. The completed method will be in Step 4.

The Winner() method has two parameters: user and computer. It returns the winner. It checks only one simple case. A more detailed check will be performed in Step 3.

Next, add the following anywhere outside any methods:

```
bool playAgain = true;
while (playAgain)
{
    string userShape = UserShape();
    string computerShape = ComputerShape();
    string winner = Winner(userShape, computerShape);
    Console.WriteLine($"User shape: {userShape}");
    Console.WriteLine($"Computer shape: {computerShape}");
    Console.WriteLine($"The winner is: {winner}");
    Console.WriteLine("Play again? y/n");
    string choice = Console.ReadLine().ToUpper();
    if (choice == "Y" || choice == "YES")
        playAgain = true;
    else
    {
        Console.WriteLine("Thanks for playing.");
        playAgain = false;
    }
}
```

Explanation:

The first line declares a Boolean variable to control the loop, initializing it to true so the loop starts. Near the end of the block, the code prompts the user again, potentially updating this value -- a common pattern for loop control.

The while loop that allows a user to play as many times as he or she desires.

The first line inside the loop calls the UserShape() method. It stores the returned value in a string variable named userShape. The second line inside the loop calls the ComputerShape() method. It stores the returned value in a string variable named computerShape. The third line inside the loop calls the Winner() method. It includes two arguments, userShape and computerShape, and returns a string. The returned value is stored in a string variable named winner.

A string has a built-in ToUpper() method which converts user input to all uppercase (so that user input will be case insensitive).

Save and run the application. The user always shows ROCK, and the computer always shows PAPER, thus making the computer the guaranteed winner. You can play as many times as desired.

Step 2: Player can choose to draw or lose

Update the UserShape() method with the code below:

```
string str;
str = "ROCK";
bool isCorrectSpelling = false;
while (!isCorrectSpelling)
{
    Console.WriteLine("Enter Rock, Paper, or Scissors:");
    str = Console.ReadLine().ToUpper();
    if (str == "ROCK" || str == "PAPER" || str == "SCISSORS")
        isCorrectSpelling = true;
}
return str;
```

Explanation

A Boolean variable, isCorrectSpelling is used to control the while loop. If the user did not spell ROCK, PAPER, or SCISSORS correctly, the loop would prompt for another input.

The ToUpper() method of a string makes the user input case insensitive.

Save and run the application.

Even though the user can enter any one of the three shapes, the result will either be a loss or a tie: if the user enters ROCK, he or she will lose; if the user enters any other shape, it will be a tie. This is due to our currently incomplete winner checking method.

Step 3: Player can choose to win, lose, or draw

Update the Winner() method with the code below:

```
string winner = "Nobody";
if (user == "ROCK" && computer == "PAPER"
    || user == "PAPER" && computer == "SCISSORS"
    || user == "SCISSORS" && computer == "ROCK")
    winner = "computer";
else if (user == "ROCK" && computer == "SCISSORS"
    || user == "PAPER" && computer == "ROCK"
    || user == "SCISSORS" && computer == "PAPER")
    winner = "Player";
return winner;
```

Explanation

The method checks only if the computer wins or the player wins. Everything else counts as nobody winning (a draw).

Save and run the application. Since the computer still only shows PAPER, you can easily play to win. Try playing, and see if you can get the expected results.

Step 4: It's a real game

Update the ComputerShape() method with the code below:

```
string str;
str = "PAPER";
Random random = new Random();
int randomNumber = random.Next(1, 4);
switch (randomNumber)
{
    case 1:
        str = "ROCK";
        break;
    case 2:
        str = "PAPER";
        break;
    case 3:
        str = "SCISSORS";
        break;
}
return str;
```

Explanation

A `Random` object named `random` is created using the built-in `Random` class. Its `Next()` method generates a random integer from 1 (inclusive) to 4 (exclusive). A `switch` statement then converts this number into the corresponding shape name -- though an `if` statement could be used instead.

Save and run the application. Test it multiple times to see if there are any logical errors (e.g. paper wins over scissors).

Test Your Understanding 4.25
What is the purpose of the following statement by using ToUpper() method?

```
string str = Console.ReadLine().ToUpper();
```

A. To enforce the user to enter text in all upper cases.
B. To display prompt in all upper cases.
C. User input will be case insensitive.
D. Cannot have a dot operator after a method like ReadLine()

Test Your Understanding 4.26
What is "Random" in the following statement?

```
Random random = new Random();
```

A. A class
B. An object
C. A method
D. A random number

Test Your Understanding 4.27
What is "random" in the following statement?

```
Random random = new Random();
```

A. A class
B. An object
C. A method
D. A random number

Programming Challenge 4.6
Modify the Rock-Paper-Scissors game so that a player can choose to play 'best two out of three games' or 'best three out of five games'.

4.5 Agile Events

As you learned in Chapter 2, there are three roles, five events, and three artifacts in Scrum. You learned the three roles in Chapter 3. You will learn the five events in this chapter. Scrum founders want you to use prescribed events to create consistency and to avoid any extra meetings. There are five events defined in the 2020 Scrum Guide (Schwaber and Sutherland, 2020). All scrum events are time-boxed, meaning the duration of the events have been predetermined and agreed upon by all members of the scrum team.

Every event within Scrum is a formal occasion to scrutinize and fine-tune Scrum artifacts (a topic in the next chapter). These events have been purposefully designed to facilitate the necessary transparency. Neglecting to conduct events as instructed may lead to missed chances for examination and adjustment. The use of events in Scrum serves to establish a routine and to reduce the necessity for meetings outside of Scrum's framework. Ideally, all events should be held at the same time and location to simplify matters.

Test Your Understanding 4.28
Is it recommended to hold Scrum events at the same times and locations?
A. Yes, to increase transparency
B. Yes, to simplify matters
C. No, it is not necessary
D. No, it can only lead to confusion

Test Your Understanding 4.29
The purpose of having regular scrum event meetings is to ______.
A. avoid additional meetings
B. control meeting time
C. train new members
D. communicate with customers

Test Your Understanding 4.30
All scrum events are time-boxed, which means ____.
A. all events have the same length
B. all events have their own predetermined length
C. all event lengths are recorded
D. all events can take as much time as they require

4.5.1 The Sprint

In Chapter 1, we introduced the concept of sprints when we compared the similarities and differences between waterfall and agile approaches. A sprint is a container event that includes all tasks that are necessary to achieve a delivery. From our toy retailer example, outlined in Chapter 1, a sprint might include the events for the development of features that allow the owner to check inventory levels and add new arrivals. At the end of the sprint, the development team will deliver the components of the application that allow the owner to check inventory and update inventory when new shipments arrive. Such a delivery is called an *increment.*

A sprint starts with sprint planning. Then, on a daily basis, the team should have brief scrum meetings. And, of course, sprints involve the actual work of completing the delivery. At the end of the sprint, the team should have a sprint review and sprint retrospective. You will learn each of these events in more detail.

A sprint duration is typically two weeks, but can be as long as a month. The purpose of limiting the duration is to increase the predictability of the software. During this short sprint, the delivery scope is less likely to be changed, and the risk of abandoning the delivery is lower.

The sprint duration should be the same for all sprints in the project. The length is agreed upon at the beginning of the project between the product owner, scrum master, and the scrum team. On rare occasions, a sprint duration may be longer in order to complete a delivery (e.g. when the delivery cannot fit into a sprint).

A sprint can be canceled if the goal of the delivery is no longer valid. In our toy retailer example, if you have a sprint working on a shopping cart software, and the owner decided to purchase the shopping cart software, then there's no longer a reason to continue the sprint. The product owner decides whether to cancel or not. When a sprint is canceled, any completed items are reviewed and may be released if the product owner desires so.

There are basic rules to sprints. During the sprint, changes are not allowed to user stories already in the sprint. If the product owner wants to make any changes, they can update the product backlog (a concept that will be explained in the next chapter), which contains all the user stories. This allows the team to focus on the current tasks.

During the sprint, the development team is not allowed to lower the quality of the goal either. This is to protect the benefits of the customer. However, as the product owner and the development team learn more about the product, a sprint clarification of the scope is allowed.

Test Your Understanding 4.31
The sprint duration should be the same for all sprints in the project. A sprint duration is typically ______.
A. one week or less
B. between one and two weeks
C. between two and four weeks
D. four weeks or more

Test Your Understanding 4.32
Which of the following statements about agile sprint is correct?
Statement1: A sprint delivers a software increment.

Statement2: Shorter sprints make the delivery scope less likely to be changed.
A. Statement1 only.
B. Statement2 only.
C. Both Statement1 and Statement2.
D. Neither Statement1 nor Statement2.

Test Your Understanding 4.33
Which of the following statements about agile sprint is correct?
Statement1: The length of a sprint is always determined by the user story. The longer the story, the longer the sprint.
Statement2: The product owner is the only person allowed to make changes to stories already in a sprint.
A. Statement1 only.
B. Statement2 only.
C. Both Statement1 and Statement2.
D. Neither Statement1 nor Statement2.

Test Your Understanding 4.34
Which of the following is NOT a sprint event?
A. sprint planning
B. daily scrum meeting
C. sprint review
D. scrum mastering

Test Your Understanding 4.35
Which of the following statements about agile is correct?
Statement1: An agile team can slightly lower the quality of the product in order to meet the sprint deadline.
Statement2: A product owner can make changes to the user stories in the product backlog.
A. Statement1 only.
B. Statement2 only.
C. Both Statement1 and Statement2.
D. Neither Statement1 nor Statement2.

4.5.2 Sprint Planning

A sprint starts with a plan meeting. The main purpose of the meeting is to pick stories from the product backlog that can be completed in one sprint (Sutherland, 2014). There are three agenda items to a sprint plan meeting:

1. Which user stories should be included in this sprint? This is determined by the priority list of the user stories in the product backlog and the projected capacity of the team for the sprint (velocity). To accomplish this task, all team members should have a thorough understanding of the user stories in the product backlog. Every story in the product backlog has a priority ranking (set by the product owner) and story points (estimated by the team members). The story points for a story indicate how much effort is needed. The team picks stories by their rankings from high to low. How many stories they pick is based on how

many story points the team can complete in one sprint. The total story points selected should not be greater than that the team can complete in one sprint. Deviating slightly in terms of priority ranking and total story points is allowed.

2. After the stories are picked, it is time to write the sprint goal. The sprint goal explains the reasons for the work and provides motivation for running the sprint. A sprint goal must be specific, measurable, and attainable (Pichler, 2012). In our toy retailer example, one sprint goal could be "Mr. Lincoln can update the inventory when a new shipment arrives".

3. The development team decides how to achieve the goal and successfully deliver the software increment in this order: first, the user stories will be broken down into more manageable individual tasks. Next, each member picks the tasks he or she is comfortable completing. Lastly, each member reports an estimate of when he or she will finish. This estimate is usually measured in hours.

Three items above are collectively called the sprint backlog. A sprint planning meeting is suggested to last 8 hours for a month-long sprint. Shorter sprints should correspond with shorter time-boxes.

Test Your Understanding 4.36
Which factor(s) determine(s) the inclusion of user stories in a sprint?
A. The priority list of user stories in the product backlog
B. The projected capacity of the team for the sprint
C. Both the priority list of user stories in the product backlog and the projected capacity of the team for the sprint
D. The project manager

Test Your Understanding 4.37
Which of the following is NOT an agenda item on a sprint planning meeting?
A. take attendance
B. pick stories from product backlog
C. write sprint goal
D. decide how to achieve the goal

Test Your Understanding 4.38
Suppose there are five stories in the product backlog:
Story 1: 20 points
Story 2: 40 points
Story 3: 40 points
Story 4: 13 points
Story 5: 20 points
If the team can complete 70 story points per sprint (their 'velocity'), and the priority is the same as the story number (meaning 1 is of highest priority, and 5 the lowest), which stories will probably be picked by the

team?
A. Story 1, Story 3, and Story 5
B. Story 1, Story 2, and Story 4
C. Story 2, Story 4, and Story 5
D. Story 1, Story 3, and Story 4

4.5.3 Daily Scrum

Daily scrum is a meeting amongst the development team, time-boxed at 15 minutes. To avoid long meetings, members are required to stand up. Every member answers the following three questions.

1. What did I do yesterday?
2. What will I do today?
3. Do I see any impediments for me or the team?

Daily scrum meetings are not simple status updates. The daily scrum is a time to make commitments. If a member states he or she will complete the “Add new inventory” feature today, you should expect to see that done by tomorrow’s meeting.

Compared to the status update meeting, which is typically held once a week or once a month, daily scrum has the advantage of identifying problems early (Hoogendoorn, 2014). Members may delay reporting problems or issues due to laziness or shyness if they only meet once a month. With daily scrum, slow progress is immediately visible.

The meeting also helps members know what others are doing. It can show who needs help. It also provides transparency. The scrum master should help resolve any issues raised by a member. If a member does not know how to make something work, the scrum master helps.

Test Your Understanding 4.39
Daily scrum is a meeting amongst the development team, time-boxed at ______.
A. 15 minutes
B. 30 minutes
C. 60 minutes
D. It depends on the topics covered in the meeting

Test Your Understanding 4.40
Daily scrum meetings should have members standing to ______.
A. make it formal
B. avoid prolonging the meeting
C. keep members healthy

D. facilitate communication

Test Your Understanding 4.41
Which of the following questions is NOT asked in the daily scrum meeting?
A. What did I do yesterday?
B. What will I do today?
C. What do I plan to do tomorrow?
D. Do I see any impediments for me or the team?

4.5.4 Sprint Review Meeting

At the end of the sprint, the team meets to inspect the increment, usually accompanied by a live software demo to show to the business users. The meeting will also update the product backlog according to feedback.

The meeting is time-boxed at four hours for a month-long sprint. The meeting is informal, and any stakeholder can attend. The key value is to get feedback from the business users. To enforce the informality, some teams forbid the use of PowerPoint slides.

The key purpose is to compare the completed increment with the sprint goal set up from the sprint planning meeting, and to see how close the goal is to being achieved.

The review can be a bit daunting, since it is one of few events where multiple stakeholders are directly involved. Stakeholders may ask questions the team is not prepared for. Features may not work as planned. However, team members should remember that this is not a status check. The purpose of the review is to elicit feedback and nurture collaboration.

There are four keys to the success of a sprint review (Lacey, 2016).

1. *Take time to plan.* Planning can increase the team's confidence. Take time to set up the software so that customers can interact with the product.

2. *Document decisions.* People tend to forget things. Keeping track of customer statements in print makes everyone accountable.

3. *Ask for acceptance.* Customers may or may not accept the product on the spot at the review meeting. It

never hurts to ask, particularly for what can be improved. It is important that the team meet the "definition of done" in the first place.

4. *Be brave.* The review meeting can be intimidating, since the customer may not accept the increment. Members may panic. The team should try their best to communicate with the customers and work closely with the product owner to reach their goal.

Test Your Understanding 4.42
Which of the following is NOT a key to success in a sprint review meeting?
A. Take time to plan
B. Document decisions
C. Ask for acceptance
D. Make it a formal meeting with customers

Test Your Understanding 4.43
Which of the following is NOT a purpose of the sprint review?
A. Customers can check the status of the project.
B. The team can check how close they are to the sprint goal.
C. The team elicits feedback from the customers.
D. The team and the customers get to collaborate.

4.5.5 Sprint Retrospective

Sprint retrospective is a three-hour meeting for a one-month long sprint. It is held after the sprint review meeting and before the new sprint. All members, including the scrum master and the product owner, should attend the meeting. It has three purposes:

1. To examine how well the last sprint went.
2. To list what went well and what did not go well.
3. To plan for improvement.

There are many ways to achieve the three purposes (Cohn, 2010). One way is to let every member in the team voice what should be implemented in the next sprint, what should be continued in the next sprint, and what should be stopped. After a list is made, the team votes. Based on the results and possibly further discussion, a plan for the next sprint is created.

Retrospectives are often omitted by scrum teams that believe the meetings are optional and don't directly add value to the product (Lacey, 2016). This omission is often the beginning of a failed scrum practice. Recall the three foundations of scrum you learned in Chapter 2: transparency, inspection, and adaptation. All other events discussed in this section focus on the product delivery. This is the only event that can support all three foundations. This meeting helps team members know how to work more efficiently and productively. This is also the only time the team learns about new techniques in the field that they can utilize.

There are four keys to the success of a sprint retrospective (Lacey, 2016).

1. *Show them the way*: The retrospective schedule should be brief enough to avoid schedule conflicts. Right before the meeting, a reminder should be sent out that includes the meeting agenda, the benefits of the meeting, and how to prepare for the meeting.

2. *Build a good environment*: One major problem with the retrospective meeting is the endless discussion on one issue and inability to reach an agreement. You can either remove chairs and/or use a timer for each agenda item to limit the discussion. In addition, make necessary artifacts available so that the team can inspect and adapt. These items include "burn-down" charts (which indicate how many stories are left in the backlog; agile metrics will be discussed in Chapter 6) and the team's vision for the product and sprint (sprint artifacts will be discussed in detail in the next chapter).

Even though members should trust each other and are allowed to work with a lot of freedom, some ground rules will help. These rules should be made available to all participants before the meeting. Example rules include being respectful, putting away laptops/phones, and not interrupting while others speak.

3. *Hold them when you need them*: Retrospectives are not just held at the end of a sprint. It can be held anytime a big issue arises, like if there is a major defect, or a change in team membership. It can also be held after a major release, or when the customers demand one. This is analogous to a time out in a basketball game.

4. *Set high priority*: You should not hold a retrospective only when there's a problem for the team. It is good for supporting scrum foundations and team self-organization. Many beginner agile teams realize this too late.

Test Your Understanding 4.44

The sprint ________ meeting is a time when the team can see what they did well and what needs improvement from the past sprint.
A. daily scrum
B. retrospective
C. review
D. improvement

Test Your Understanding 4.45
Which of the following is NOT a purpose of sprint retrospectives?
A. Examining how well the last sprint went.
B. Listing what went well and what did not go well.
C. Planning for improvement.
D. To demo the software to the customers.

Test Your Understanding 4.46
Which of the following is NOT a key to the success of a sprint retrospective?
A. Show them the way.
B. Product owner should not be present.
C. Build a good environment.
D. Hold them when you need them.

Test Your Understanding 4.47
When should a team hold a sprint retrospective?
A. After the sprint review.
B. Any time a big issue arises.
C. At the end of the sprint, plus any time a big issue happens.
D. When a new user story is added to the product backlog.

4.6 Chapter Summary

In this chapter, you learned how to organize logically related C# statements into a method. A method can have parameters that receive arguments from the caller. A method can also return a value. A method makes your code better organized. Better-organized code makes maintenance much easier, and thus saves money for the business. You also learned the five events for scrum. They are the sprint, sprint plan meeting, daily scrum, sprint review meeting, and sprint retrospective. These meetings make the scrum practice more consistent, and prevent additional unnecessary meetings.

4.7 References

Cohn, M. (2010), Succeeding with Agile: Software Development Using Scrum, Addison-Wesley Professional PTG.
Hoogendoorn, S., (2014), This Is Agile, Beyond the Basics, Beyond the Hype, Beyond Scrum, Dymaxicon, Sausalito, CA.

Lacey, M. (2016), The Scrum Field Guide, 2nd Edition, Addison-Wesley, Boston.
Pichler, R., (2012), Effective Sprint Goals, Available at http://www.romanpichler.com/blog/effective-sprint-goals/ Visited November 20, 2016.
Schwaber, K. and Sutherland, J. (2020), The Scrum Guide, available at www.scrumguides.org Visited April 9, 2021.
Sutherland, J. (2014), Scrum the Art of Doing Twice the Work in Half the Time, Crown Business, New York.

4.8 Solutions to Selected Programming Challenges

Programming Challenge 4.5

```
Console.WriteLine("Enter an integer:");
int m = int.Parse(Console.ReadLine());
Square(m);

static void Square(int n)
{
    if (n > 0 || n <= 20)
    {
        for (int i = 0; i < n; i++)
        {
            for (int j = 0; j < n; j++)
            {
                Console.Write("* ");
            }
            Console.WriteLine();
        }
    }
}
```

4.9 Solutions to Test Your Understanding

4.1 A; 4.2 A; 4.3 C; 4.4 B; 4.5 C; 4.6 B; 4.7 A; 4.8 C; 4.9 D; 4.10 C; 4.11 C; 4.12 C; 4.13 A; 4.14 B; 4.15 D; 4.16 C; 4.17 C; 4.18 A; 4.19 D; 4.20 B; 4.21 D; 4.22 B; 4.23 A; 4.24 A; 4.25 C; 4.26 A; 4.27 B; 4.28 B; 4.29 A; 4.30 B; 4.31 C; 4.32 C; 4.33 D; 4.34 D; 4.35 B; 4.36 C; 4.37 A; 4.38 B; 4.39 A; 4.40 B; 4.41 C; 4.42 D; 4.43 A; 4.44 B; 4.45 D; 4.46 B; 4.47 C;

Chapter 5: C# Classes and Agile Artifacts

Chapter Learning Outcomes

5.1 Recognize a class as a logical group of methods and fields
5.2 Exemplify class usage with instantiating
5.3 Explain components of a class
5.4 Recall types of artifacts in agile
5.5 Summarize different types of agile artifacts

5.1 A Class Is a Logical Group of Methods and Fields

In the last chapter, you learned how to group a block of statements with a common goal into a method. In this chapter, you will learn how to group a set of related methods into a class. Because methods usually need data to work on, a class will also contain the related data. In Object Oriented Programming (OOP) terminology, data is termed *fields*. As a result, a class contains fields and methods of the same type of objects.

A class is a conceptual category, like students, employees, cars, or houses. A class is not an object; an object is a specific instance that belongs to a class. So, if you had the class 'student', 'Alice' may be an object of that class. Or, as another example, a class could be the blueprints to a certain model of house, and the house built from that is the object of that class. When you program the object-oriented way, you create a class first. When you need to use an object, you use the class to instantiate an object. In Chapter 4, you declared a random object from the built-in Random class in order to use its 'Next' method for a random number.

A class keeps track of a certain status. For example, all students have a name and GPA. Therefore, the student class includes name and GPA as statuses. As another example, all cars have a make and color. The car class would have make and color as statuses. In OOP, the statuses of a class are called 'fields.'

A class also has behaviors. Students can take a course, or convert a numeric grade to a letter grade. A car can speed up or down, or change tires. In OOP, these behaviors are called 'methods'.

In short, a class is a conceptual category. A class can have fields to keep track of statuses and methods to carry out actions. In most cases, you will create an object to use the methods.

The OOP is a mindset. It is a new way of thinking. Before this chapter, you think about what you want the computers to do. In OOP, you should think what classes you need and what status and behaviors of these classes have.

Test Your Understanding 5.1
Which of the following statements about C# class is correct?
Statement1: A class is a logical group of methods and fields.
Statement2: In OOP, classes and objects are the same thing.
A. Statement1 only.
B. Statement2 only.
C. Both Statement1 and Statement2.
D. Neither Statement1 nor Statement2.

Test Your Understanding 5.2
In OOP, a class is like a ______, and an object is like a ______ built out of that ______.
A. house, blueprint, construction materials
B. house, room, construction materials
C. house, room, house
D. blueprint, house, blueprint

Test Your Understanding 5.3
John Doe is a student. In OOP terminology, which of the following statements is correct?
A. John Doe is a class
B. John Doe is an object
C. Student is an object
D. Both John Doe and students are objects

Test Your Understanding 5.4
A class can have ______ to keep track of statuses and _______ to carry out actions.
A. objects, fields
B. fields, methods
C. objects, methods
D. methods, objects

Test Your Understanding 5.5
A class keeps track of a certain ______, such as student name and GPA.
A. status
B. name
C. GPA
D. behaviors

Test Your Understanding 5.6
A class has _____, such as students take courses, or convert numeric grades to letter grades.
A. status
B. name
C. GPA
D. behaviors

Test Your Understanding 5.7
The OOP is a mindset. It is a new way of thinking. Before learning OOP, you ______.
A. don't know how to write programs
B. think what you want the computers to do
C. think what classes you need
D. don't know how to organize the code

Test Your Understanding 5.8
The OOP is a mindset. It is a new way of thinking. In OOP, you ______.
A. don't know how to write programs
B. think what you want the computers to do
C. think what classes you need
D. don't know how to organize the code

Test Your Understanding 5.9
The OOP is a mindset. It is a new way of thinking. In OOP, you think of a class in terms of ______.
A. status and behaviors
B. names and behaviors
C. status and objects
D. objects and behaviors

Example 5.1

Problem:

A student has a name and a numerical grade/score. The numerical score can be converted to a letter grade. Create a class called Student with those fields (name and numeric score) and a method (change numeric score to letter grade). Then demonstrate the class by instantiating the two student objects shown below.

Name: Lynn, numeric score: 97

Name: Bob, numeric score: 87

Finally, print the two students' names and letter grades on the console screen.
The formula for converting a numeric score to a letter grade is 90-100 A; 80-89 B; 70-79 C; 60-69 D; 0-59 F.

Analysis:

You can easily program this problem with what you have learned so far. However, you should learn how to code in OOP so you can handle more difficult problems as they come along and build more robust applications.

The student class has two fields: student name and student score. These fields will store individual names and numeric scores. The student class also has the method GetLetterGrade(), which will return a letter grade based on the student score field value.

Solution:

By following this solution, you will learn how to solve the problem in OOP. Create a console app called Chapter5Example1. In the "Solution Explorer" window (you may need to click on the tab located on bottom right), right click on the Chapter5Exampe1 Project (not the solution). In the pop-up context menu, point to "Add" then "Class" in the submenu.

The "Add new item" dialog will pop up. Type in the new name 'Student.cs' and make sure the "Class" type is highlighted then click on the "Add" button. This will create a new class called Student in the project with default code, as shown below. Note the Solution Explorer window now has a Student.cs file.

```
using System;
using System.Collections.Generic;
using System.Text;

namespace Chapter1Example1
{
    internal class Student
    {
    }
}
```

You will add all components of the Student class inside the class braces, { and }, shown above. Move the cursor to the line after the beginning brace {. Push enter a few times and type in the code below:

```
        // fields
        private string name;
        private int score;
        // properties
        public string Name
        {
            get { return name; }
            set { name = value; }
        }
        public int Score
        {
            get { return score; }
            set { score = value; }
        }
        // constructor(s)
        public Student(string name, int score)
        {
            Name = name;
            Score = score;
        }
        // method(s)
        public char GetLetterGrade()
        {
            char letterGrade;
            if (Score >= 90)
```

```
            letterGrade = 'A';
        else if (Score >= 80)
            letterGrade = 'B';
        else if (Score >= 70)
            letterGrade = 'C';
        else if (Score >= 60)
            letterGrade = 'D';
        else
            letterGrade = 'F';
        return letterGrade;
    }
    // ToString
    public override string ToString()
    {
        string str;
        str = $"Name: {Name} Letter Grade: {GetLetterGrade()}";
        return str;
    }
```

Explanation:

The field section declares two private variables called fields: one to store student name, and the other to store student score. The first one should be a string data type, and the second one should be an int data type. The private modifier allows this variable to be used only inside this class. In OOP terminology, this is called *encapsulation*, which prevents outside objects from accessing the implementation details of a class.

The next section includes two properties. A property provides controlled access to a field -- typically, one public property corresponds to one private field. Properties allow you to retrieve a field's value (through a 'get' accessor) or store a value to it (through a 'set' accessor). Within the setter, the keyword `value` represents the incoming value being assigned to the property.

For example, outside the class you cannot write `name = "Lynn"` because `name` (lowercase) is a private field. Instead, you use the public property `Name = "Lynn"` (uppercase first letter). Following C# convention, field names begin with a lowercase letter while property names begin with an uppercase letter.

Even inside the class, it's good practice to access data through properties rather than using fields directly. In the Student class, each of the two private fields has a corresponding public property that follows this naming convention.

The constructor section can have one or more constructors. A constructor is a special method that is called every time a new object is created. Usually, you use a constructor to initialize the field values. The assignment assigns the value from the parameter to the variable in the field through the properties. The left side of the equal sign is the property and the right side is the parameter variable.

A constructor does not have a return type (not even the "void" keyword). A constructor must have the same name as the class, including the case. In this example, both the constructor and the class are called Student. Often times, you need more than one constructor. They still use the same name, but with different parameters. This is called method *overload* (remember constructor is a method). If you don't define any constructors in your class, C# automatically provides a default parameterless constructor for you. However, once you define your own constructor (even one with parameters), the compiler no longer supplies this default constructor—you must explicitly define a parameterless one if you need it.

The method section includes zero or more methods. The GetLetterGrade() method in the Student class evaluates the student's numeric score and returns the corresponding letter grade as a char. A char literal consists of a single character enclosed in single quotation marks, for example, 'A' or 'B'.

The ToString section has the ToString() method. It is a special method that returns a string value of an object. You can modify it so that it returns different values or returns the same values in a different format. Every class has a ToString() method by default inherited from the "Object" class. C# makes all classes automatically inherited from the "Object" class. The keyword "override" simply means that this class won't use the default ToString() method implementation of the Object class and will use this new one. ToString() is very convenient, and you should get used to having one for every class you create. It is a good practice to use properties instead of fields inside the ToString method.

Let's summarize. A class typically has zero or many fields. Each field has a corresponding property. A class also has one or many constructors. Additionally, a class has zero or many methods for class behavior. All classes come with a ToString() method, which you should override to have a meaningful outcome when an object of the class is printed.

Test Your Understanding 5.10
By convention, a field name begins with a(n) _______ case letter while a property name begins with a(n) _______ case letter.
A. lower, upper
B. upper, lower
C. lower, lower
D. upper, upper

Test Your Understanding 5.11
A(n) _______ of a class allows the retrieval of the field value or the storage of a value to the field.
A. property

B. constructor
C. object
D. ToString method

Test Your Understanding 5.12
A ________ of a class is a special method that is called every time a new object is created.
A. field
B. property
C. constructor
D. ToString method

Test Your Understanding 5.13
In the following code snippet, what is wrong?
```
public class Student
{
    private string name;
    private int score;
    public Student(string name, int score)
    {
        name = name;
        score = score;
    }
}
```
A. The body of the constructor does not do anything
B. The Student class misses methods
C. The Student class misses properties for the fields
D. A syntax error

Test Your Understanding 5.14
Which of the following is NOT a component of a class?
A. fields
B. properties
C. methods
D. repeating statements

Test Your Understanding 5.15
Can you have two methods with the same name in the same class?
A. Yes, as long as they have different return type.
B. Yes, as long as they have different body part.
C. Yes, as long as they have different parameters.
D. No, only constructors allowed to do that.

Test Your Understanding 5.16
Two methods in the same class with the same name is called ______
A. method duplication
B. method overriding
C. method overloading
D. constructors

Next, go to the "Solution Explorer" window and click on the "Program.cs" file to display it in the code window. Replace the default code with the following:

```
namespace Chapter5Example1
{
    public class Program
    {
        static void Main()
        {
            // create two student instances
            Student student1 = new Student("Lynn", 97);
            Student student2 = new Student("Bob", 87);
            // display the student data
            Console.WriteLine(student1);
            Console.WriteLine(student2);
        }
    }
}
```

Explanation:

So far, you've written C# statements directly in the `Program.cs` file -- and you can continue to do so. However, it's now time to introduce the full program structure, which includes a namespace, a class, and the `Main()` method.

In C#, you have two options: 1) Use the *top-level statements* style (just writing code directly in `Program.cs`, without explicitly declaring a class or `Main` method), or 2) Write the complete structure with an explicit `namespace`, `class`, and `Main()` method containing your statements. Visual Studio supports both approaches and will compile either one correctly.

The first line inside the Main() method creates a student object, called student1, by calling the constructor of the Student class and passing two arguments, "Lynn" for name and 97 for her score. A Student type variable called student1 is declared and assigned the reference to the newly created Student object.

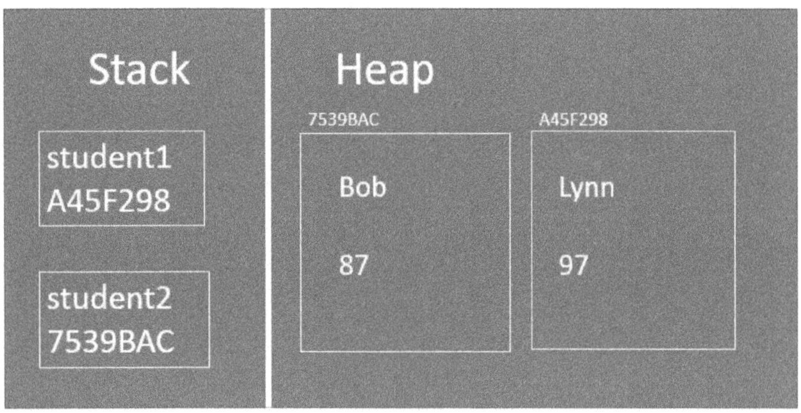

Figure 5.1 Memory storage of an object.

There are three things that happen in that line of the statement. First, in the heap area of computer memory, an unnamed object with a string value of "Lynn" and an int value of 97 is created. Second, in the stack area of computer memory, a Student type variable called student1 is created. Third, the memory address of that unnamed object is stored in the student1. If skipping the "Third", the student1 will store null. The memory address is often referred to as "reference". For now, just need to know the heap area is the slower area in memory and the stack area is the faster area in memory. You can think of computer memory like a parking lot in a shopping mall: the spaces closest to the entrance represent the stack, while the more distant areas represent the heap.

When you print an object like `student1`, C# automatically calls the `ToString()` method of its class (`Student` in this case) to get a string representation of the object. For learning purposes, you are encouraged to make some changes to the ToString() method of the Student class. You can see how the console display changes when you run the program again.

A namespace is a container which starts with the keyword, namespace, followed by a name and a pair of curly braces. A namespace can contain one or more classes. A class is also a container that can have zero or more methods. Finally, a method is a container that can have zero or more instructions. All containers have a container header followed by a pair of curly braces. All code for the rest of the book will follow the structure of namespace, class, and method.

Test Your Understanding 5.17
Some areas in a computer memory are faster than the others. The slower areas are often called ______
A. sluggish
B. back-burner
C. heap
D. stack

Test Your Understanding 5.18
Some areas in a computer memory are faster than the others. The faster areas are often called ______
A. fleet
B. front burner
C. heap
D. stack

Test Your Understanding 5.19
What happens in a computer memory when the following line is executed, assuming the 'Student' is a class?
Student s;

A. A Student type variable called s is created.
B. A Student name is created.
C. A student with a name of s is created.
D. It is an error, the s should be student.

Test Your Understanding 5.20
What happens in a computer memory when the following line is executed, assuming the 'Student' is a class with name and score fields?

```
new Student("Lynn", 97);
```

A. It is an error because "Lynn" is a string and 97 is an int. They must be the same data type.
B. A Student name and score are added to the current student.
C. A named object with a string value of "Lynn" and an int value of 97 is created
D. An unnamed object with a string value of "Lynn" and an int value of 97 is created.

Test Your Understanding 5.21
What is the equal sign in the following statement, assuming the 'Student' is a class with name and score fields?

```
Student s = new Student("Lynn", 97);
```

A. It is an error because "Lynn" is a string and 97 is an int. They must be the same data type.
B. A Student name and score are added to the current student.
C. The memory address of an unnamed object is stored in the s variable.
D. A named object with a string value of "Lynn" and an int value of 97 is stored in the s variable.

Test Your Understanding 5.22
Suppose s1 is an object of the Student class. What will the following statement do?

```
Console.WriteLine(s1);
```

A. s1 will be displayed on the console screen.
B. the ToString() method of the Student class will be called.
C. the constructor of the Student class will be called if defined.
D. a compiler error will result if the ToString() method of the Student class is not defined.

Test Your Understanding 5.23
Which of the following statements about C# class is correct?
Statement1: When creating a new object of a class, a constructor of the class is called.
Statement2: When creating a new object of a class, the object's name is always "new".
A. Statement1 only
B. Statement2 only
C. both Statement1 and Statement2
D. neither Statement1 nor Statement2

Test Your Understanding 5.24
You cannot live in a blueprint. You have to build a house to live in it. Similarly, for most classes, you cannot use it directly, you have to create a(n) ______ of the class before calling its methods.
A. instance
B. object
C. instance or object
D. house

Programming Challenge 5.1
An employee has a name, a payrate, and an hoursWorked. The pay amount can be calculated by multiplying

payrate and hoursWorked. Create a class called Employee with three fields (name, payrate, and hoursWorked). The data type for the name should be a string. The data type for payrate and hoursWorked should be double. The class should have a method called GetPayAmount that returns pay amount. The return data type must be double. The class should also include properties, constructor(s), and the ToString method. The ToString method must display employee name and pay amount. The amount must be currency formatted. Make sure you use properties instead of fields in a method. The class must be in its own cs file. Then, inside the Main method of the Program class, demonstrate the Employee class by instantiating two employee objects with made up data. One of the employees must be you. Next print both employees.

Example 5.2

Problem: Tic Tac Toe

Develop a console application of the Tic Tac Toe game. The Tic Tac Toe board includes nine squares in three rows by three columns. The game starts with all empty squares each marked with an "E". Two players take turns declaring squares. Whoever claims three consecutive squares first wins. The first player is "X". The second player is "O". A player claims a square by marking the square with either "X" or "O", depending whose turn it is.

A player declares a square by entering a row number (with the top row as 0, middle row as 1, and bottom row as 2) followed by a column number (with the left column as 0, middle column as 1, and right column as 2). If a player declares a square that is already declared, the game will display "invalid move" and the player should enter another choice. The game is over when one player wins or when all squares have been declared.

Solution:

Step 1: Display the board.

Start a new project called Chapter5Example2. Add a new class called Board to the project (You should see Board.cs in the Solution Explorer window). Type the code as shown below:

```
namespace Chapter5Example2
{
    public enum CellValue { E, X, O }
    internal class Board
    {
        // field
        private CellValue[,] allCells;
        // property
        public CellValue[,] AllCells
        {
            get { return allCells; }
            set { allCells = value; }
        }

        // constructor
```

```
        public Board()
        {
            AllCells = new CellValue[3, 3];
        }

        // ToString
        public override string ToString()
        {
            string str;
            str = AllCells[0, 0] + " | " + AllCells[0, 1] + " | " + AllCells[0, 2]
                + "\n-----------\n" +
                AllCells[1, 0] + " | " + AllCells[1, 1] + " | " + AllCells[1, 2]
                + "\n-----------\n" +
                AllCells[2, 0] + " | " + AllCells[2, 1] + " | " + AllCells[2, 2];
            return str;
        }

    }
}
```

Explanation:

The line of code right above the class definition creates an enum type called CellValue, with possible values of E, X, and O. Enumeration (enum) is a programmer defined type. It works like a constant variable, which you learned earlier can be more meaningful than a numeric literal. Enumeration prevents errors by not allowing programmers to type in anything other than what is defined. Declaring an enumeration is similar to declaring a class. Just replace the "class" keyword with the "enum" keyword. The content of an enum is much simpler. Just include all allowed values in a pair of curly braces.

The Board class has only one field called allCells, which is a two-dimensional array. This corresponds to the 3 by 3 game board. A two-dimensional array uses two indices to access an element of the array.

The constructor creates a two-dimensional array of CellValue type. The size of the array is 3 by 3, meaning it has three rows and three columns. The rows count from 0 to 2. The same is true for columns. The memory address of this new array is assigned to the AllCells property. The default value of this array is E, because that's the first one on the CellValue enum type.

The Board class has a ToString() method that will display the board with the content from allCells. AllCells[0, 0] holds the value of row 0 (the first row) and column 0 (the first column). Similarly AllCells[0, 1] holds the value of row 0 (the first row) and column 1 (the second column). The "\n" is a new line symbol. It works like pressing the "Enter" key.

Next, in the default Program.cs file, type in the code as shown below:

```
namespace Chapter5Example2
{
    class Program
    {
        static void Main()
        {
            Board board = new Board();
            Console.WriteLine(board);
        }
    }
}
```

Save and run the program. You should see a console output as shown here:

```
E | E | E
-----------
E | E | E
-----------
E | E | E
```

Step 2: Play until all squares are declared.

We are going to change the letter E to X or O based on which player plays. After the first player (X) chooses the row and column numbers, that position will be replaced with X. Next, the second player (O) chooses a position to put O. The two players take turns to play forever. After all squares are declared, no valid play is possible.

Add a class called Player to the project (You should see Player.cs in the Solution Explorer window). Replace the default code with the following:

```
namespace Chapter5Example2
{
    internal class Player
    {
        // fields
        private CellValue playerName;
        private int row;
        private int column;
        // properties
        public CellValue PlayerName
        {
            get { return playerName; }
            set { playerName = value; }
        }
        public int Row
        {
            get { return row; }
            set { row = value; }
        }
        private int Column
        {
            get { return column; }
```

```
            set { column = value; }
        }
        // constructor
        public Player(CellValue playerName, int row, int column)
        {
            PlayerName = playerName;
            Row = row;
            Column = column;
        }
        // method
        public void PlayerMove(Board board)
        {
            board.AllCells[Row, Column] = PlayerName;
        }
    }
}
```

Explanation:

The playerName field value can only be E, X, or O because it is the CellValue type.

The PlayerMove() method updates the two dimensional array for the specific player on the specified row and column position.

Next, update the Main() method so that the body part now looks like:

```
    Board board = new Board();
    Console.WriteLine(board);
    CellValue playerName = CellValue.X;
    int row;
    int col;
    bool playerWins = false;
    bool stalemate = false;
    bool validCell;
    while (!(playerWins || stalemate))
    {
        do
        {
            Console.WriteLine($"Player {playerName} moves.");
            Console.WriteLine("Enter row number (0, 1, 2):");
            row = int.Parse(Console.ReadLine());
            Console.WriteLine("Enter column number (0, 1, 2):");
            col = int.Parse(Console.ReadLine());
            validCell = row < 3 && row >= 0 && col < 3 && col >= 0
                        && board.AllCells[row, col] == CellValue.E;
            if (!validCell)
                Console.WriteLine("Invalid move");
        } while (!validCell);
        Player player = new Player(playerName, row, col);
        player.PlayerMove(board);
        Console.WriteLine(board);
        playerName = (playerName == CellValue.X) ?
                     CellValue.O : CellValue.X;
    }
```

Explanation:

The playerName variable is initialized to the first player (player X). Two int variables are declared to hold the row and column numbers entered by a player.

The while loop will keep running until the game is over. The game is over when one player wins or all squares on the board are declared (stalemate). Because we don't know how to check if a player wins or if all squares on the board are declared, this loop will run forever. However, the inner do while loop will stop iterating when all cells are occupied. This inner loop will run until the player enters a valid row and column number. A valid row and column number is a square that has the E value (empty).

A player object is instantiated with the row and column chosen by the player. Then the PlayerMove() method of the Player class is called to update the array value. After that the new board is displayed.

Finally, we change the player name with a ternary expression. The ternary expression is the same as the following:

```
if (playerName == CellValue.X)
   playerName = CellValue.O;
else
   playerName = CellValue.X;
```

Save and run the program to see the X and Os replacing Es. You will not see the winner.

Step 3: Game over

You need to check if a player has won, or if all squares on the board have been declared (not E).

First, open the Player class in code view and add the IsPlayerWin() method to the class with the code below (anywhere inside the class, but outside any other methods):

```
public bool IsPlayerWin(Board board)
{
    bool isWin = false;
    if (board.AllCells[0, 0] != CellValue.E &&
        board.AllCells[0, 0] == board.AllCells[1, 1] &&
        board.AllCells[1, 1] == board.AllCells[2, 2])
    {
        isWin = true;
    }
    if (board.AllCells[0, 2] != CellValue.E &&
        board.AllCells[0, 2] == board.AllCells[1, 1] &&
        board.AllCells[1, 1] == board.AllCells[2, 0])
    {
        isWin = true;
    }
    for (int r = 0; r < 3; r++)
    {
```

```
            if (board.AllCells[r, 0] != CellValue.E &&
                board.AllCells[r, 0] == board.AllCells[r, 1] &&
                board.AllCells[r, 1] == board.AllCells[r, 2])
            {
                isWin = true;
            }
        }
        for (int c = 0; c < 3; c++)
        {
            if (board.AllCells[0, c] != CellValue.E &&
                board.AllCells[0, c] == board.AllCells[1, c] &&
                board.AllCells[1, c] == board.AllCells[2, c])
            {
                isWin = true;
            }
        }
        return isWin;
    }
```

Explanation:

There are four situations in which a player wins: 1) the diagonal, from top left to bottom right are the same letter; 2) the diagonal, from top right to bottom left are the same letter; 3) any of the three rows are the same letter; 4) any of the three columns are the same letter. The IsPlayerWin() does exactly that.

Next, add the HasNoMoreE() method, as shown below, inside the Board class (recommended between the constructor and the ToString()):

```
public bool HasNoMoreE()
{
    bool hasNoMoreE = true;
    for (int r = 0; r < 3; r++)
    {
        for (int c = 0; c < 3; c++)
        {
            if (allCells[r, c] == CellValue.E)
                hasNoMoreE = false;
        }
    }
    return hasNoMoreE;
}
```

Finally, add the code, as shown below, inside the Main() method towards the end of the method right before the following line: `playerName = (playerName == CellValue.X)?`

Here's the code to add:

```
playerWins = player.IsPlayerWin(board);
stalemate = board.HasNoMoreE();
if (playerWins)
    Console.WriteLine($"Player {playerName} wins.");
```

```
if (stalemate)
    Console.WriteLine("Stalemate!");
```

Save and run the application to see how your Tic Tac Toe game works.

Test Your Understanding 5.25
In C#, the ______ is a new line symbol. It works like pressing the "Enter" key.
A. "n"
B. "\n"
C. "nl"
D. "\nl"

Test Your Understanding 5.26
What will be displayed on the console screen?

```
int x = 0;
int y= (x == 0) ? 1:2;
Console.WriteLine(y);
```

A. 0
B. 1
C. 2
D. 3

Test Your Understanding 5.27
What will be displayed on the console screen?

```
int x = 3;
int y= (x == 0) ? 1:2;
Console.WriteLine(y);
```

A. 0
B. 1
C. 2
D. 3

5.2 Agile Artifact: Product Backlog

As you learned in Chapter 2, there are three roles, five events, and three artifacts in scrum. You learned the agile roles and events in the previous two chapters. In this chapter, you will learn the three artifacts. The agile artifacts include product backlog, sprint backlog, and increments.

5.2.1 Product Backlog Definition

The product backlog contains all software requirements in the form of user stories. The product backlog starts with rough software requirements in varying degrees of detail. Some stories are very specific while others are general. Over time, when more about the software is known and more increments are completed, the product backlog evolves.

Product Backlog
User Story 1 (most valuable and detailed)
User Story 2 (next valuable and detailed)
....
Epic (less detailed)
....
Theme (least detailed)

Figure 5.2 Product backlog.

User stories in the product backlog are organized with those of higher priority at the top and those of lower priority at the bottom (Figure 5.2). The stories at the top are in more detail. Priority is based on how much value the completed user story will add to the business. The product owner decides which user stories are the most valuable based on the value analysis.

Let us consider the characteristics of a good product backlog, according to the DEEP principle (Cohn, 2010).

Detailed appropriately: Higher priority stories contain more details than lower priority stories.

Estimated: User stories in the product backlog should be estimable by the development team. This indicates the team can understand the stories. At the very least, stories at the top should be estimable.

Emergent: Stories in the product backlog are constantly evolving. When more about the marketplace is known, or technology advancement takes place, the product backlog should be updated. The product backlog is also updated between the sprints.

Prioritized: All stories should be prioritized based on the business value a story provides.

Test Your Understanding 5.28
The priority of the user stories in the product backlog is based on ______.
A. how much value the completed story will add to the business
B. how many features the completed story will add to the business
C. how fast the team can complete the story
D. how much the story cost when completed

Test Your Understanding 5.29
The ______ decides which user stories are the most valuable based on the value analysis.
A. CEO
B. product owner
C. scrum master
D. team

Test Your Understanding 5.30
The product backlog contains ______.

A. product
B. product details
C. user stories
D. increments

Test Your Understanding 5.31
The User stories are ______.
A. product
B. product details
C. user experiences
D. software requirements

Test Your Understanding 5.32
User stories with higher priority should be ______ of the product backlog.
A. at the top
B. in the middle
C. at the bottom
D. anywhere

Test Your Understanding 5.33
User stories at the top of the product backlog are in ______ details.
A. normal
B. more
C. less
D. least

Test Your Understanding 5.34
Which of the following is an agile artifact explained in the book?
A. product backlog
B. user stories
C. software requirements
D. kanban

Test Your Understanding 5.35
In product backlog, higher priority stories contain more details than lower priority stories. This is a property of _______.
A. detailed appropriately
B. estimate
C. emergent
D. prioritized

Test Your Understanding 5.36
User stories in the product backlog should be estimable by the development team. This indicates the _____.
A. story can be completed in time
B. story can be completed within the budget
C. team can understand the stories
D. team can complete the stories as promised

Test Your Understanding 5.37
All stories should be prioritized based on the ______ a story provides

A. features
B. business value
C. story points
D. simplicity

Test Your Understanding 5.38
Which of the following is NOT a characteristic of a good product backlog?
A. Detailed appropriately
B. Length appropriately
C. Estimate
D. Prioritized

Test Your Understanding 5.39
Stories in the product backlog are constantly evolving. This is a property of _______.
A. detailed appropriately
B. estimate
C. emergent
D. prioritized

5.2.2 Value Analysis

To determine business values, first determine the area the completed user story will affect (Marchewka, 2015). The following are potential areas affected:

1. *Customer.* These values are related to customers. For example, if the software functions or features can reduce product price, then the business value is in the customer area.
2. *Strategic.* If the completed user story can create new markets or increase the market share of the company, then the value is in the strategic area.
3. *Financial.* If the software can increase the return on investment or reduce the cost, then the value is in the financial area.
4. *Operational.* If the software can increase the efficiency and effectiveness of the company operation, the value is in the operational area.
5. *Social.* If the software can benefit society, such as dissemination of knowledge, or reduction of pollution, the value is in the social area.

Next, develop an appropriate metric to measure the business value. Not all values can be easily quantified, though business values in the financial area are relatively easy to quantify. Value analysis alone is insufficient for prioritization -- you must combine value assessment with implementation effort to make rational sequencing decisions. The core relationship follows this principle: Prioritize user stories that deliver the highest value relative to their cost/effort first.

After identifying which value areas a user story affects (customer, strategic, financial, operational, social), teams typically:

Score the value (e.g., 1–10 scale) across relevant dimensions

Example: A payment feature might score:

- Customer value: 9 (reduces checkout friction)
- Financial value: 8 (reduces transaction fees)
- Strategic value: 6 (supports market expansion)

Composite value score = 23

Estimate effort (story points explained later in the chapter): 8 story points

Calculate value-to-effort ratio: 23 ÷ 8 = 2.88 (high priority candidate)

Test Your Understanding 5.40
If the software can increase the return on investment or reduce the cost, then the business value is in the ______ area.
A. customer
B. financial
C. strategic
D. operational

Test Your Understanding 5.41
If the software can increase the efficiency and effectiveness of the company operation, the business value is in the _______ area.
A. customer
B. financial
C. strategic
D. operational

Test Your Understanding 5.42
If the software can benefit society, such as dissemination of knowledge, or reduction of pollution, the business value is in the _______ area.
A. customer
B. social
C. strategic
D. operational

Test Your Understanding 5.43
Which of the following is NOT a business value area?
A. customer
B. financial
C. social

D. technical

Test Your Understanding 5.44
If the completed feature of the user story can create new markets for the company, the business value is in ________ area.
A. customer
B. financial
C. strategic
D. technical

Test Your Understanding 5.45
If the completed feature of the user story can reduce product price, the business value is in ________ area.
A. customer
B. social
C. strategic
D. technical

5.2.3 The MoSCow Method

Another prioritization method is called MoSCow, outlined in the Dynamic Systems Development Method (DSDM) (Craddock et al., 2012), which is one of many agile approaches. MoSCoW includes four priority levels:

1. Must haves: Requirements in this category must be implemented, otherwise the solution won't work or will be useless. These are the minimum components the team must deliver. Examples might include:

    The ability for users to create an account and log in.

    Basic CRUD (create, read, update, delete) functionality for core data objects in the application.

    Reliable error handling and logging to ensure problems can be identified and resolved quickly.

2. Should haves: Requirements in this category are important, but can be omitted if the schedule or budget won't permit. Examples might include:

    Advanced search functionality to make it easier for users to find specific information.

    Integration with third-party APIs to provide additional functionality or data sources.

    Automated testing and deployment processes to ensure high quality and efficiency.

3. Could haves: These requirements enhance the solution, but can be left out or are not critical. Examples might include:

    Additional customization options for users to personalize their experience.

    Support for multiple languages or currencies to accommodate international users.

    Advanced analytics and reporting features to help users understand trends and insights.

4. Want to haves: These requirements are nice to have and can be included in later development. They are not included in the initial delivery. Examples might include:

Gamification features like badges or achievements to encourage user engagement.

Social media integration to allow users to share content or connect with friends.

Test Your Understanding 5.46
The MoSCoW is a(n) ______ method, outlined in the Dynamic Systems Development Method (DSDM).
A. agile
B. business analytic
C. kanban
D. prioritization

Test Your Understanding 5.47
In MoSCoW, which category includes requirements that are important, but can be omitted if the schedule or budget won't permit?
A. Must haves
B. Should haves
C. Could haves
D. Want to haves

Test Your Understanding 5.48
In MoSCoW, which category includes requirements that are nice to have and can be included in the next development?
A. Must haves
B. Should haves
C. Could haves
D. Want to haves

Test Your Understanding 5.49
In MoSCoW, which category includes the requirements that can enhance the solution, but can be left out or are not critical?
A. Must haves
B. Should haves
C. Could haves
D. Want to haves

Test Your Understanding 5.50
In the MoSCoW examples in the book, which of the following examples is most likely to be in the 'Must haves' category?
A. The ability for users to create an account and log in
B. Advanced search functionality to make it easier for users to find specific information
C. Integration with third-party APIs to provide additional functionality or data sources.
D. Automated testing and deployment processes to ensure high quality and efficiency.

Test Your Understanding 5.51
In the MoSCoW examples in the book, which of the following examples is most likely to be in the 'Should haves' category?
A. The ability for users to create an account and log in
B. Advanced search functionality to make it easier for users to find specific information

C. Basic CRUD (create, read, update, delete) functionality for core data objects in the application.
D. Reliable error handling and logging to ensure problems can be identified and resolved quickly

Test Your Understanding 5.52
In the MoSCoW examples in the book, which of the following examples is most likely to be in the 'Could haves' category?
A. The ability for users to create an account and log in
B. Advanced search functionality to make it easier for users to find specific information
C. Additional customization options for users to personalize their experience
D. Reliable error handling and logging to ensure problems can be identified and resolved quickly

5.3 Story, Epic, and Theme

As shown in Figure 5.2, not all user stories in the product backlog are in the same granularity (Patton, 2014). For those at the top of the list, greater detail is needed. Those at the bottom of the list may not even count as stories. They may instead be referred to as 'epics' or 'themes'. An epic is a user story that is too big to be designed, coded, or tested within a single sprint. A theme is a very general story or a big idea, sometimes containing the whole release or even multiple releases. Most requirements start out as themes or epics, since the first idea customers have for their software tends to be abstract. As the project progresses, stories will become more detailed to fit the work.

Here are some examples of epic:
Example 1: Implement a mobile app for a healthcare provider that allows patients to view their medical records and schedule appointments. This user story is too big to be designed, coded, or tested within a single sprint, so it would be broken down into smaller, more manageable stories.

Example 2: Develop a new e-commerce website for a retailer that sells a wide range of products. This user story is too big to be completed within a single sprint, and would likely involve multiple sub-teams working on different aspects of the project such as designing the user interface, integrating with payment systems, or implementing search and filtering functionality.

Example 3: Develop a cloud-based CRM system for a sales team. This epic could include many user stories, such as designing a customizable dashboard, implementing lead management tools, developing reporting and analytics features, and integrating with other software systems. Each of these user stories would need to be broken down into smaller, more manageable pieces.

Here are some examples of theme:

Example 1: Improve the user experience of a social media platform. This is a very general story or a big idea that could span multiple releases, and would likely involve a variety of specific user stories such as enhancing the search functionality, improving the comment system, or adding new features like video sharing.

Example 2: Enhance the security of a financial services application. This is a broad idea that could encompass a variety of specific user stories such as adding two-factor authentication, implementing SSL encryption, or conducting security audits to identify vulnerabilities. The theme of improving security could also extend across multiple releases as new threats emerge and new features are developed.

Example 3: Improve the performance of a web application. This theme could encompass a variety of specific user stories, such as optimizing page load times, reducing server response times, and minimizing data transfer between the client and server. The theme of performance improvement could also extend across multiple releases as new performance metrics are identified and new features are developed.

Test Your Understanding 5.53
With examples from the book, which of the following user requirements is more likely to be an epic?
A. Implement a mobile app for a healthcare provider that allows patients to view their medical records and schedule appointments.
B. Improve the user experience of a social media platform.
C. Enhance the security of a financial services application
D. Improve the performance of a web application

Test Your Understanding 5.54
With examples from the book, which of the following user requirements is more likely to be a theme?
A. Implement a mobile app for a healthcare provider that allows patients to view their medical records and schedule appointments.
B. Improve the user experience of a social media platform.
C. Develop a new e-commerce website for a retailer that sells a wide range of products
D. Develop a cloud-based CRM system for a sales team

Test Your Understanding 5.55
A(n) ______ is a user story that is too big to be designed, coded, or tested within a single sprint.
A. requirement
B. increment
C. epic
D. product backlog

Test Your Understanding 5.56
A(n) ______ is a very general story or a big idea, sometimes containing the whole release or even multiple releases.

A. major requirement
B. theme
C. epic
D. product backlog

Test Your Understanding 5.57
User stories in the product backlog have different ____; stories with higher priority should have ___ details.
A. length, less
B. priority, less
C. details, less
D. granularity, more

Test Your Understanding 5.58
List items in the product backlog from least to most detailed.
A. user story, epic, theme
B. theme, epic, user story
C. epic, user story, theme
D. epic, theme. User story

5.4 User Story

A user story is a lightweight, user-centered requirement description used in agile development to capture who needs a feature, what they need to accomplish, and why. Rather than specifying technical implementation details, it focuses on delivering value to end users through concise, collaborative narratives. This section introduces the standard structure for writing user stories and explores the qualities that make them effective tools for guiding development and fostering shared understanding among teams and stakeholders.

5.4.1 Story Structure

You have seen the term "user story" many times, but what exactly is a user story? A user story includes a statement of the requirements and any acceptance criteria. A user story takes this format:

As a <type of user>, I want <some goal>, so that <some reason>

In our toy retailer example outlined in Chapter 1, a possible user story can be:
As a manager, I want to check the inventory level at any time so that I know when to place a replenishment.

A user story is written on an index card, implying it shouldn't be too long or complicated.

Acceptance criteria is written on the back of the user story (Cohn, 2004). The criteria include assumptions made by the customers. In the retailer example, the manager may state that he wants to be able to check the inventory by product id, product name, and partial product name, and be able to view all products on one screen.

The criteria can also be used to determine if a story is fully implemented. From the same example, the manager may simply want all inventory information to be displayed on one screen and be able to print it off onto paper.

Earlier in the chapter, you see the following epic: "Implement a mobile app for a healthcare provider that allows patients to view their medical records and schedule appointments." Here are a few user stories that could be derived from the given epic:

User Story Example 1:
As a patient, I want to view my medical records on my mobile device, so that I can easily access my health information from anywhere.

Acceptance Criteria:

The app must allow patients to securely log in using their unique credentials.
The app must display the patient's medical records, including test results, prescriptions, and medical history.
The app must provide the ability to filter and search for specific information within their medical records.
The app must maintain patient privacy by complying with all relevant data privacy regulations.

User Story Example 2:
As a patient, I want to schedule appointments with my healthcare provider through the mobile app, so that I can easily manage my healthcare appointments.

Acceptance Criteria:

The app must allow patients to view their provider's availability for appointments.
The app must provide patients with the ability to book, reschedule, or cancel appointments within the app.
The app must send notifications to patients regarding their upcoming appointments, including reminders and any changes made to the appointment schedule.
The app must allow patients to provide additional information or notes regarding their appointments.

User Story Example 3:
As a healthcare provider, I want to access patient medical records and appointment schedules through the mobile app, so that I can manage my patients' healthcare more efficiently.

Acceptance Criteria:

The app must allow providers to securely log in using their unique credentials.
The app must display the provider's schedule, including patient appointments and availability.
The app must provide providers with the ability to access patient medical records within the app.
The app must allow providers to add notes and updates to patients' medical records.
The app must maintain patient privacy by complying with all relevant data privacy regulations.

Note: These stories are just a starting point and there may be several more user stories that can be derived from the given epic. The acceptance criteria may also vary depending on the specific needs of the healthcare provider and the mobile app's intended users.

Test Your Understanding 5.59
Which of the following is NOT a part of a user story?
A. type of user
B. some goal
C. some reason
D. some benefit

Test Your Understanding 5.60
Which component of a user story is missing in the following story?
"As a manager, I want to check the inventory level at any time. The manager wants to be able to check the inventory by product id, product name, and partial product name, and be able to view all products on one screen."
A. type of user
B. some goal
C. some reason
D. acceptance criteria

Test Your Understanding 5.61
Which component of a user story is missing in the following story?
"As a manager, I want to check the inventory level at any time so that I know when to place a replenishment."
A. type of user
B. some goal
C. some reason
D. acceptance criteria

Test Your Understanding 5.62
The acceptance criteria of a user story include ______ made by the customers.
A. type of user
B. some goal
C. some reason
D. assumptions

Test Your Understanding 5.63
The ______ can be used to determine if a story is fully implemented.
A. type of user
B. some goal
C. some reason
D. acceptance criteria

Test Your Understanding 5.64
Which of the following is NOT a component of a user story?
A. user
B. goal
C. platform
D. reason

5.4.2 What Is a Good User Story

To write a good user story, you must follow the INVEST acronym (Cohn, 2010):

Independent: A user story must be able to stand alone. Ideally, user stories can be delivered in any order. By independent, it means that a user story should not depend on any other user story or feature to be completed first. Each user story should be self-contained and able to be implemented and tested independently, without requiring any other user stories to be delivered first.

For example, consider a user story that involves allowing users to create a profile on a website. This user story should be independent of other user stories, such as allowing users to reset their password or upload a profile picture. It should be possible to implement and test the "create a profile" user story without any dependencies on other features.

In addition, independent user stories can be delivered in any order, which is one of the benefits of Agile development. This means that the development team can prioritize user stories based on their importance, complexity, or other factors, without being constrained by dependencies between them.

Negotiable: A user story is a conversation, not a specification. Collaboration and discussion about the best way to solve the business problem should happen between the product owner and the development team. When we say that a user story is negotiable, it means that it is flexible and subject to change. The user story is not a rigid specification that must be followed to the letter. Instead, it serves as a starting point for a conversation between the product owner and the development team.

This conversation should be collaborative, with both parties contributing their expertise and ideas to find the best solution to the business problem at hand. The product owner provides the context and the vision of what needs to be accomplished, while the development team offers technical insight and expertise.

For example, suppose a product owner wants to build an e-commerce website. A user story might be "As a customer, I want to be able to filter search results by price." However, during the discussion between the product owner and the development team, they might realize that filtering by price alone might not be sufficient. The development team might suggest adding additional filters such as product category or brand.

By being negotiable, the user story can be adjusted and refined to reflect the evolving understanding of the business problem and the technical considerations that need to be taken into account. Ultimately, this collaborative approach leads to a better solution that meets the needs of both the business and the end-users.

Valuable: A user story should provide value to stakeholders, as you learned earlier in this chapter. When we say that a user story should be valuable, it means that it should deliver tangible benefits -- whether to end users, the business, or the system's long-term health. While user stories ideally focus on user-facing outcomes, technical work can and should be captured as user stories when necessary -- provided the business rationale or value is clearly articulated. For example, instead of "Upgrade the database," a valuable technical story explains why: "To reduce system downtime by 30% and prevent $50K in monthly lost revenue, we need to upgrade the database infrastructure." The key is that even technical requirements should connect to a meaningful outcome rather than existing as isolated implementation tasks.

For example, a product owner might identify a business problem, such as low customer retention rates. They might create a user story that addresses this problem, such as "As a customer, I want to receive personalized recommendations based on my past purchases, so that I am more likely to make additional purchases and remain a loyal customer." This user story is valuable because it directly addresses a business problem and has the potential to increase customer retention rates, which is a valuable outcome for the company.

Estimable: When we say that a user story must be estimable, it means that it should be detailed enough to allow the development team to estimate the amount of effort, time, and resources required to complete it. This estimation is essential for effective project planning and management, as it helps the team to allocate resources appropriately, set realistic deadlines, and prioritize work.

For example, suppose a product owner creates a user story that says, "As a customer, I want to be able to add items to my shopping cart, so that I can purchase them later." This user story is too broad and lacking in detail to be estimable. The development team would have difficulty estimating the amount of effort needed to complete it, as it does not specify important details such as the type of items that can be added to the shopping cart, the design of the shopping cart interface, or the necessary backend infrastructure to support the feature.

On the other hand, a more detailed user story might be, "As a customer, I want to be able to add multiple sizes and colors of a product to my shopping cart, so that I can easily compare and purchase them at a later time." This user story provides more details that allow the development team to estimate the amount of effort needed to implement the feature.

In order to be estimable, a user story should provide sufficient information about the desired functionality, acceptance criteria, and any technical requirements or constraints. This information allows the development team to make informed estimates about the effort required to complete the user story and to plan accordingly.

Small: When we say that a user story should be small, it means that it should be small enough to be completed within a single sprint, which is a time-boxed period of development typically lasting between two and four weeks. Small user stories are important because they allow the development team to make steady progress, maintain momentum, and deliver value to the product owner and end-users in a timely manner. This approach also allows the product owner to provide feedback and make adjustments along the way, which ultimately leads to a better product.

For example, suppose a product owner wants to create a new feature for an e-commerce website that allows customers to leave product reviews. Instead of creating a single user story that encompasses all aspects of the feature, such as designing the review interface, creating a backend database, and implementing review moderation features, the product owner could create multiple small user stories. Each small user story would focus on a specific aspect of the feature and would be small enough to be completed within a single sprint.

Testable: When we say that a user story should be testable, it means that it should be specific and detailed enough to allow for testing and verification. A user story that is not testable is typically too vague or lacks clear acceptance criteria, which can lead to misunderstandings and delays in the development process. For example, suppose a product owner creates a user story that says, "As a customer, I want the website to be fast." This user story is not testable because it is too vague and does not provide any specific criteria for measuring speed. The development team would have difficulty verifying whether the story has been successfully completed, and the product owner would not have a clear idea of what to expect.

On the other hand, a more testable user story might be, "As a customer, I want the website to load in under three seconds, even on slow internet connections so that I can quickly access content without frustration and stay engaged with my task." This user story provides specific criteria that can be measured and verified through testing. The development team can ensure that the website meets these criteria, and the product owner can be confident that the story has been successfully completed.

In order to be testable, a user story should provide clear acceptance criteria that define what the user expects to see or experience as a result of the story being completed. Acceptance criteria should be specific, measurable, and verifiable, and they should be agreed upon by both the product owner and the development team. This ensures that there is a shared understanding of what is expected and that the story can be completed successfully.

Test Your Understanding 5.65
A user story must be able to stand alone. Ideally, user stories can be delivered in any order. This is ______ in the INVEST acronym.
A. independent
B. negotiable
C. valuable
D. estimable

Test Your Understanding 5.66
A story should be small enough to fit into a single sprint. This is ________ in the INVEST acronym.
A. independent
B. negotiable
C. small
D. estimable

Test Your Understanding 5.67
A user story is a conversation, not a specification. This is ________ in the INVEST acronym.
A. independent
B. negotiable
C. valuable
D. estimable

Test Your Understanding 5.68
A user story should not be vague. This is _____ in the INVEST acronym.
A. independent
B. negotiable
C. small
D. testable

5.5 Story Time

User stories in the product backlog must be estimated. If not all stories are estimated, at least those stories at the top should be estimated. Estimation is about predicting how much effort will be required to complete the story by the development team. It is measured by story points and determined by the development team. Many development teams estimate effort by using the *planning poker game* (Rubin, 2013):

Each team member has a stack of cards with the numbers ½, 1, 2, 3, 5, 8, 13, 20, 40, and 100. A story is then picked. The team reads the story and discusses it. Then, independently, team members place a card face down indicating how much effort they think the story will be. Values correspond to difficulty level. All cards are flipped over at the same time. The members with the smallest and largest values should explain their reasoning. The game is repeated until all numbers are relatively similar. Then, the team can select a number for the story.

Note that the numbers on planning poker cards are not simply consecutive, like 1, 2, 3, 4, 5. This is because larger efforts are more difficult to estimate accurately. For instance, if you want to estimate the distance between where you stand and an object right in front of you, you can be quite accurate. However, if you want to estimate the distance to an object that is farther away from you, the accuracy is reduced.

Using a range of story points in planning poker allows the team to express greater granularity in their estimates, which can help to more accurately reflect the complexity of a particular task or user story. The larger the gap between two consecutive numbers, the greater the uncertainty and variability in the estimated effort required to complete a task or story.

The use of non-consecutive numbers also helps to prevent the team from getting bogged down in detailed discussions of small differences in effort. For example, if the team were using consecutive numbers like 1, 2, 3, 4, 5, it might be difficult to distinguish between a 3-point story and a 4-point story, and the team might waste time debating the difference between the two. By using non-consecutive numbers, the team can better communicate the differences in complexity between stories and focus on discussing the most significant differences.

Story points reflect the team's estimate for how much effort is needed to complete the story. It is a relative number. In other words, the story points for one team cannot be compared to the story points of another team.

Test Your Understanding 5.69
Why are non-consecutive numbers used in planning poker?
A. To make the estimation process more challenge and fun
B. To reflect the complexity of a task or user story more accurately
C. To prevent the team from discussing topics not related to the story
D. To increase the technical estimation skills

Test Your Understanding 5.70
How does the use of non-consecutive numbers in planning poker help prevent the team from getting bogged down in detailed discussions?
A. By making the estimation process more challenge
B. By ignoring the details
C. By allowing for greater range of story points
D. By making it difficult to distinguish between similar estimates

Test Your Understanding 5.71
When estimating a user story with the planning poker game, the ______ of all members' card face values is used as the team story points.
A. average
B. smallest
C. largest
D. relatively similar number

Test Your Understanding 5.72
If Team A estimates 40 points, and Team B estimates 20 points for the same user story, ______
A. one can conclude that Team B can complete the story in about half the time of Team A
B. one can conclude that Team A can complete the story in about half the time of Team B
C. one can conclude that Team B can complete the story faster than Team A
D. no conclusion can be made

5.6 Agile Artifact: Sprint Backlog

The sprint backlog contains items from the product backlog selected by the development team for the current sprint. It also includes any items added in the sprint planning meeting, such as the sprint goal. It is a forecast by the development team about what features will be included in the next increment, and the work needed to complete the features. The stories from the product backlog are picked based on their business values and the team velocity (the number of story points the team can complete in one sprint). Stories in the product backlog can be updated as needed while stories in the sprint backlog should not be changed so that the team can complete the sprint.

The stories in the sprint backlog are broken down into sprint tasks, which are small enough to be assigned to one member as a day's work or less. Every sprint task is then estimated for the number of hours needed to complete it. User stories in the product backlog are estimated for effort in story points, while tasks in the sprint backlog are estimated by hours. As a result, each story in the sprint backlog also has a time estimate. Note that the relationship between story points and time estimates are not linear. In other words, if a 20 points story takes 200 hours, it does not mean that a 40 points story will take 400 hours. Story points are relative numbers while task estimates are absolute.

Items	Product Backlog	Sprint Backlog
Scope	Project	Sprint
Detail	Less	More
Measurement	Story point	Hour
Ownership	Product owner	Team
Update Frequency	Weekly	Daily

Table 5.1 Comparison between Product Backlog and Sprint Backlog

Test Your Understanding 5.73
The sprint backlog contains items from the ______ selected by the development team for the current sprint.
A. user stories
B. requirements
C. product backlog
D. product inventory

Test Your Understanding 5.74
The stories from the product backlog are often picked into a sprint backlog based on the team ______.
A. agreement
B. contract
C. charter
D. velocity

Test Your Understanding 5.75
The team ______ is the number of story points the team can complete in one sprint.
A. agreement
B. contract
C. charter
D. velocity

Test Your Understanding 5.76
The stories in the sprint backlog are broken down into sprint ______, which are small enough to be assigned to one member as a day's work or less.
A. tasks
B. events
C. stories
D. velocities

Test Your Understanding 5.77
User stories in the product backlog are estimated for effort in ______, while tasks in the sprint backlog are estimated by ______.
A. story points, sprint points
B. sprint points, story points
C. hours, story points
D. story points, hours

Test Your Understanding 5.78
The stories in the product backlog ______ while stories in the sprint backlog ______.
A. can be updated as needed, should not be changed
B. should not be changed, can be updated as needed
C. is called epic, is called theme
D. is called theme, is called theme epic

Test Your Understanding 5.79
The product backlog is owned by ______ while the sprint backlog is owned by ______.
A. the team, the scrum master
B. the scrum master, the team
C. the product owner, the team
D. the team, the product owner

5.7 Agile Artifact: Increment

The increment is the piece of software containing all currently completed and tested items. All increments must be completed to be 'done' and accepted by the product owner. Thus, the increment gets larger and larger as more sprints are completed. The increment of the last sprint of the project is the whole, completed software the customer asked for.

Test Your Understanding 5.80
An increment is all the items completed in _____ sprint(s).
A. one
B. two
C. three
D. the current and previous

Test Your Understanding 5.81
The increment of the last sprint of a project is ________.
A. a milestone
B. a closure
C. the final sprint
D. the software the customer wants

5.8 Chapter Summary

In this chapter, you learned that a C# class is a logical group of methods and the data that these methods work on. When you think of a class, you think of its status and behavior. The status is the fields, and the behavior is the methods. Most classes will include fields, properties, constructors, normal methods, and ToString() methods. You also learned the three artifacts of scrum: product backlog, sprint backlog, and increment. The product backlog contains all user stories, epics, and themes. The sprint backlog are stories picked from the product backlog by the team to be in the current sprint backlog, plus additional items agreed upon by the team during the sprint planning. The increment is the accumulated parts of software after each sprint.

5.9 References

Cohn, M. (2004). User Stories Applied for Agile Software Development, Addison-Wesley. Boston.
Cohn, M. (2006). Agile estimating and planning. Prentice Hall. Upper Saddle River, NJ.
Cohn, M. (2010). Succeeding with Agile: Software development using Scrum. Addison-Wesley. Boston, MA.
Craddock, A., Roberts, B., Richards, K. Godwin, J., and Tudor, D. (2012), The DSDM Agile Project Framework for Scrum. DSDM consortium.
Marchewka, J. T. (2015), *Information Technology Project Management*, 5th Edition. Wiley.
Patton, J. (2014), User Story Mapping Discover the whole story, Build the Right Product. O'Reilly. Sebastopol, CA.
Rubin, K.S. (2013). Essential Scrum A Practical Guide to the Most Popular Agile Process, Addison-Wesley. Boston.

5.10 Solutions to Test Your Understanding

5.1 A; 5.2 D; 5.3 B; 5.4 B; 5.5 A; 5.6 D; 5.7 B; 5.8 C; 5.9 A; 5.10 A; 5.11 A; 5.12 C; 5.13 A; 5.14 D; 5.15 C; 5.16 C; 5.17 C; 5.18 D; 5.19 A; 5.20 D; 5.21 C; 5.22 B; 5.23 A; 5.24 C; 5.25 B; 5.26 B; 5.27 C; 5.28 A; 5.29 B; 5.30 C; 5.31 D; 5.32 A; 5.33 B; 5.34 A; 5.35 A; 5.36 C; 5.37 B; 5.38 B; 5.39 C; 5.40 B; 5.41 D; 5.42 B; 5.43D; 5.44 C; 5.45 A; 5.46 D; 5.47 B; 5.48 D; 5.49 C; 5.50 A; 5.51 B; 5.52 C; 5.53 A; 5.54 B; 5.55 C; 5.56 B; 5.57 D; 5.58 B; 5.59 D; 5.60 C; 5.61 D; 5.62 D; 5.63 D; 5.64 C; 5.65 A; 5.66 C; 5.67 B; 5.68 D; 5.69 B; 5.70 C; 5.71 D; 5.72 D; 5.73 C; 5.74 D; 5.75 D; 5.76 A; 5.77 D; 5.78 A; 5.79 C; 5.80 D.5.81 D;

Chapter 6: C# Inheritance and Agile Metrics

Chapter Learning Objectives

6.1 Recognize the benefits of inheritance
6.2 Exemplify UML class diagrams
6.3 Use abstract classes and interfaces
6.4 Explain polymorphism in object oriented programming
6.5 Recall types of metrics in agile

6.1 Inheritance

In the last chapter, you learned how to create your own custom classes and how to instantiate a class to use its methods. What if the two classes you need to create are very similar? While you can still create two classes, it's important to note that having many duplicated fields and methods can lead to maintenance issues in the future, especially as the number of classes increases. There is a better way to do it. Put all those common fields and methods from those two classes in a third class called 'super type' and let the two classes, known as "sub type", inherit all elements from the super type.

Instead of creating two classes, you end up with writing three classes. Since all common members are now in the super class, the two sub classes are now simpler. This also enhances the maintenance. If you need to update one common member while using the two classes approach, you would have to update in two places. If you use the three classes approach, you only have to update in one location.

Example 6.1

Problem:

At Tiny College, both undergraduate and graduate students have a student ID, a student name, and a numeric grade score between 0 and 100. However, undergraduates have letter grades (A, B, C, D, and F) with pluses and minuses, while graduates only have a letter. Create a class hierarchy with three classes: a superclass, also known as a base class, named Student, and two subclasses, also known as derived classes, named Undergraduate and Graduate respectively.

Demonstrate the classes you created with four students, two undergraduates and two graduates inside the Main() method. The output should look like:

```
Name: Lynn Score: 98 Letter grade: A
Name: Bob Score: 88 Letter grade: B+
Name: Chuck Score: 76 Letter grade: C
Name: Dan Score: 56 Letter grade: F
```

Analysis:

In this example, the two-class approach appears manageable. However, with many fields and methods, significant duplication arises. Duplication increases development effort and complicates maintenance. For instance, if Tiny College separates student names into first and last fields, every related class must be updated, making omissions likely and errors costly. Organizations often pay consultants to resolve these accumulated technical debts. A better solution is to create a `Student` superclass containing shared attributes and behaviors, with `Undergraduate` and `Graduate` subclasses inheriting from it. This eliminates redundancy and centralizes changes. A Unified Modeling Language (UML) class diagram is displayed below.

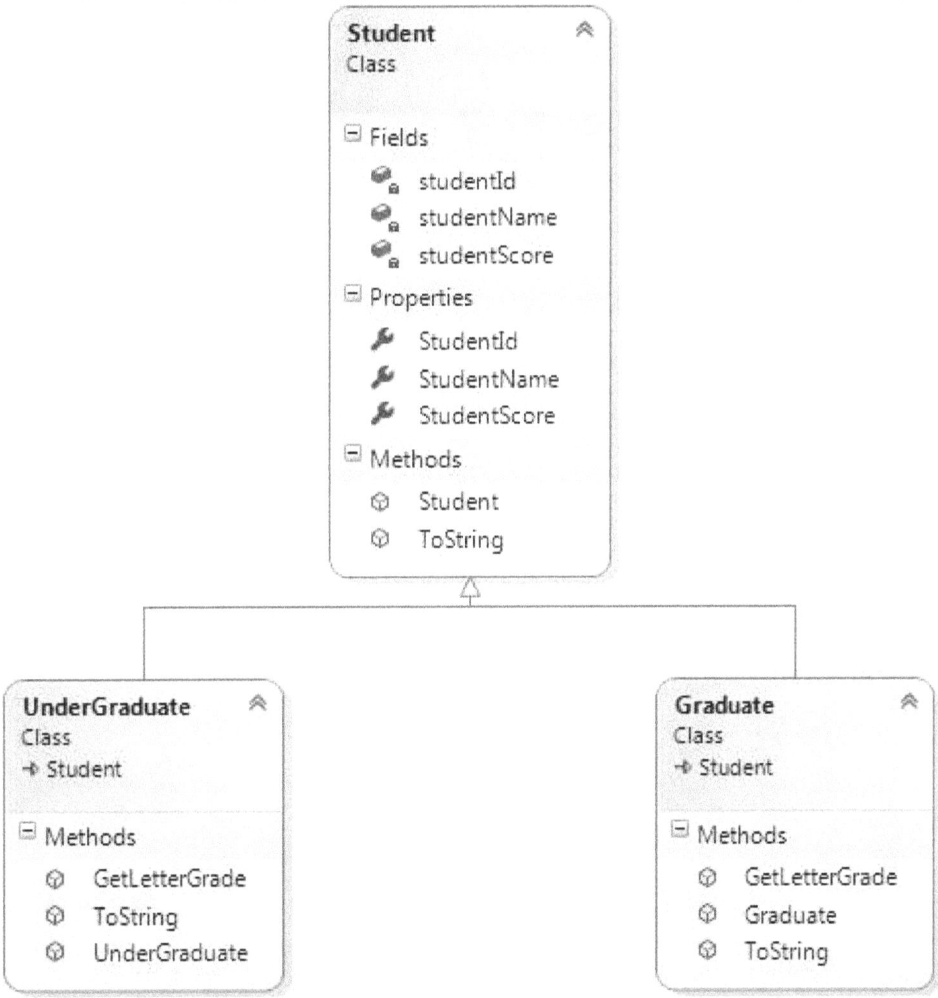

Figure 6.1 UML class diagram.

UML is a standardized visual notation for modeling software systems, particularly object-oriented designs. Class diagrams specifically illustrate classes, their attributes and methods, and relationships like inheritance, making complex hierarchies easier to design, communicate, and maintain.

A class diagram uses a rectangle box to represent a class, with all fields, properties, and methods inside the box. It uses the empty arrow head to show the inheritance relationship. The arrow points to the super class from the sub class. The inheritance relationship is often called an "is-a" relationship, because a sub type "is-a" super type.

The super class is often called base class and the sub class is often called derived class in C# community.

As you can see from the diagram, neither Undergraduate nor Graduate classes need to repeat the common fields and properties. They just need those unique member elements. When a change is needed for student name, only the Student class needs to be updated. This avoids many potential errors.

Solution:

Step 1. Add the Student class:

Create a console app called Chapter6Example1. Right click on the project in the "Solution Explorer" window, and add a new class called "Student". In the Student Class, nothing new is introduced. Just type the code as shown below after removing the default code:

```
namespace Chapter6Example1
{
    internal class Student
    {
        // fields
        private string studentId;
        private string name;
        private int score;
        // properties
        public string StudentId
        {
            get { return studentId; }
            set { studentId = value; }
        }
        public string Name
        {
            get { return name; }
            set { name = value; }
        }
        public int Score
        {
            get { return score; }
            set { score = value; }
        }
        // constructor
```

```
        public Student(string studentId, string name, int score)
        {
            StudentId = studentId;
            Name = name;
            Score = score;
        }
        //ToString
        public override string ToString()
        {
            string str;
            str = $"Name: {Name} Score: {Score}";
            return str;
        }
    }
}
```

Step 2. Add the Undergraduate class:

Next, right click on the project Chapter6Example1 in the "Solution Explorer" window again to add a new class called "Undergraduate.cs". Add the code as shown below after removing the default code:

```
namespace Chapter6Example1
{
    internal class Undergraduate : Student
    {
        // constructor
        public Undergraduate(string studentId, string name, int score)
            : base(studentId, name, score)
        {
        }
        // method
        public string GetLetterGrade()
        {
            string letterGrade;
            if (Score >= 94)
                letterGrade = "A";
            else if (Score >= 90)
                letterGrade = "A-";
            else if (Score >= 87)
                letterGrade = "B+";
            else if (Score >= 84)
                letterGrade = "B";
            else if (Score >= 80)
                letterGrade = "B-";
            else if (Score >= 77)
                letterGrade = "C+";
            else if (Score >= 74)
                letterGrade = "C";
            else if (Score >= 70)
                letterGrade = "C-";
            else if (Score >= 67)
                letterGrade = "D+";
            else if (Score >= 64)
                letterGrade = "D";
            else if (Score >= 60)
                letterGrade = "D-";
            else
                letterGrade = "F";
            return letterGrade;
```

```
        }
        //ToString
        public override string ToString()
        {
            string str;
            str = base.ToString() + $" Letter grade: {GetLetterGrade()}";
            return str;
        }
    }
}
```

Explanation:

To make Undergraduate class a derived class of the Student class, add :Student to the Undergraduate class header, like this:

```
internal class Undergraduate: Student
```

Additionally, the Undergraduate class constructor can call the base class constructor by :base. The constructor of the Undergraduate class is:

```
public Undergraduate(string studentId, string name, int score)
    : base(studentId, name, score)
{
}
```

This indicates the three arguments are passed to the base class constructor. In other words, the current constructor will not do anything to those three parameters. The base class constructor will handle it. It calls the base class constructor by passing arguments for the fields in the base class. If any fields that are in the derived class and not in the base class, the derived class should still handle them.

Inside the ToString method, the base.ToString() will call the ToString() method in the base class and add content there.

Test Your Understanding 6.1
Which of the following statements about inheritance is correct?
Statement1: A super class contains all the common fields and methods of the sub classes so that the sub classes don't need to include those members.
Statement2: A super class is often called derived class and a sub class is often called base class.
A. Statement1 only.
B. Statement2 only.
C. both Statement1 and Statement2.
D. neither Statement1 nor Statement2.

Test Your Understanding 6.2

The relationship between the super type and sub type in an inheritance is often called an _____ relationship.
A. super-sub
B. belongs to
C. has-a
D. is-a

Test Your Understanding 6.3
A diagram with rectangles to represent classes with fields, properties, and methods inside the box and arrows showing the relationships is a(n) _______ class diagram.
A. UML
B. CML
C. UCL
D. UMC

Test Your Understanding 6.4
Which of the following statements about class inheritance is correct?
Statement1: If Class A inherits from Class B, you don't need to do anything on Class B.
Statement2: If Class A inherits from Class B, you should add :B in the Class A header to indicate Class A inherits from Class B.
A. Statement1 only.
B. Statement2 only.
C. both Statement1 and Statement2.
D. neither Statement1 nor Statement2.

Test Your Understanding 6.5
Constructors in a sub class often need to call the super class constructor by using :______.
A. base()
B. super()
C. sub()
D. derived()

Step 3. Add the Graduate class:

Next, right click on the project Chapter6Example1 in the "Solution Explorer" window again to add a new class called "Graduate.cs". Replace the default code with the code below:

```
namespace Chapter6Example1
{
    internal class Graduate : Student
    {
        // constructor
        public Graduate(string studentId, string name, int score)
            : base(studentId, name, score)
        {

        }
        // method
        public string GetLetterGrade()
        {
            string letterGrade;
```

```
            if (Score >= 90)
                letterGrade = "A";
            else if (Score >= 80)
                letterGrade = "B";
            else if (Score >= 70)
                letterGrade = "C";
            else if (Score >= 60)
                letterGrade = "D";
            else
                letterGrade = "F";
            return letterGrade;
        }
        public override string ToString()
        {
            string str;
            str = base.ToString() + $" Letter grade: {GetLetterGrade()}";
            return str;
        }
    }
}
```

Step 4. Demonstrate the classes in the Main() method.

Finally, in the "Solution Explorer" window, open the "Program.cs" in code view, replace the default code with the following:

```
namespace Chapter6Example1
{
    public class Program
    {
        static void Main()
        {
            List<Student> students = new List<Student>();
            Undergraduate ud1 = new Undergraduate("111", "Lynn", 98);
            students.Add(ud1);
            Undergraduate ud2 = new Undergraduate("222", "Bob", 88);
            students.Add(ud2);
            Graduate g1 = new Graduate("333", "Chuck", 76);
            students.Add(g1);
            Graduate g2 = new Graduate("444", "Dan", 56);
            students.Add(g2);
            foreach (Student student in students)
            {
                Console.WriteLine(student);
            }
        }
    }
}
```

Explanation:

The following line:

```
List<Student> students = new List<Student>();
```

declares a variable named students. The variable is assigned an instance of the List<Student> class, which creates an empty list that can store Student objects. In this book, we treat instances and objects the same.

Here's a breakdown of the line:

List<Student> is a List<Student> type.

The "students" is the name of the variable being declared of the List<Student> type.

The "new List<Student>()" creates a new instance of the List<Student> class, which initializes an empty list of Student objects. The memory address of the new list is then assigned to the "students" variable.

A List is similar to an array, but it offers more convenience due to its additional methods and ability to expand dynamically. The class name in the bracket <Student> indicates the List will hold only the Student type. Because both undergraduate and graduate inherits from Student, we say the relationship is an "is a" relationship. In other words, an undergraduate is a student, and a graduate is a student too. As a result, both Undergraduate and Graduate can be stored in the students list.

Using Student to represent both undergraduate and graduate is called *polymorphism* in object-oriented programming. Polymorphism means "multiple forms". In this example, Student can have "two forms", an undergraduate or a graduate.

The following line:

```
students.Add(ud1);
```

Add an undergraduate object to the list by using the pre-built method "Add" of the List class.

Test Your Understanding 6.6
The statement, List<Student> students = new List<Student>(); will create a list called students that can only hold references to ______.
A. a student type, not any other types
B. an undergraduate type only
C. a graduate type only
D. a student type and its derived types

Test Your Understanding 6.7
If the Graduate class inherits from the Student class, then, anywhere in the code, when a Student object is expected, a Graduate object can be used. This is called ________.
A. encapsulation
B. polymorphism
C. inheritance
D. representation

Test Your Understanding 6.8

A List in C# is similar to an array that can be used to hold a group of values. However, a List is more convenient because ________.
A. it has more methods, and it runs faster
B. it can expand as needed, and it runs faster
C. it has more methods, and it can expand as needed
D. it is more concise

Test Your Understanding 6.9
To add an element to a List, you can use the _____ method of the List class.
A. Add()
B. Include()
C. Element()
D. AddElement()

Test Your Understanding 6.10
According to the author of the textbook, what is the differences between an instance and an object?
A. They are the same.
B. The instance is more specific
C. The object is more specific
D. They are different during the application analysis and design stage.

Test Your Understanding 6.11
What does the following line of code do, assuming Student is a class?
List<Student> students;
A. Declares a variable called students that can hold an object of List<Student> class.
B. Declares a variable called students that can hold student data.
C. Declares a variable called students that can hold any type of students.
D. Declares a variable called students of Student type.

Test Your Understanding 6.12
What does the following line of code do, assuming Student is a class?
new List<Student>();
A. Create an object of List<Student> class.
B. Create an object of Student class.
C. Declare a new variable of List<Student> type.
D. Declares a new variable of Student type.

Test Your Understanding 6.13
What is an instance of List<Student> class, assuming Student is a class?
A. The instance contains a list of Student objects.
B. The class contains a list of Student objects.
C. The List<Student> class is the same as the Student class when there is only one student in the list.
D. The List<Student> object is the same as the Student object when there is only one student in the list.

Programming Challenge 6.1
The Tiny Company has two types of employees: fulltime and parttime. Both types have an employee ID and employee name. Fulltime employees have a salary, and parttime employees have an hourly wage and hours worked.
A full time employee gets paid weekly by dividing the salary by 52 while a part time employee gets paid by

the product of hourly wage and hours worked.
Specifically, you will create an Employee class with the common elements (employee ID, employee name, ToString() method). Then create a Fulltime employee class with a salary field and the GetWeeklyPaid() method. Similarly, create a Parttime employee class with hourly wage and hours worked fields and the GetWeeklyPaid() method. Add appropriate properties, constructors, and ToString() methods. Output must be formatted appropriately. Each class should be in its own cs file.
Finally, demonstrate the classes in the Main() method of the Program class with data made up for two full time employees and two part time employees in a List of Employee. Display the employee's payment data in a foreach loop.

6.2 Abstract Method and Abstract Class

In Example 6.1, you may notice that both Graduate and Undergraduate sub classes have a GetLetterGrade() method that is not in the super class. Why is a common method not in the super class? This is because they have different implementations. However, a better design is to put the GetLetterGrade() method in the super class as an abstract method.

We have to make the GetLetterGrade() method in the super class as abstract because we don't have any implementations for that method. The implementation depends on whether a student is a graduate or undergraduate. An abstract method has only a method header without a method body, not even the pair of curly braces. The abstract method terminated with a semicolon.

If a class has one or more abstract methods, the class itself must be abstract. You cannot instantiate an abstract class like you do with a normal concrete class.

Example 6.2

Problem:

Continue to work on Example 6.1 by adding an abstract method called GetLetterGrade to the Student class. Make necessary modification to the code so that the app works as Example 6.1

Solution:

Make a copy of Chapter6Example1 project folder. Rename the folder to Chapter6Example2. Do not rename anything inside the folder. Open the app in the new folder in Visual Studio. Inside the Student class, add the following abstract method right before the ToString() method:

```
public abstract string GetLetterGrade();
```

You will notice that the method name has a red squiggly line. If you point your mouse over it, you will see why. The error message tells you that you must make the class abstract because you now have an abstract method. Therefore, add the keyword "abstract" right before the "class Student" in the class header, like this:

```
internal abstract class Student
```

Note that an abstract class cannot be instantiated, or cannot have objects. In other words, Tiny College can have graduate or undergraduate students, but cannot have any categorized as simply 'students'.

The Student class is now free of errors. However, both the UnderGraduate and Graduate classes have errors. This is because when a sub class inherits from an abstract super class, all abstract methods in the super class must be overridden or kept abstract. Go to both derived classes and add the "override" keyword to the GetLetterGrade() methods:

```
public override string GetLetterGrade()
```

In C#, a method override is a feature that allows a subclass to provide its own implementation of a method that is already defined in its parent class. Method overriding is useful for creating more specialized behavior in a subclass, and for implementing polymorphism in object-oriented programming.

Save and run the program. You should see the same output as Example 6.1 on the console screen.

The benefit of adding an abstract method in the super class without implementation is that you can be sure that all sub classes have that method with its own implementation. In our example, you can be sure that all sub classes from the Student class have a GetLetterGrade() method. No programmers can "forget" to add that method in a sub class.

In class inheritance, you must override an abstract method in the base class. Can you override an ordinary method in the base class in order to have a different implementation? No. If you have such a need, you can set the method in the base class as virtual. Suppose you have a method in the base class:

```
public virtual string Greeting()
{
    return "Good morning.";
}
```

You can override it in the derived class like this:

```
public override string Greeting()
{
    return "Good afternoon.";
}
```

The keyword "override" in the Greeting method allows the Greeting method to behave differently than its parent's method with the same name, same parameters (this is called method signature), same access modifier, and covariant (more derived/specific) return type (must be the same before C# 9.0).

An abstract method in the base class must be overridden in the derived class or kept abstract. A virtual method in the base class can be overridden in the derived class. A normal method in the base class cannot be overridden in the derived class.

Test Your Understanding 6.14
Which of the following statements about override is correct?
Statement1: In C#, a virtual method in the super class can be overridden by a method in the sub class if a different implementation is used in the sub class.
Statement2: In C#, an abstract method in the super class can be overridden by a method in the sub class if a different implementation is used in the sub class.
A. Statement1 only.
B. Statement2 only.
C. both Statement1 and Statement2.
D. neither Statement1 nor Statement2.

Test Your Understanding 6.15
Which of the following statements about override is correct?
Statement1: In C#, a virtual method in the super class must be overridden by a method in the sub class.
Statement2: In C#, any method in the super class can be overridden by a sub class if a different implementation is used in the sub class.
A. Statement1 only.
B. Statement2 only.
C. both Statement1 and Statement2.
D. neither Statement1 nor Statement2.

Test Your Understanding 6.16
When a method in the sub class overrides a method in the super class (in the same assembly), the two methods must have the same method header except ______.
A. signature
B. return type
C. parameter list
D. access modifier

Test Your Understanding 6.17
A method's name and parameter lists are often called a method's _______.
A. header

B. Main
C. signature
D. method body

Test Your Understanding 6.18
If a class in C# has an abstract method, the class must _______.
A. have a corresponding overloaded method
B. have a corresponding overridden method
C. have no other method(s)
D. be abstract

Test Your Understanding 6.19
A benefit of adding an abstract method in the super class without implementation is ______.
A. for the backward compatibility
B. flexibility
C. that you can be sure that all sub classes have that method with its own implementation.
D. code brevity

Test Your Understanding 6.20
Unlike a concrete class, an abstract class cannot _____.
A. be instantiated
B. be updated
C. have fields
D. have non abstract methods

Test Your Understanding 6.21
When a sub class inherits from an abstract super class, all abstract methods in the super class must be ______.
A. overridden
B. overloaded
C. overridden or kept abstract.
D. overloaded or kept abstract

Programming Challenge 6.2
Make a copy of the Program Challenge 6.1 project folder. Open the app of the new folder in Visual Studio. With Employee class in code view, add GetWeeklyPaid() abstract method to the class. Make all necessary changes so that the program can still run as expected.

6.3 Interface

Interface is similar to an abstract class, but it plays a very different role. A superclass defines common behavior for related subclasses. For example, a superclass called Student can be used for all types of students to inherit, but not for faculty. An interface, on the other hand, can be used to define common behaviors for any classes (including unrelated classes; for example, both students and faculty can set up an email account). Additionally, a class can only inherit from one other class, but can implement many interfaces.

An interface is like a contract that if a class implements this interface, it meets all the requirements of the interface. In everyday life, suppose you want to buy a plug for an outlet of a new house. You would need to find out about the pins, voltages, etc. Or, if you know the type follows the US Department of Commerce International Trade Administration (ITA) standard, you can buy the same type of plug and be sure they will match. You can think of the type by ITA as an interface. Even though ITA does not make any outlets or plugs, if a plug and an outlet meet the ITA's type standard, you can be sure they will match.

Interfaces define a specific set of functionalities without having to provide any details. Any class that implements the interface has to provide the details and make the methods work. Different classes implementing the same interface can have different implementations of the same functionality. For example, both credit cards and debit cards have a "make a purchase" functionality, but credit card purchases increase balance while debit card purchases decrease balance.

Example 6.3

Problem:

Continue Example 6.1 for Tiny College. Create an interface called IRegistration with two properties: parttimeMaxHours and fulltimeMaxHours , and two methods: checkPrerequisite() and addClass().
Next, create a class called ParttimeStudent that inherits from the Graduate class and implements the IRegistration interface. Finally, demonstrate the ParttimeStudent in the Main() method.

Solution:

Copy Chapter6Example1 project folder and rename it to Chapter6Example3. Open the app of the new folder in Visual Studio. In the "Solution Explorer" window, right click on the "Chapter6Example1" project. Select "Add", then select "New Item". In the middle panel of the popup "Add new item" window (you may need to click "show all templates"), select "Interface", then type in "IRegistration.cs" in the "Name" field at the bottom.

Click on the "Add" button to have a blank interface. Use the code below for the IRegistration interface.

```
namespace Chapter6Example1
{
    internal interface IRegistration
    {
        int ParttimeMaxHours { get; set; }
        int FulltimeMaxHours { get; set; }
        bool CheckPrerequisite();
        string AddClass();
```

```
    }
}
```

Explanation:

You may notice that there is no access modifier for any property or method in an interface. Also, a method does not have a body as an abstract method does. All members of an interface are public and abstract by default. Additionally, interfaces cannot have data fields. By convention, all interface names begin with the capital letter "I".

Next, add a class called ParttimeStudent to the project. Use the code below:

```
namespace Chapter6Example1
{
    internal class ParttimeStudent : Graduate, IRegistration
    {
        // constructor
        public ParttimeStudent(string studentId, string name, int score)
            : base(studentId, name, score)
        {
        }
        public int ParttimeMaxHours { get; set; } = 6;
        public int FulltimeMaxHours { get; set; } = 18;
        public string AddClass()
        {
            if (CheckPrerequisite())
                return "Class added.";
            else
                return "Prerequisite not met.";
        }
        public bool CheckPrerequisite()
        {
            if (GetLetterGrade() == "A")
                return true;
            return false;
        }
    }
}
```

Explanation:

The following line:

```
internal class ParttimeStudent:Graduate, IRegistration
```

indicates that the ParttimeStudent class inherits from the Graduate class and implements the IRegistration interface.

The following line:

```
public int ParttimeMaxHours { get; set; } = 6;
```

sets the default value for ParttimeMaxHours property at 6.

Finally, update the Main() method of the Program class by adding two part time students and display if they can add a class. Replace the foreach loop with the following code:

```
ParttimeStudent p1 = new ParttimeStudent("555", "Franklin", 88);
ParttimeStudent p2 = new ParttimeStudent("666", "Gray", 99);
students.Add(p1);
students.Add(p2);
foreach (Student student in students)
{
    Console.WriteLine(student);
    if (student is ParttimeStudent)
        Console.WriteLine(((ParttimeStudent)student).AddClass());
}
```

Explanation:

The following lines:

```
if (student is ParttimeStudent)
   Console.WriteLine(((ParttimeStudent)student).AddClass());
```

Check if the student object is a ParttimeStudent type. If yes, then include the AddClass() method.

The `(ParttimeStudent)student` down casts the student object to ParttimeStudent type from a Student type so that you can use the AddClass() method.

Save and run the program. A sample output looks like:

```
Name: Lynn Score: 98 Letter grade: A
Name: Bob Score: 88 Letter grade: B+
Name: Chuck Score: 76 Letter grade: C
Name: Dan Score: 56 Letter grade: F
Name: Franklin Score: 88 Letter grade: B
Prerequisite not met.
Name: Gray Score: 99 Letter grade: A
Class added.
```

Test Your Understanding 6.22
A superclass defines common behavior for ______ subclasses. An interface, on the other hand, can be used to define common behaviors for ______ classes.
A. concrete, unconcrete
B. related, unrelated
C. abstract, non-abstract.
D. abstract, concrete

Test Your Understanding 6.23
A class can inherit from ______ other class. A class can implement ______ interfaces.
A. one, one
B. one, many
C. many, one

D. many, many

Test Your Understanding 6.24
An interface is like a ____. If a class implements this interface, it meets all the requirements of the interface.
A. method
B. contract
C. window
D. field

Test Your Understanding 6.25
All members of an interface are _________ by default.
A. public and abstract
B. private and abstract
C. public and static
D. private and static

Test Your Understanding 6.26
In C#, an interface cannot have _________.
A. data fields
B. properties
C. methods
D. both properties and methods in the same interface

Test Your Understanding 6.27
Which of the following statements about interface naming is correct?
A. all interface names must begin with a lowercase "i"
B. all interface names must begin with the uppercase "I"
C. by convention, all interface names begin with a lowercase "i"
D. by convention, all interface names begin with the uppercase "I"

Programming Challenge 6.3
Copy Programming Challenge 6.1 project folder and rename it to Programming Challenge 6.3. Open the app of the new folder in Visual Studio. Add an interface called IMinimumWage with a property for state minimum hourly wage and a method called MetMinimum that returns true if the wage meets the minimum. Next, add a class called CommissionEmployee that inherits from ParttimeEmployee and implements an IMinimumWage interface. A commission employee has a name, weekly sales amount, commission rate, and weekly hours worked. A commission employee is paid by weekly sales amount multiplied by the commission rate.

Finally, update the Main method to demonstrate the CommissionEmployee class by creating two commission employees: one that meets the minimum wage and one that does not.

6.4 Agile Metrics

Metrics are good communication tools that allow both stakeholders and team members to know where they are and how well they are doing (Broadus, 2013). Such communication is a success factor for agile project management (Tilk, 2016). In this section, we introduce three metrics. They are the Kanban board, burn down chart, and information radiator.

6.4.1 Kanban Board

You learned the concept of Kanban in Chapter 2. Every user story is written on one card, and each card is posted under one category to indicate the current status of that user story. A card will be rearranged after the status changes. This Kanban provides a visual representation of the software development status.

Agile teams often use a white board or simply the wall with sticky notes. The board is separated into five regions as shown in Figure 6.2:

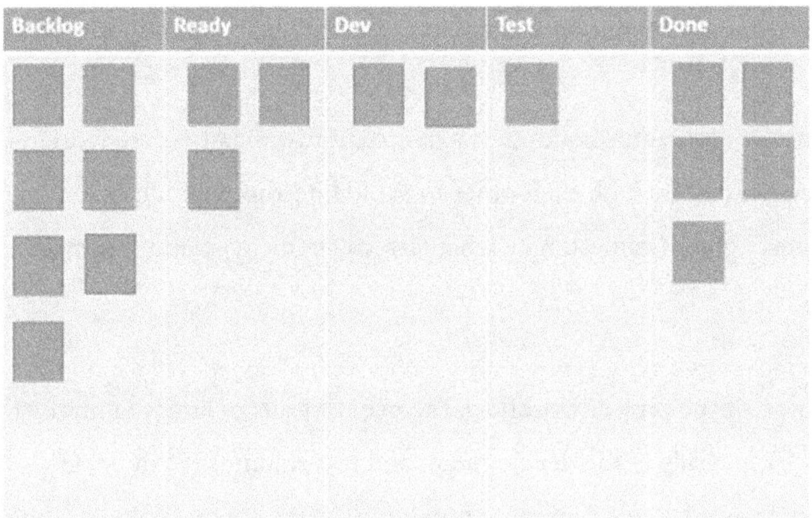

Figure 6.2 A Sample Kanban Board

Backlog category: The product owner is in charge of this category. A user story is written on a sticky note and posted in the order of priority. Each story also contains a story point estimated by the development team. Depending on the size of the project, the list can be long and the product owner may update the category as needed, usually between the sprints.

Ready category: Stories in this category are in the hands of the development team. The stories are picked from the backlog category and are for the current sprint. Because each story usually should be broken down into multiple tasks, a sticky note from this column and any notes to the right of the same row will represent the different tasks of the same story. Estimation of the story is also changed from story points to time units, such as hours. There can be multiple tasks (sticky notes) on each row to represent the tasks for that story.

Development category: The development team is working on these tasks.

Test category: The development team is testing on these tasks to make sure the code is working as expected.

Done category: The tasks in this column are considered ready to be delivered to a customer. When all tasks of a user story are in this column, the sticky note that represents the user story is moved to this column.

Each column identifies a key hand-off or milestone for the tasks as a story is moved from one column to the next. Holding daily scrum meetings in front of the Kanban board makes the meeting more effective and also facilitates information sharing among the team members (Dinsmore and Cabanis-Brewin, 2014). Each member can easily see what the rest of the team are working on.

The Kanban board allows for quick feedback on potential issues. For example, if two members are working on the same column of the same row, they can discuss with each other to avoid interrupting each other's work. Also, the member working on the next column can estimate what task will come next and thus plan ahead.

In addition to providing a visual presentation of the project workflow, the major idea is to limit the number of stories that are a work-in-process (WIP), especially in the development and test columns (Ordysinski, 2013) so that bottlenecks can be identified. If more than a minimum number of WIPs are in a column, other members should take the opportunity to step up and assist.

Test Your Understanding 6.28
The major ______ of Kanban is to limit the number of stories that are a work-in-process (WIP)
A. idea
B. advantage
C. disadvantage
D. issue

Test Your Understanding 6.29
Why does Kanban limit the number of stories that are in WIP?
A. To identify the bottleneck
B. To fit stories in a sprint
C. To fit the work in a single day
D. To make sure one member can complete a task in one day

Test Your Understanding 6.30
Which of the following is NOT a category of a Kanban board listed in the text?
A. Backlog
B. Ready
C. Start
D. Development

Test Your Understanding 6.31
In which category of a Kanban board, a sticky note always represents a story?
A. Backlog
B. Ready
C. Start
D. Development

Test Your Understanding 6.32
A sticky note on the "ready" category of a Kanban board usually represents a ______.
A. category
B. brief note
C. task
D. user story

Test Your Understanding 6.33
Which of the following is NOT an agile metric listed in the text?
A. Kanban board
B. Burn-down chart
C. information radiator
D. user stories

Test Your Understanding 6.34
Metrics are good _________ that allow both stakeholders and team members to know where they are and how well they are doing.
A. status checks
B. measurements
C. reporting tools
D. communication tools

Test Your Understanding 6.35
Which of the following is NOT a direct benefit of using Kanban?
A. visual representation of the status
B. identifying any bottlenecks
C. code transparency
D. communication metrics

6.4.2 Burn-Down Charts

A burn-down chart has two axes. The horizontal axis displays the number of days in the sprint, with larger numbers on the left and smaller numbers on the right. The vertical axis displays the number of hours left.

Some teams display the number of hours left for the whole project, while some teams just display it for one sprint. This book follows the latter.

Let us explain how to draw a burn-down chart with an example. Suppose a team has 3 members, and each member works 8 hours a day, 5 days a week, and a sprint is time-boxed at 2 weeks. The team has 10 days marked on the horizontal axis and 240 hours (3x8x10 = 240) on the vertical axis. When there are 10 days left, there are 240 hours' worth of tasks left. When there are 9 days left, there are 216 (3x8x9=216) hours' worth of tasks left. When there are 8 days left, there are 192 (3x8x8 = 192) hours' worth of tasks left. Continuing with this trend, when there is 1 day left, there are 24 (3x8x1 = 24) hours' worth of tasks left. When there are zero days left, there are zero hours' worth of tasks left. This is called a perfect burn down line or a planned burn down line. This line represents the ideal situation and is used for comparison purposes. Figure 6.3 displays the planned burn down chart.

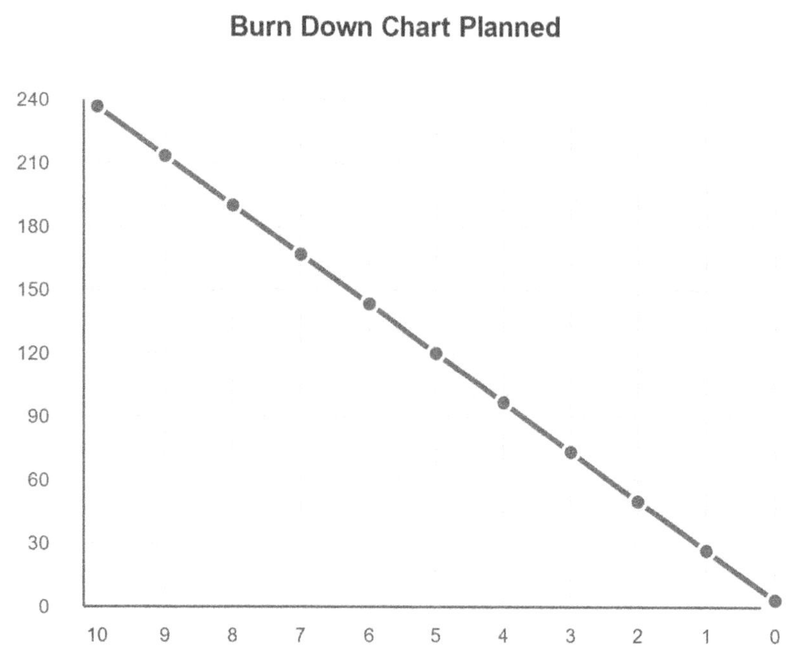

Figure 6.3 Planned Burn Down Chart

On the same chart, let's draw another line to reflect the team's actual burn down. Suppose after the first day of work, the team completes 30 hours' worth of tasks. Mark the chart with (9, 210). Then there are two points on the chart. In the beginning of the sprint, there are always 240 hours' worth of tasks left (10, 240), and on 9 days left, there are 210 hours' worth of tasks left. Figure 6.4 shows the result after one day's work.

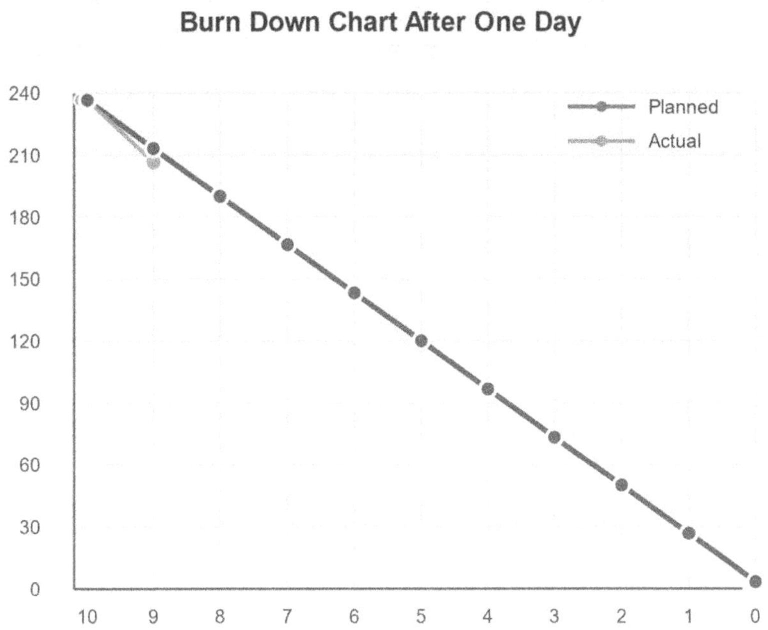

Figure 6.4 The burn down chart after one day's work.

Continue to draw the burn down chart for the team. Suppose on the second day (8 days left), the team completes another 35 hours' worth of tasks. Now there are only 175 (210-35) hours left. The new point is (8, 175). Figure 6.5 displays the burn down chart after two days' work.

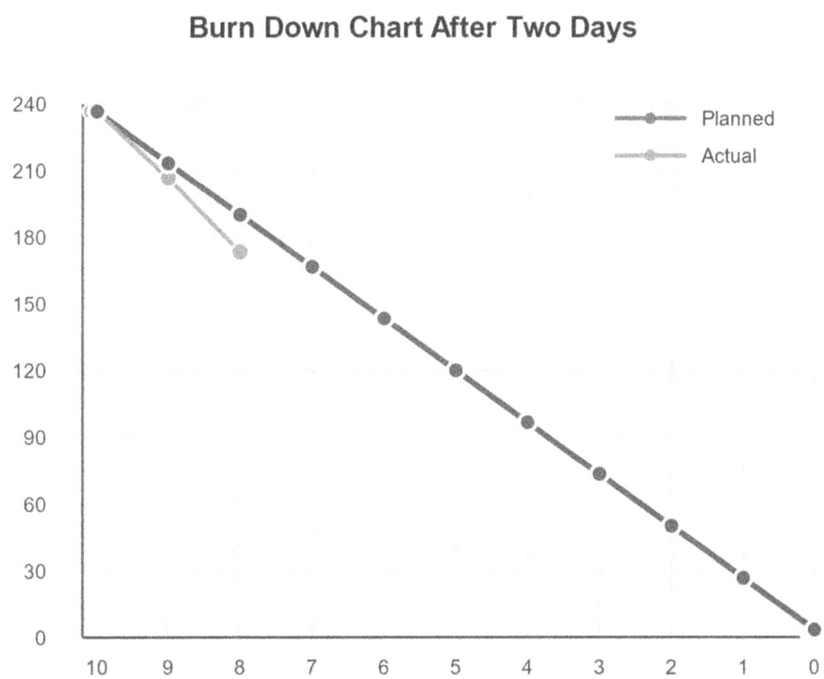

Figure 6.5 The burn down chart after two days' work.

Suppose, on the third day (7 days left), the team completes only 20 hours' worth of tasks. Now there are only 155 (175-20) hours left. The new point is (7, 155). Figure 6.6 displays the burn down chart after three days' work by the team.

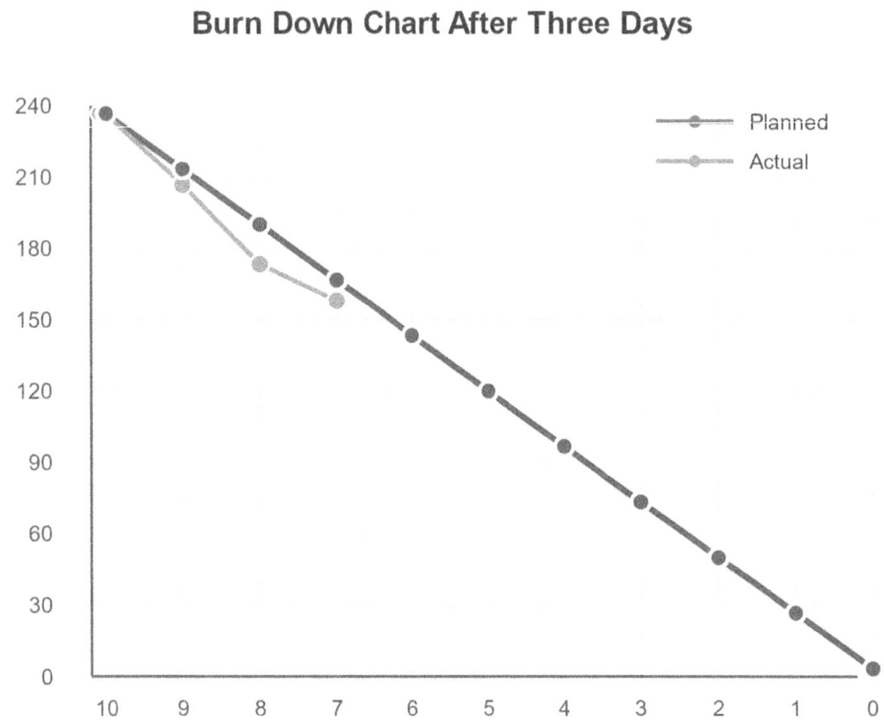

Figure 6.6 The burn down chart after three days' work.

You should have no difficulty completing the chart as the team completes more work until the end of the sprint.

A word of warning: it is possible for the actual line to go up when something went wrong (Vanderjack, 2015). For example, a task might've been underestimated. In general, if the "actual" line is under the "planned" line, the team is ahead of schedule, as shown in the figures. However, if the "actual" line is above the "planned" line for several days, the team must determine if they are able to finish the planned amount of work within the sprint.

Test Your Understanding 6.36
Which of the following statements about burn down charts is correct?
Statement1: In a burn down chart, the horizontal axis represents the number of hours left, and the vertical axis represents the number of days left in the sprint.
Statement2: The perfect burn down line is a straight line from top left to bottom right.

A. Statement1 only.
B. Statement2 only.
C. both Statement1 and Statement2.
D. neither Statement1 nor Statement2.

Test Your Understanding 6.37
Which of the following statements about burn down charts is correct?
Statement1: To draw the burn down chart, at the end of each day, the team finds a point that represents how many days are left and how many hours' worth of work are left and connect that point to the existing trend.
Statement2: If the team burn down chart is above the planned burn down line, this indicates that the team will complete the sprint as scheduled.
A. Statement1 only.
B. Statement2 only.
C. both Statement1 and Statement2.
D. neither Statement1 nor Statement2.

Test Your Understanding 6.38
What do you know if the actual burn down line is above the planed burn down line?
A. The team is behind the schedule
B. The team is ahead the schedule
C. The team is on schedule
D. The burn down chart reflects cost, not schedule

Test Your Understanding 6.39
What do you know if the actual burn down line is under the planed burn down line?
A. The team is behind the schedule
B. The team is ahead the schedule
C. The team is on schedule
D. The burn down chart reflects cost, not schedule

6.4.3 Information Radiators

One communication limitation is that the result is not readily available (Koch, 2005). For example, the result of face-to-face communication is stored in our memory, which may not last long. Written documents filed away in a cabinet may never be seen again. Even files in a computer may not be easily found (do you remember the file name for your last homework assignment?). Even if a file in the computer is easy to find, you may not open it every day. "Information radiator" in agile was invented to solve this problem.

Information radiator is a low-tech metric used in agile software development. It keeps all useful information posted around the team's physical workspace so that they will see it on a regular basis. It is persistent and will be there at all times. It is up to date and reflects the team's current status. It is easy to locate when a member needs it. It is simple to use, since one just raises their head to see the team's progress. In short, the information radiator provides a simple and effective way for any stakeholder to understand the exact status of the development project.

The radiator also helps reinforce important philosophies and principles among the team members. Like TV commercials that are on screen all the time, the radiator can affect team subconscious with information that promotes team morale. Teams can decide what to post and how often to update the posts.

Examples of information radiators can include any project information that is easily understood and provides the team with the information they need to make informed decisions and work efficiently. For instance, a sprint burn down chart, which shows the remaining work in a sprint or release, can be displayed on an information radiator. Other examples of information radiators include a release calendar or a team performance dashboard that shows metrics such as team velocity, cycle time, and defect rates. The key is to create visual displays that are easily understood and help the team stay on top of important project information.

Test Your Understanding 6.40
In agile, information posted around a team's physical working space is called a(n) ________.
A. valuable data
B. team domain
C. information posted
D. information radiator

Test Your Understanding 6.41
An information radiator can help ______.
A. enhance team moral
B. room temperature
C. information flow
D. information distribution

Test Your Understanding 6.42
Information radiators were invented to solve a major limitation of communication. What was the limitation?
A. Not everyone in an agile team spoke English
B. Not everyone had a computer open at all time
C. The result of communication was not readily available
D. The result of communication was not signed by a manager

Test Your Understanding 6.43
Which of the following is an example of an information radiator?
A. A bug tracking tool
B. A sprint retrospective meeting
C. A team performance dashboard
D. A code repository

Test Your Understanding 6.44
What is the key to creating effective information radiators in agile software development?
A. Displaying as much information as possible
B. Using the latest technology
C. Creating visual displays that are easily understood
D. Only displaying information to certain team members

6.5 Chapter Summary

In this chapter, you learned that if two or more classes have common members (fields and methods), a super class can be created to include those common members and allow other classes to inherit the super class and add their own unique members. This is not just to save typing time. It is one of the most important aspects of object-oriented programming. In class inheritance, if different sub classes have different implementations of the same method, then you can use an abstract method in the super class. Similar to an abstract class, an interface can be used to define behaviors for a group of classes as long as they all implement the interface. You also learned the common communication techniques used in agile. They are the Kanban board, burn down chart, and information radiator. These are just some techniques for you to start with. In the real world, you may modify and enhance them for your own team.

6.6 References:

Broadus III, W. A. (2013). Stakeholder Needs and Expectations: Planning Your Agile Project and Program Metrics. Defense AT & L. Vol.42, Issue 6, Nov/Dec, p 50-54.
Dinsmore, P. C., & Cabanis-Brewin, J. (2014). The AMA Handbook of Project Management. New York: AMACOM.
Koch, A. S. (2005). Agile Software Development : Evaluating the Methods for Your Organization. Boston, MA: Artech House, Inc.
Ordysinski, T. (2013). Kanban Based Information Management in Organization, Studies & Proceedings Polish Association for Knowledge Management, 63, p. 76-85.
Tilk, D. (2016). Five Steps to Agile Project Success, Internal Auditor. Apr. Vol. 73 Issue 2, p57-61.
Vanderjack, B. (2015). The Agile Edge : Managing Projects Effectively Using Agile Scrum. New York: Business Expert Press.

6.7 Solutions to Test Your Understanding:

6.1 A; 6.2 D; 6.3 A; 6.4 C; 6.5 A; 6.6 D; 6.7 B; 6.8 C; 6.9 A; 6.10 A; 6.11 A; 6.12 A; 6.13 A; 6.14 A; 6.15 D; 6.16 B; 6.17 C; 6.18 D; 6.19 C; 6.20 A; 6.21 C; 6.22 B; 6.23 B; 6.24 B; 6.25 A; 6.26 A; 6.27 D; 6.28 A; 6.29 A; 6.30 C; 6.31 A; 6.32 C; 6.33 D; 6.34 D; 6.35 C; 6.36 B; 6.37 A; 6.38 A; 6.39 B; 6.40 D; 6.41 A; 6.42 C; 6.43 C; 6.44 C;

Chapter 7: C# Exception Handling and Agile Quality Assurance

Chapter Learning Objectives

7.1 Recognize the need for exception handling
7.2 Exemplify exception handling in a program
7.3 Recall the characteristics of software quality
7.4 Interpret quality philosophies and principles and their relationships with pair programming

7.1 What Is C# Exception?

So far, you focused on learning how to make the code run. It is time for you to learn that having an application that solves business problems is only half of the story. The other half, or perhaps more than half, is quality software.

Example 7.1

Problem:

Write an application that calculates the retail price based on the wholesale price plus mark ups. The program prompts the user for the wholesale price and management markup percentage, then displays the retail price. For example, if the wholesale price is \$10.00 and the markup percentage is 45%, then the retail price will be \$14.50

Solution:

Create a console app project called Chapter7Example1. Type the code below inside the Program.cs file.

```
namespace Chapter7Example1
{
    class Program
    {
        static void Main()
        {
            //Prompt user for wholesale price and markup
            Console.WriteLine("Enter Wholesale Price:");
            double wholesalePrice = double.Parse(Console.ReadLine()!);
            Console.WriteLine("Enter Markup Percentage:");
            double markupPercentage = double.Parse(Console.ReadLine()!);
            // calculate retail price
            double retailPrice = wholesalePrice * (1 + markupPercentage / 100);
            // display result
```

```
            Console.WriteLine($"Retail Price: {retailPrice:C}");
        }
    }
}
```

Explanation:

These statements solve the problem. If a user enters 10 as the wholesale price and 45 for the markup percentage, the console will display $14.50 as the retail price. That's correct. However, if the user enters "ten" for the wholesale price, the program will halt and display the following exception:

"**System.FormatException:** 'The input string 'ten' was not in a correct format.'"

This is an example of a run time error. A FormatException was thrown. You cannot convert "ten" to a double value. It's an error that C# caught (Common Language Runtime (CLR) to be exact), so an exception is thrown. An exception is C#'s response to any programming bug, invalid user input, or external issues (such as a connection to a nonexistent file). An exception is often a built-in class.

The above exception was thrown because of invalid user input. Usually, this type of exception can be fixed by the programmer. You can use C# flow control to make sure that the user enters the correct format. You can use an 'if' statement to accomplish this.

You may notice the ! operator used in Console.Readline(). The postfix ! is the null-forgiving operator. It has no effect at run time. It only affects the compiler's static flow analysis (green underline gone).

Example 7.2

Problem:

Use the 'if' statement to handle the exceptions in Example 7.1. If the user enters a non-numeric value for the wholesale price or percentage, display an error message.

Solution:

Copy Chapter7Example1 project folder. Rename the folder to Chapter7Example2. Do not rename the files inside. Open the new project in Visual Studio, Modify the Main method with this code:

```
//declare variables to hold user values
double wholesalePrice;
double markupPercentage;
// prompt the user for wholesale price
```

```
Console.WriteLine("Enter Wholesale Price:");
if (!(double.TryParse(Console.ReadLine(), out wholesalePrice)))
{
    Console.WriteLine("Wholesale price must be numeric.");
}
else
{
    // wholesale price is good
    // prompt for markup
    Console.WriteLine("Enter markup percentage:");
    if (!(double.TryParse(Console.ReadLine(), out markupPercentage)))
    {
        Console.WriteLine("Markup must be numeric.");
    }
    else
    {
        // markup is also good
        // calculate retail price
        double retailPrice = wholesalePrice * (1 + markupPercentage / 100);
        // display result
        Console.WriteLine($"Retail price: {retailPrice:C}");
    }
}
```

Explanation:

The TryParse() method converts the first argument (what the user enters) to the second argument (the wholesalePrice variable). If the conversion succeeds, the TryParse() method will return true. Otherwise, it will return false. The ! operator is NOT in logic, so if the conversion failed, the condition in the if statement is true (thanks to !). It will then display to the user the feedback, "Wholesale price must be numeric."
You can think of the TryParse() method as doing two things: 1) Converting the first argument to the second argument; 2) Returning true if the conversion is successful, or false if otherwise.

Note that the TryParse() method uses the modifier "out" for the second parameter. This is because a method can only return one value or reference without using the "out" parameter modifier (see Chapter 4 for more details). You want this method to return two values, one Boolean value and one wholesale price. An almost identical validation for the markup percentage is nested inside the else block.

Test Your Understanding 7.1
Which of the following statements about exception is correct?
Statement1: An exception is C#'s response to a programming error.
Statement2: An exception is the same as a programming bug.
A. Statement1 only.
B. Statement2 only.
C. both Statement1 and Statement2.
D. neither Statement1 nor Statement2.

Test Your Understanding 7.2
Which of the following statements about exceptions is correct?
Statement1: An exception in C# is a class.
Statement2: If an invalid user input is not handled in the code, it can cause an exception.
A. Statement1 only.
B. Statement2 only.
C. both Statement1 and Statement2.
D. neither Statement1 nor Statement2.

Test Your Understanding 7.3
Which of the following is a C# built-in exception class? This exception will be thrown when the user enters 'ten' when the application expects the number '10'.
A. UserInputException
B. FormatException
C. RuntimeErrorException
D. Number10Exception

Test Your Understanding 7.4
What are the two things the TryParse() method does?
A. Returning two values to the caller.
B. Accepting one value and returning a bool value.
C. Accepting two values and returning a bool value.
D. Passing a value from the first parameter to the second and returning a bool value.

Test Your Understanding 7.5
What is the ! operator used in the following C# statement?
Console.Readline()!;
A. It is the "NOT" logic operator
B. It is the null-forgiving operator
C. It is the emphasis operator
D. It enforce the line of code to be executed without any exception

Test Your Understanding 7.6
What is the ! operator used in the following C# statement?

```
if(!(double.TryParse(Console.ReadLine(),
            out wholesalePrice)))
```

A. It is the "NOT" logic operator
B. It is the null-forgiving operator
C. It is the emphasis operator
D. It enforce the line of code to be executed without any exception

Test Your Understanding 7.7
Which of the following statements about the null-forgiving operator in C# is correct?
A. It has no effect at run time
B. It checks if the value is null
C. It allows a variable to accept a null value
D. It won't allow a variable to accept any null values

Test Your Understanding 7.8

Suppose you have two variables string x = “2”; double y = 3;. How do you use TryParse() method to convert x to y?
A. TryParse(x, y);
B. double.TryPrse(x, y);
C. TryParse(x, out y);
D. double.TryParse(x, out y);

Test Your Understanding 7.9
What will be displayed on the console screen after the following lines of C# code are executed?

```
string x = "2";
double y = 3;
double.TryParse(x, out y);
Console.WriteLine(y);
```

A. “2”
B. “3”
C. 2
D. 3

Test Your Understanding 7.10
What will be displayed on the console screen after the following lines of C# code are executed?

```
    int x = 5;
    if(!(x>1)){
        Console.WriteLine("C# is fun.");
    }
    else{
        Console.WriteLine("C# is NOT fun.");
    }
```

A. C# is fun.
B. C# is NOT fun.
C. Blank screen.
D. Run-time error.

Programming Challenge 7.1
Modify the program in Example 7.2 so that it also won’t accept a negative number for the wholesale price nor for the markup percentage.

Example 7.3

Problem:

Example 7.2 fixed the exception issues with the if statements and TryParse() method. However, the user does not get a chance to enter a correct value after an error. Rewrite the program so that the application keeps prompting the user for a value until a value in the correct format is entered.

Analysis:

This program prompts the user to enter the wholesale price as a numeric value. If the user enters a value in an incorrect format, the program will prompt them to enter it again. This process continues until the user enters a value in the correct format.

Because we don't know how many times the user will enter an incorrect format, a while loop is a suitable way to handle this scenario. Essentially, if the user enters an incorrect format, the program displays a feedback message and prompts them to enter the data again until they provide it in the correct format.

Solution:

Create a console app called Chapter7Example3. Replace the default code in Program.cs with the following:

```
namespace Chapter7Example3
{
    class Program
    {
        static void Main()
        {
            // declare variables to hold user values
            double wholesalePrice;
            double markupPercentage;
            //Prompt user for wholesale price and markup
            Console.WriteLine("Enter Wholesale Price:");
            while (!double.TryParse(Console.ReadLine(), out wholesalePrice)
                || (wholesalePrice < 0))
            {
                Console.WriteLine("Wholesale price must be numeric and positive.");
            }
            // wholesalePrice is valid
            Console.WriteLine("Enter markup percentage:");
            while (!double.TryParse(Console.ReadLine(), out markupPercentage)
                    || markupPercentage < 0)
            {
                Console.WriteLine("Markup must be numeric and positive.");
            }
            // markup percentage is valid
            // calculate retail price
            double retailPrice = wholesalePrice * (1 + markupPercentage / 100);
            // display result
            Console.WriteLine($"Retail Price: {retailPrice:C}");
        }
    }
}
```

Explanation:

Each while loop in the Main() method does only two things: 1) Give feedback to the user, and 2) Receive new input from the user.

The while loop has a condition that checks whether the value entered by the user can be successfully converted to a double data type using the `double.TryParse()` method. If the conversion fails, the condition also checks whether the value is a negative number. If either of these conditions is true, the input is considered invalid, and the loop continues to prompt the user for a valid input. The || symbol in the code represents the logical OR operator, which evaluates to true if either of the conditions is true.

Test Your Understanding 7.11
Because we don't know how many times the user will enter an incorrect format, a(n) ______ is a suitable way to handle this scenario.
A. if statement
B. switch statement
C. for loop
D. while loop.

Test Your Understanding 7.12
What is the || operator used in the following C# statement?

```
if(7>5 || 7< 5)
```

A. It is the "NOT" logic operator
B. It is the null-forgiving operator
C. It is the emphasis operator
D. It is the "OR" logic operator

Test Your Understanding 7.13
The double.TryParse() method converts a _____ value to a ______ and returns a ______ value.
A. double, string, bool
B. string, double, bool
C. double, bool, string
D. string, bool, double

Programming Challenge 7.2
Write a console application that lets the user enter a student name and an integer score between 0 and 100. Then the application displays the student name and the letter grade by using the formula: 90 or above A; between 80 and 89 B; between 70 and 79 C; between 60 and 69 D; below 60 F. If the user enters an invalid score, prompt the user to enter again until a valid score is entered.

7.2 Exception Handling with Try ... Catch Statement

Example 7.4

Problem:

Write a console app that asks the user to enter two whole numbers then divides the first number by the second number and displays the quotient.

Analysis:

You can use the same technique in the previous example so that only valid data is accepted. This example uses a different approach. Use the C# built in Exception classes to catch different types of exceptions. Note that in the real world, you should write more robust code to remove the bugs and validate user input. The Exception classes should be used to handle external errors that are rare and unexpected. An example of an external error might be a file that is missing or a database that cannot be reached. These types of errors cannot be anticipated by the program, and they require a special type of handling.

For instance, let's say you are developing a program that reads data from a file. If the file is missing, an IOException exception will be thrown. In this case, you should catch the exception using a try-catch block and provide appropriate error handling, such as displaying an error message to the user or logging the error.

Solution 1:

This first solution will not include any exception handling.

Create a project called Chapter7Example4a. Replace the default code in Program.cs with the following:

```
namespace Chapter7Example4a
{
    class Program
    {
        static void Main()
        {
            // prompt the user for dividend
            Console.WriteLine("Enter dividend:");
            int dividend = int.Parse(Console.ReadLine()!);
            // prompt the user for divisor
            Console.WriteLine("Enter divisor:");
            int divisor = int.Parse(Console.ReadLine()!);
            // calculate the quotient
            int quotient = dividend / divisor;
            // display the result
            Console.WriteLine($"{dividend} divided by {divisor} is {quotient}");
        }
    }
}
```

Explanation:

This program will run if the user enters all valid input. For example, if you enter 10 for dividend and enter 3 for divisor, you will get the correct quotient.

Now try this:

Run the program by entering 5.4 as the dividend. You will see "FormatException"

Next, run the program again by entering 5 as the dividend and 0 as the divisor. You will see

"DivideByZeroException".

Finally, run the program by entering 2345678901. You will see "OverflowException." This is because the largest int allowed is 2,147,483,647, and you just entered a whole number larger than that.

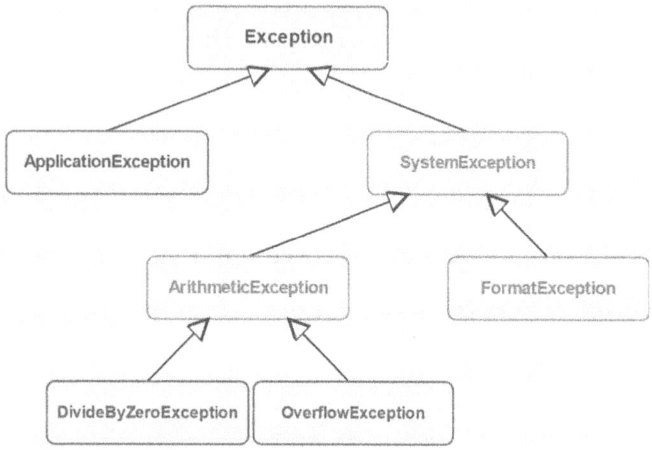

Figure 7.1 Sample built-in exception classes.

C# programming has many built in Exception classes. Figure 7.1 shows a small part of the tree in the UML class diagram. All built in exceptions are inherited from the "SystemException" class, which in turn is inherited from the Exception class. All custom build exception classes should inherit from the "ApplicationException" class, which in turn is inherited from the Exception class. The arrows in Figure 7.1 point from a sub class to the super class.

There are many more built-in exception classes under the "SystemException" class. For a complete list, visit https://msdn.microsoft.com/en-us/library/z4c5tckx%28v=vs.110%29.aspx.

Test Your Understanding 7.14
If a user enters 1.23 when an int data type value is expected by the program, what type of exception will it throw?
A. ApplicationException
B. FormatException
C. OverflowException
D. DivideByZeroException

Test Your Understanding 7.15
The Exception classes should be used to handle external errors that are rare and unexpected. An example of an external error might be ______. These types of errors cannot be anticipated by the program, and they require a special type of handling.
A. a file that is missing
B. a variable receives wrong value
C. a variable is in wrong type
D. a variable from another program is incorrect

Test Your Understanding 7.16
The Exception classes should be used to handle external errors that are rare and unexpected. An example of

an external error might be ______. These types of errors cannot be anticipated by the program, and they require a special type of handling.
A. a database that cannot be reached
B. a variable receives wrong value
C. a variable is in wrong type
D. a variable from another program is incorrect

Test Your Understanding 7.17
If you want to write a custom exception class, it should be inherited from the _______ class.
A. Exception
B. ApplicationException
C. SystemException
D. CustomException

Test Your Understanding 7.18
In the UML class diagram, an arrow points from ClassA to ClassB, indicating _______.
A. ClassA is a super class
B. ClassB is a super class
C. neither ClassA nor ClassB is a super class
D. both ClassA and ClassB are super classes

Test Your Understanding 7.19
Which of the following is NOT a built-in exception class in C#?
A. Exception
B. ApplicationException
C. SystemException
D. BuiltInException

Test Your Understanding 7.20
If a user enters 2345678901 when an int data type value is expected by the program, what type of exception will it throw?
A. ApplicationException
B. FormatException
C. OverflowException
D. DivideByZeroException

Solution 2:

The second solution to the problem is to use the Try ... Catch statement to handle the exceptions. Create a project called Chapter7Example4b. Replace the default code in Program.cs with the following:

```
namespace Chapter7Example4b
{
    class Program
    {
        static void Main()
        {
            try
            {
                // prompt the user for dividend
```

```
                Console.WriteLine("Enter dividend:");
                int dividend = int.Parse(Console.ReadLine()!);
                // prompt the user for divisor
                Console.WriteLine("Enter divisor:");
                int divisor = int.Parse(Console.ReadLine()!);
                // calculate the quotient
                int quotient = dividend / divisor;
                // display the result
                Console.WriteLine($"{dividend} divided by {divisor} is {quotient}");
            }
            catch (DivideByZeroException ex)
            {
                Console.WriteLine(ex.Message);
            }
            catch (OverflowException ex)
            {
                Console.WriteLine(ex.Message);
            }
            catch (ArithmeticException ex)
            {
                Console.WriteLine(ex.Message);
            }
            catch (FormatException ex)
            {
                Console.WriteLine(ex.Message);
            }
            catch (SystemException ex)
            {
                Console.WriteLine(ex.Message);
            }
            catch (Exception ex)
            {
                Console.WriteLine(ex.Message);
            }

            finally
            {
                Console.WriteLine("Thank you!");
            }
        }
    }
}
```

Explanation:

You put all the statements that may throw an exception inside the try block. When an exception is thrown, the execution will jump to one of the catch blocks and end up in the finally block.

You may notice how the sequence of catch blocks is organized. All catch blocks should be organized from specific to general, with more specific exceptions first and more general exceptions later. By examining the class diagram in Figure 7.1, you can see a super class is more general and a sub class is more specific. This is because when an exception is thrown, the runtime checks the catch blocks in sequence and executes only the first catch block whose type matches the exception (or is a superclass of it); once a match is found and handled, the remaining catch blocks are skipped entirely. If you put the most general exception class first, it will catch any exception and prevent more specific catch blocks later in the sequence from ever being reached. After the execution of either the try or catch block, the finally block will follow. The "finally" block is optional.

Test Your Understanding 7.21
Which of the following exceptions is the most general?
A. Exception
B. SystemException
C. ArithmeticException
D. OverflowException

Test Your Understanding 7.22
Which of the following exceptions is the most specific?
A. Exception
B. SystemException
C. ArithmeticException
D. OverflowException

Test Your Understanding 7.23
Which of the following statements about try … catch is correct?
Statement1: When using the try … catch statement to handle the exception, only one catch block will be executed at most, even if you put multiple catch blocks in the application.
Statement2: When using the try … catch … finally statement, the finally block will always be executed whether an exception is thrown or not.
A. Statement1 only.
B. Statement2 only.
C. both Statement1 and Statement2.
D. neither Statement1 nor Statement2.

Test Your Understanding 7.24
When using the try ... catch statement to handle the exception, in the catch blocks, you should put more ______ exception classes before the more ______ exception classes.
A. general, specific
B. specific, general
C. frequent, rare
D. rare, frequent

Programming Challenge 7.3
Write an application that can calculate a trip's gas usage in miles per gallon. The application prompts the user for the number of miles of a trip and how many gallons of gas was used for the trip. Then the application should display the miles per gallon. Use the try ... catch ... finally to handle the exceptions.

7.3 Software Quality

Quality is in the eyes of the beholder. Different people see the same software with differing levels of quality. Even the same person may see the same software at different times with differing quality. Furthermore, the definition of software quality may be different among experts. We believe that quality is about fulfilling requirements (Marchewka, 2015). To understand quality, you need to know the nine characteristics of software quality defined by the ISO/IEC 25010 (2023):

Functional suitability: A high-quality application should meet the stated and implied needs of the users when used under specified conditions.

Performance efficiency: A high-quality application should perform its functions within specified time and throughput parameters and not require excessive resources.

Compatibility: A high-quality application should be able to exchange information with other applications and perform its functions while sharing the same environment.

Interaction capability: A high-quality application should allow specified users to interact effectively via the user interface to complete specific tasks in various contexts (formerly known as Usability).

Reliability: A high-quality application should perform specified functions under specified conditions for a defined period without failure.

Security: A high-quality application should protect information and data so that users and other systems have the degree of access appropriate to their authorization.

Maintainability: A high-quality application should allow for effective and efficient modifications by maintainers to improve, correct, or adapt the software.

Flexibility: A high-quality application should be adaptable to changes in requirements, contexts of use, or system environments (formerly known as Portability).

Safety: A high-quality application should ensure that it does not pose acceptable risks to human life, health, property, or the environment during operation.

Test Your Understanding 7.25
A marketing team adopts a new customer relationship management (CRM) system intended to track leads, automate follow-up emails, and generate campaign reports. After deployment, users discover that while the interface looks modern, the system cannot generate the required campaign performance reports promised during procurement. Which software quality characteristic is primarily lacking?
A. Performance efficiency
B. Functional suitability
C. Interaction capability
D. Maintainability

Test Your Understanding 7.26
A hospital implements an electronic health record (EHR) system. During peak hours, physicians experience long delays when accessing patient charts, even though all features are available and correct. The system consumes excessive server resources and slows down clinical workflows. Which quality characteristic is most directly affected?
A. Reliability
B. Compatibility
C. Performance efficiency
D. Security

Test Your Understanding 7.27
A logistics company deploys a new inventory management application. While it works well on its own, it cannot exchange data with the company's existing warehouse management and accounting systems, requiring manual data entry. Which software quality characteristic is being violated?
A. Maintainability
B. Compatibility
C. Flexibility
D. Interaction capability

Test Your Understanding 7.28
A university introduces an online learning platform with all required features. However, students struggle to submit assignments because navigation is confusing, instructions are unclear, and tasks require unnecessary steps. Which quality characteristic best explains this issue?
A. Functional suitability
B. Interaction capability
C. Reliability
D. Safety

Test Your Understanding 7.29
A bank's risk assessment application needs frequent updates to comply with new regulations. Each small change requires significant effort, introduces new bugs, and takes weeks to deploy. Which quality characteristic is most clearly deficient?

A. Maintainability
B. Flexibility
C. Reliability
D. Security

Test Your Understanding 7.30
A manufacturing company uses software to control robotic arms on an assembly line. A flaw in the system

occasionally causes unexpected movements, posing a risk of injury to nearby workers. Which software quality characteristic is most critical in this situation?
A. Reliability
B. Performance efficiency
C. Safety
D. Compatibility

7.4 Quality Philosophies and Principles

Software quality depends a lot on the development team. There are four general philosophies and principles that can guide a team through its journey in software development (Marchewka, 2015).

1. *Focus on customer satisfaction*: Software development is not to show off how smart the team is. It is to satisfy the customers' requirements. Only when this philosophy is a part of the team norm can the agile principles be implemented. Another reason for meeting customer and stakeholder requirements is because the customer is the ultimate judge of the quality (Ginac, 1998).

2. *Prevention, Not Inspection*: The cost of quality depends on its four components —prevention, inspection, internal failure, and external failure. The most efficient way to reduce the quality cost is through prevention (Lewis, 2008). The business rule of ten can be applied here. When a quality issue is identified by a team member, the cost may be $1. When the same issue is noticed by a customer, the cost can be $10.

3. *Quality Is Everyone's Responsibility*: Achieving quality is not a free endeavor. It demands time, effort, and a comprehensive and purposeful process of planning, executing, and assessing work to meet or surpass the standards and expectations of both the organization and its stakeholders. This process involves identifying and addressing potential risks and issues, continually enhancing processes and practices, and providing constructive feedback to colleagues to help them improve their work. All team members should be accountable and empowered to ensure quality and encouraged to take pride in their work. Each member should pledge to prioritize quality (McKay, 2007; Jyothi and Rao, 2012). A software development team that adheres to agile methodologies expects every team member to assume responsibility for the quality of their code and actively participate in code reviews, testing, and continuous integration processes.

4. *Fact-Based Management*: Numbers, pictures, and charts should be used for ease of understanding and quick references. Data collected can be used for evaluating and improving the process (Kloppenborg and Petrick. 2002).

Test Your Understanding 7.31
What does ensuring quality require?
A. money
B. time
C. Both time and effort
D. Neither time nor effort

Test Your Understanding 7.32
'The goal of software development is to satisfy the customers' requirements' describes which quality philosophy?
A. Fact-Based Management
B. Focus on customer satisfaction
C. Prevention, not inspection
D. Quality is everyone's responsibility

Test Your Understanding 7.33
'Team members should be responsible and empowered for ensuring quality and encouraged to take pride in their work' describes which quality philosophy?
A. Fact-Based Management
B. Focus on customer satisfaction
C. Prevention, not inspection
D. Quality is everyone's responsibility

Test Your Understanding 7.34
Which of the following is NOT a quality philosophy discussed in the book?
A. Quality is not tangible
B. Focus on customer satisfaction
C. Prevention, not inspection
D. Quality is everyone's responsibility

7.5 Pair Programming

As you learned in Chapter 1, a non-agile team typically has a very clear line between the roles of developer and quality assurance (QA). This can be a problem.

Let's use an example. A developer is working on feature A and a QA may be working on something else. After the developer completes feature A and moves on to Feature B, the QA will start to test on feature A and may find some bugs. Now the developer has to stop working on feature B, reset up the environment for working on feature A, and fix the bugs of feature A. This will repeat for every feature, making the process inefficient and of low quality.

The pair programming approach will start with both the developer and the QA working on the test case before the developer starts coding. This will help the developer better understand the case and write better code. Once the developer starts to code, the QA can follow with the testing. This kind of teamwork ensures higher quality with less time spent on setting up the environment.

In short, agile requires a cross functional team which means the developer understands how the QA works, and the QA knows the programming. They should both know the analysis and design. By physically sitting together and working together, they can test the code as it is written. This increases the quality of software.

Pair programming involves two team members working on one computer with just one keyboard and mouse. The member who works at the keyboard with the mouse is called the "driver", and the other member who is also actively participating in the current work is called the "navigator". The two members take turns controlling the keyboard and mouse.

Pair programming allows team members with different expertise to code together, take turns controlling the keyboard, and learning from each other (Beck and Andres, 2005). There can be different flavors of pair programming. For example, peer review or peer code review is similar to pair programming.

Researchers have identified many benefits of pair programming (Hannay, 2009; Vanhanen and Mantyla, 2013). Improved quality is at the top of the list. Pair programming can result in higher quality products due to team effort. Also, "programming out loud" helps programmers think more clearly about the requirements.

When a development team is not physically located in one place, communication and collaboration may be more difficult and can negatively impact the performance of the pair programming. There are positive reports that benefits are still possible in the virtual team, even in the asynchronous mode (Zin, 2006). Carefully selected communication tools that are comfortable to use for all participants and sufficient training of team members will minimize the failure of pair programming in a distributed environment (Canfora et al, 2006).

Test Your Understanding 7.35
Which of the following statements about pair programming is correct?
Statement1: Pair programming works with two team members working together on one computer with two sets of keyboard and mouse.

Statement2: Pair programming helps programmers think more clearly about the requirements.
A. Statement1 only.
B. Statement2 only.
C. both Statement1 and Statement2.
D. neither Statement1 nor Statement2.

Test Your Understanding 7.36
In pair programming, the member who works at the keyboard with the mouse is called the _______.
A. navigator
B. warrior
C. active coder
D. driver

Test Your Understanding 7.37
In pair programming, the member who is away from the keyboard and the mouse is called the ________.
A. navigator
B. warrior
C. active coder
D. driver

Test Your Understanding 7.38
According to the author of this book, which of the following statements about pair programming is correct?
Statement1: Pair programming allows team members to learn from each other.
Statement2: The only concern of pair programming is the efficiency with two members working on one task.
A. Statement1 only.
B. Statement2 only.
C. both Statement1 and Statement2.
D. neither Statement1 nor Statement2.

7.6 Code Debugging

Debugging is an essential part of software development, and it allows developers to identify and fix issues in their code. In this section, we will guide you through the steps to debug C# code in Visual Studio. Mastering debugging will help you write better code and improve your productivity. Remember to always test your code thoroughly and use debugging tools to identify and fix any issues.

Example 7.5

Problem:

Write a console app that calculates the average of an integer array.

Analysis:

We purposely make a bug in the following code and see if you can see by reading the code. Assume you cannot see the bug. We will demonstrate how to debug by using Visual Studio.

Solution:

Create a project called Chapter7Example5. Replace the default code in Program.cs with the following:

```
int[] numbers = new int[] {1, 2, 3, 4};
int sum = 0;
foreach (int number in numbers)
{
    sum += number;
}
Console.WriteLine($"The sum is: {sum}");
Console.WriteLine($"Numbers in the array {numbers.Length}");
double average = sum / numbers.Length;
Console.WriteLine($"The average is: {average}");
```

Output:

```
The sum is: 10
Numbers in the array 4
The average is: 2
```

However, the correct average is 2.5, not 2. Let's debug the issue.

Step 1: Set a breakpoint

To debug our code, we need to set a breakpoint. A *breakpoint* is a marker that tells the debugger to pause the program's execution at a particular line of code, allowing us to inspect the state of the program at that point. To set a breakpoint, click on the gray margin to the left of the line number where you want to pause the execution. In our case, let's set a breakpoint at the line where the incorrect average is displayed. You can set the breakpoint by clicking on the margin next to the line number.

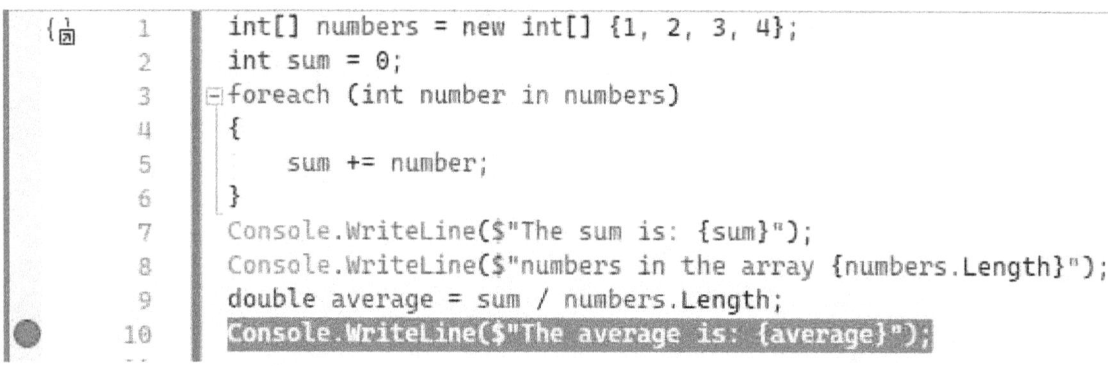

Figure 7.2 Set breakpoint on Visual Studio.

Step 2: Start the debugger

Now that we have a breakpoint, let's start the debugger. To do this, click on "Debug" -> "Start Debugging" in the top menu. You will see the program run.

Step 3: Inspect the program's state

When the program reaches the breakpoint, it will pause its execution, and the Visual Studio interface will change to show the Debugging Tools window. This window allows you to inspect the program's state, including variables, call stack, and threads.

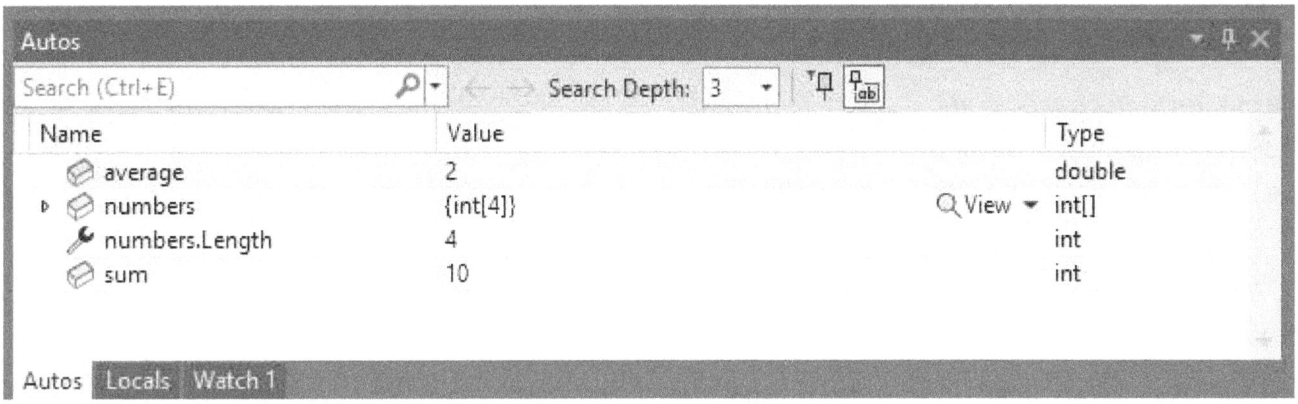

Figure 7.3 Program states window in debugging.

Step 4: Fix the issue:

In our case, we can see that the value of sum is 10, and the value of numers.Length is 4. We expect the average to be 2.5 (10/4 = 2.5). However, we see a 2 as average. Something is wrong in the calculation. You can recall that we learned integer division and that is the issue. Just convert the int sum to double like this, (double) sum. We can also see that the program has stopped at the line where we set the breakpoint.

Step 5: Step through the code

Now that we are paused at the breakpoint, we can step through the code to see what happens next. In our case, click on the "step into" icon or press F11 to finish the execution.

Step 6: Run the program again

Now that we have fixed the issue (change Line 9 "sum" to "(double) sum"), let's run the program again. You can do this by clicking on "Debug" -> "Start Debugging" in the top menu. You should see the correct average of 2.5.

Step 7: Clean up

Once you have finished debugging, you should remove the breakpoint and any other debugging code you added. To remove the breakpoint, click on the margin to the left of the line number where the breakpoint is set or press F9.

Test Your Understanding 7.39
What is the purpose of debugging in software development?
A. To write code faster
B. To identify and fix issues in code
C. To create new features in code
D. To optimize code for faster performance

Test Your Understanding 7.40
What is a breakpoint in debugging?
A. A line where you want to pause the execution
B. A line where the code may break.
C. A line where the error statement will break.
D. A line where the programmer wants to take a break.

Test Your Understanding 7.41
How to set a breakpoint in debugging in Visual Studio?
A. Click on the gray margin to the left of the line number
B. Click on the number
C. Click on the breakpoint from the "debug" then "start debugging" on the nemu.
D. Triple click on the line.

Test Your Understanding 7.42
What is 5/2 in C#?
A. 1
B. 2
C. 2.5
D. 5

Test Your Understanding 7.43
What is 5.0/2 in C#?
A. 1
B. 2
C. 2.5
D. 5

7.7 Chapter Summary

In this chapter, you learned exception handling in C#. One way to handle the exception is to write more robust code, such as using the 'if' statement. Another way is to use the Try ... Catch statement with the built-in exception classes. You also learned software quality and how agile enhances the quality of the software developed. You learned how pair programming works and how it enhances the software quality. Finally, you got hands-on experience with debugging in Visual Studio.

7.8 References

Beck, K. and Andres, C. (2005), Extreme Programming Explained: Embrace Change, 2nd Edition, Addison-Wesley.

Canfora, G., Cimitile, A., Di Lucca, G. A., Visaggio, C. A. (2006). How Distribution Affects the Success of Pair Programming. INTERNATIONAL JOURNAL OF SOFTWARE ENGINEERING & KNOWLEDGE ENGINEERING. April Vol. 16 Issue 2, p293-313

Ginac, F. P. (1998), Customer Oriented Software Qual- ity Assurance. Upper Saddle River, NJ: Prentice Hall.

Hannay, J. E., Dyba, T., Arisholm, E., and Sjoberg, D. I. K. (2009). The Effectiveness of Pair Programming: A Meta Analysis. *Information and Software Technology*. 51(7). July, p. 1110-1122.

ISO/IEC 25010:2023(en), Systems and software engineering — Systems and software Quality Requirements and Evaluation (SQuaRE) — Product quality model. https://www.iso.org/obp/ui/en/#iso:std:iso-iec:25010:ed-2:v1:en

Jyothi, V.E. and Rao, K. N. (2012). Effective Implementation of Agile Practices - Incoordination with Lean Kanban, International Journal on Computer Science and Engineering, 4(1), p. 87-91.

Kloppenborg, T. J. and J. A. Petrick. (2002), Managing Project Quality. Vienna, VA: Management Concepts.

Lewis, W. E. (2008), Software Testing and Continuous Quality Improvement. 3rd Edition, Boca Raton, FL: Auer- bach.

Marchewka, J. T. (2015), *Information Technology Project Management*, 5th Edition. Wiley.

McKay, J. (2007), "Quality Just Doesn't Happen." CIO Magazine. May 24.

Vanhanen, J. and Mantyla, M. V. (2013). A Systematic Mapping Study of Empirical Studies on the Use of Pair Programming in Industry, International Journal of Software Engineering and Knowledge Engineering, Vol. 23, Issue 9, p. 1221-1267.

Zin, A. M. Idris, S., and Subramaniam, N. K. (2006). Implementing Virtual Pair Programming in E-Learning Environment, JOURNAL OF INFORMATION SYSTEMS EDUCATION. Summer, Vol. 17 Issue 2, p113-117.

7.9 Solutions to Test Your Understanding

7.1 A; 7.2 C; 7.3 B; 7.4 D; 7.5 B; 7.6 A; 7.7 A; 7.8 D; 7.9 C; 7.10 B; 7.11 D; 7.12 D; 7.13 B; 7.14 B; 7.15 A; 7.16 A; 7.17 B; 7.18 B; 7.19 D; 7.20 C; 7.21 A; 7.22 D; 7.23 C; 7.24 B; 7.25 B; 7.26 C; 7.27 B; 7.28 B; 7.29 A; 7.30 C; 7.31 C; 7.32 B; 7.33 D; 7.34 A; 7.35 B; 7.36 D; 7.37 A; 7.38 A; 7.39 B; 7.40 A; 7.41 A; 7.42 B; 7.43 C;

Chapter 8: C# Windows Forms and Agile Summary

Chapter Learning Objectives

8.1 Implement Windows Forms Application
8.2 Work with an external text file
8.3 Search records in a List
8.4 Print data on a form

8.1 Windows Forms Application

You have acquired foundational knowledge in object-oriented programming using C# in the previous chapters. Now, it's time to apply that knowledge and create Graphical User Interface (GUI) desktop applications.

Example 8.1

Problem:

The Tiny College needs an application that allows instructors to enter student IDs, student names, and numeric test scores between 0 and 100 for the semester. They want these data to be saved in a text file that can be pulled out, displayed, searched, and printed as wanted.

User Stories:

Based on the description and interviewing with some employees at The Tiny College, you come up with the following user stories.

User Story 1: As an instructor, I want to save my student's ID, name, and score in a text file so that I can keep student's records.
Acceptance Criteria: Graphical user interface. A score is a whole number between 0 and 100.

User Story 2: As an administrator, I want to see all students' records in one screen with student ID, student name, and corresponding letter grades so that I can have an overall picture of my college.
Acceptance Criteria: Graphical user interface. All students listed on one screen. Letter grade is based on the

formula: 90-100 A; 80-89 B; 70-79 C; 60-69 D; Under 60 F.

User Story 3: As a staff member, I want to be able to search a particular student by student ID so that I can decide if the student is qualified for registration.
Acceptance Criteria: Graphical user interface. When the student ID is entered, only that student's name and letter grade are shown. The letter grade formula is the same as in story 2. The Tiny College requires all students to have a grade of C or higher to qualify for registration.

User Story 4: As a staff member, I want to be able to print the student record from the application so that I can give it to the students or for the convenience of discussion with the students.
Acceptance Criteria: Graphical user interface. The administrator wants to print all records in one document with appropriate headers and date time of printing. The staff wants to print just one student record.

Solution:
Start Visual Studio. "Create a new Project" as you did in the past, but don't use "Console Application" as you've used in the previous chapters. This time, on the "Create a new project" window, select "Windows Forms App" as shown in Figure 8.1 and click on the "next" button.

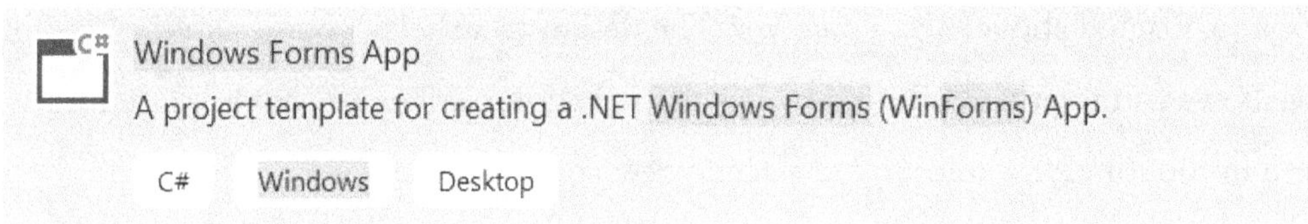

Figure 8.1 Select "Windows Forms App.

On the "Configure your new project" window, name the project "Chapter8Example1". Click on the "Next" button to move to the "Additional Information" window. Make sure ".NET 10.0(Long-term support) is selected for framework. Click on the "Create" button to start a new blank window form application. It may take a couple of minutes for the form to show in design view (double click on the Form1.cs in Solution Explorer window if necessary).

As you continue to develop the application, pay special attention to the following terms: design view window, controls and toolbox, properties window, solution explorer window, and code window.

The *Design View window* is a Windows Form used during design time. It appears by default when you start a new project. You can also open it by double-clicking the form's name in the Solution Explorer.

To find the *toolbox*, click on the "Toolbox" tab on the left side. Or "View" on the menu, then "toolbox". Controls are organized by categories. Expand a category by clicking on it and you can see controls, such as "Button" and "CheckBox". If you want to add a control to the form, you should open the form in the design view. Just double click on an item in the toolbox you want to add to the form, or drag and drop the control to the form.

Controls are object items on a form, like a button, a label, a textbox, a radio button, a checkbox and so on. Toolbox is a place where all those controls are stored.

Each control has many *properties*. Those properties can be found in the property Window, or right click on a control on the form in design view and select "properties". For example, a button has the "text" property, which will be the text shown on the button.

Solution Explorer Window is the same one you see throughout the book. All the files of the project can be found there.

Every form has a design view (explained above) and a *code view*. The design view helps you design the look of a form while the code view allows you to enter code and makes the form interactive. To see the code for a form, right click on the form in the solution explorer and select "view code"

Next, let us rename the default Form1.cs file in the project to something more meaningful. In the "Solution Explorer" window, right click on the Form1.cs. Select "Rename". Change the Form1 name to MainForm.cs (No space in the name). A popup will be displayed asking if you want to change the name for all corresponding components. Click yes.

Next, make the title/caption of the MainForm more readable instead of using the default "Form1". First, click (do not double click) on anywhere in the form to select it. You should see the "Properties" window (Bottom right corner by default). If you don't see it, you can right click on the form and then select "Properties". By default, the properties are organized by category. You can click on the "A to Z alphabetical" icon (second from left) to see a different organization.

Find the "Text" property in the properties window (left column). Change its default value (right column) from "Form1" to "Main Form" (note the use of space between words for users). If the "Text" property is not shown, you may scroll down the list.

Test Your Understanding 8.1
Every Windows Form in the development environment has a ______ view and a ______ view
A. design, code
B. user, design
C. code, user
D. developer, user

Test Your Understanding 8.2
A text field you want to add to a Windows form is called a _______.
A. design item
B. user item
C. control
D. property

Test Your Understanding 8.3
Where can you find all the controls you can add to a Windows form in a design view?
A. design view
B. Solution Explorer
C. Properties Window
D. toolbox

Test Your Understanding 8.4
If you want to change the settings of a control, such as the title/caption of a form, where can you find those settings?
A. design view
B. Solution Explorer
C. Properties Window
D. toolbox

Test Your Understanding 8.5
If you want to change the title/caption of a form, what property of the form would you change?
A. Title
B. Caption
C. either Title or Caption
D. Text

Test Your Understanding 8.6
If a windows form you are working on does not show, where can you find it by double-clicking on it?
A. Solution Explorer window
B. Properties window
C. Toolbox
D. Design view window

Test Your Understanding 8.7
Controls are ______ items on a form, like a button, a label, a textbox, a radio button, a checkbox and so on.
A. useful

B. object
C. class
D. method

Test Your Understanding 8.8
On windows forms, each control usually has ______ properties.
A. 0
B. 1
C. 2
D. many

8.2 Add Controls to the Form

In this section, you will learn how to add different controls to a Windows form in Design View. Have Chapter8Example1 project open before continuing.

With the MainForm displayed in the designer window, go to the "Toolbox". Add a "Label" control to the form, then click once on the label in the form to select it (if it is not already selected by default). Go to the properties window, change the "Text" property to "Student Records", then find the "Font" property and click once to select it. Click on the ellipsis button (small button with little dots) on the right to open the font dialogue window.

In the font dialog box, select the font, style, and size of your liking. In this project, we will select "Lucida Handwriting" for Font, "Italic" for Font style, and 24 for Size.

Next, add four buttons to the form. Make the property of each button according to the values in Table 8.1 (the & sign in front of a character makes the quick key at run time where a user press Alt+character-key on keyboard to click the button):

Click once to select	Change "Text" property to	Change "Name" property to
Button1	&Add	addButton
Button2	&Display	displayButton
Button3	&Search	searchButton
Button4	E&xit	exitButton

Table 8.1 Properties for the Main Form buttons.

The completed MainForm looks like Figure 8.2 below:

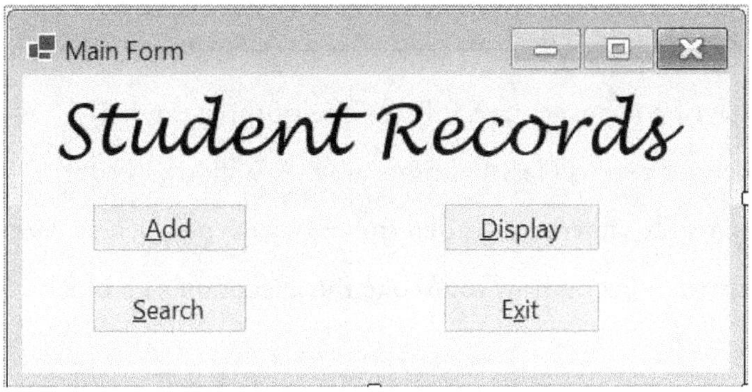

Figure 8.2 The MainForm with the controls.

Test Your Understanding 8.9
If you want to have a label on a windows form that displays "Student Records", ______.
A. you should set the label's Text property to "Student Records"
B. you just type in "Student Records" on the label
C. you should set the label's Name property to "Student Records"
D. you should set the label's display property to "Student Records"

Test Your Understanding 8.10
If you want to have a label on a windows form that displays "Student Records" in larger font size, ______.
A. you should use the label's font property
B. you should use the label's size property
C. you should use the label's font size property
D. you should use the label's larger font size property

Test Your Understanding 8.11
How do you make a button on a form display the text "Click me" on it?
A. you should use the button's font property
B. you should use the button's text property
C. you should use the button's name property
D. you should use the button's display property

Test Your Understanding 8.12
How do you make a button on a form display the text "Click me" with the character k underlined?
A. you should set the button's text property to "ClickU me"
B. you should use the button's text property to "ClicUk me"
C. you should use the button's text property to "Clic&k me"
D. you should use the button's text property to "Click& me"

Test Your Understanding 8.13
What is special about a button with a character underlined?
A. The character is a quick key at run time.
B. The character is important at run time.
C. The character is a quick key at design time.
D. The character is important at design time.

8.3 Add Event Handler to a Button

In previous chapters of the book, you learned the flow of code execution follows one of three ways: 1) sequential, 2) conditional, and 3) repeating. In this section, you will learn another way. A Windows Form application is event-driven. The flow of the execution of the statements is determined by events such as user actions (e.g. mouse click, key press). You will write instructions on how to invoke the execution of a block of statements by clicking on buttons.

Continue to work on the Chapter8Examplee1 project, open the main form in the "design view" window by double clicking on "MainForm.cs" in the "Solution Explorer" window, if it is not already open. Then double click on the "Exit" button to create a button click event handler. When the user clicks on this button at run-time, all statements inside the handler will be executed. For now, you just need to add "Close();" inside the handler to exit the application. The code will look like (You type only the single bolded line):

```
namespace Chapter8Example1
{
    public partial class MainForm : Form
    {
        public Form1()
        {
            InitializeComponent();
        }

        private void exitButton_Click(object sender, EventArgs e)
        {
            Close();
        }
    }
}
```

Next, click on the "Save all" icon in Visual Studio to save the project. Then click on the green play button on top to run the application. Your Exit button should work as expected.

Test Your Understanding 8.14
What are the three ways the flow of code execution can follow?
A. Random, sequential, repeating
B. Parallel, conditional, repeating
C. Sequential, conditional, repeating
D. Sequential, conditional, incremental

Test Your Understanding 8.15
How is the flow of execution of statements determined in a Windows Form application?
A. By user actions such as mouse click and key press

B. By the order of code written in the program
C. By the operating system
D. By the programming language used

Test Your Understanding 8.16
The flow of execution of the statements as determined by events, such as user actions, is called _____ programming.
A. sequential
B. conditional
C. repeating
D. event-driven

Test Your Understanding 8.17
The Windows Forms application is ________.
A. sequential
B. conditional
C. repeating
D. event-driven

Test Your Understanding 8.18
Which of the following statements about buttons is correct?
Statement1: With the form in the design view, double clicking on a button in the form generates the button click event handler.
Statement2: All statements inside a button click event handler will be executed when the user clicks on the button at run time.
A. Statement1 only.
B. Statement2 only.
C. both Statement1 and Statement2.
D. neither Statement1 nor Statement2.

8.4 Add Student Class to the Project

The application is about students at The Tiny College. You need a class called Student that has three fields (ID, name, and score) and a method (GetLetterGrade()). Go to the "Solution Explorer" window and right click on the "Chapter8Example1" project (not the solution) and add a new class named Student.cs as you did in the previous chapters. Add the following code inside the Student class:

```
// fields
private string studentId;
private string name;
private int score;
// properties
public string StudentId
{
    get { return studentId; }
    set { studentId = value; }
}
```

```
public string Name
{
    get { return name; }
    set { name = value; }
}
public int Score
{
    get { return score; }
    set { score = value; }
}
// constructor
public Student(string studentId, string name, int score)
{
    StudentId = studentId;
    Name = name;
    Score = score;
}
// method
public char GetLetterGrade()
{
    char letterGrade;
    if (Score >= 90)
    {
        letterGrade = 'A';
    }
    else if (Score >= 80)
    {
        letterGrade = 'B';
    }
    else if (Score >= 70)
    {
        letterGrade = 'C';
    }
    else if (Score >= 60)
    {
        letterGrade = 'D';
    }
    else
    {
        letterGrade = 'F';
    }
    return letterGrade;
}
// ToString() method
public override string ToString()
{
    string str;
    str = $"{StudentId}\n{Name}\n{Score}";
    return str;
}
```

Explanation:

The "\n" inside the ToString method indicates "new line". It is the same as pressing the "Enter" key. As a result, the str variable holds text in three lines.

Test Your Understanding 8.19
Which of the following statements about adding a class to the project is correct?
Statement1: Adding a class to a Windows Form project is the same as adding a class to a console project.
Statement2: The project typically appears as the first line in the solution explorer window.
A. Statement1 only.
B. Statement2 only.
C. both Statement1 and Statement2.
D. neither Statement1 nor Statement2.

Test Your Understanding 8.20
What is the "\n" in the following string?
```
string str = $"{StudentId}\n, {Name}\n, {GetLetterGrade()}\n";
```
A. new character
B. new variable
C. new line
D. no more

8.5 User Story 1

User Story 1: As an instructor, I want to save my student's ID, name, and score in a text file so that I can keep student's records.

Acceptance Criteria: Graphical user interface. A score is a whole number between 0 and 100.

The project needs a new form to let an instructor save student records in a text file. Similar to adding a class to a project, in the "Solution Explorer" window, right click on the Chapter8Example1 project, then "Add" and then "Form (Windows Forms)...".

The "Add New Form" dialog box will pop up. Name this new form as DataEntryForm.cs. Click on the "Add" button to add this new form.

Next, have the "Toolbox" window showing. Add the following controls to the Data Entry Form (must be in design view) by double clicking on each control in the toolbox (each double click adds only one control):

1 GroupBox, 3 Labels, 3 TextBoxes, and 3 Buttons.

Reorganize the controls in the "Data Entry Form" so they look like Figure 8.3. You can move a control by dragging and moving. Note that all controls except the buttons are inside the group box control (Just enlarge the groupbox and drag controls inside it).

With the Data Entry Form in the design view, change its Text property to "Data Entry Form" (note the space between words).

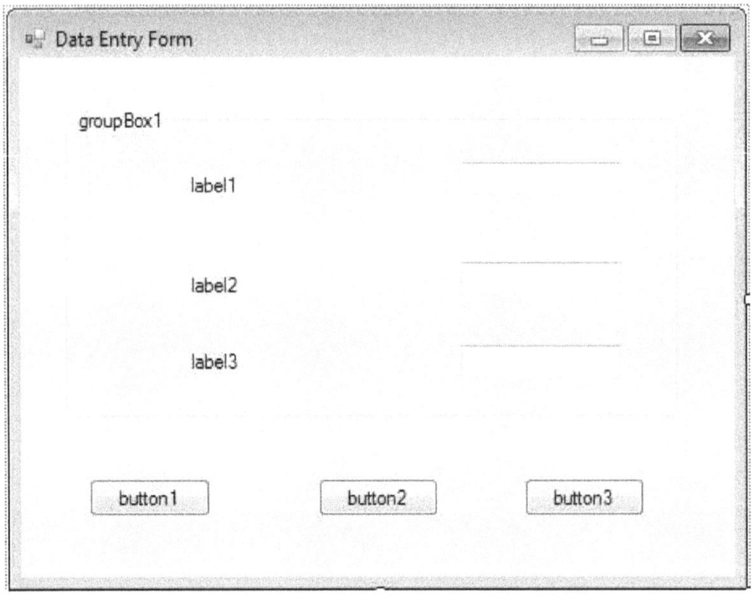

Figure 8.3 Data Entry Form with controls added

Next, we set the properties of these controls by following the property values defined in Table 8.2 below:

Click once to select	Change "Text" property to	Change "Name" property to
groupBox1	Student Data	
label1	Student ID:	
label2	Student Name:	
label3	Student Score:	
textBox1		idTextBox
textBox2		nameTextBox
textBox3		scoreTextBox
button1	&Save	saveButton
button2	&Clear	clearButton
button3	Cl&ose	closeButton

Table 8.2 Properties for Data Entry Form controls

To select groupBox1, click once on the group box itself, but not on any of the controls inside it. Then, in the Properties window, locate the Text property and change its value from "groupBox1" to "Student Data". Click anywhere outside of the Text property box to see the change. You should see the text displayed on the group box change to "Student Data".

Follow the same rule: click once on the control, go to the "Properties" window and change its properties listed in Table 8.2. The blank cell in the table means no change is necessary/just accept the default value. We don't recommend changing a control name when it is never used in the code.

The completed form should look like Figure 8.4 (name property cannot be seen; make sure you did change them).

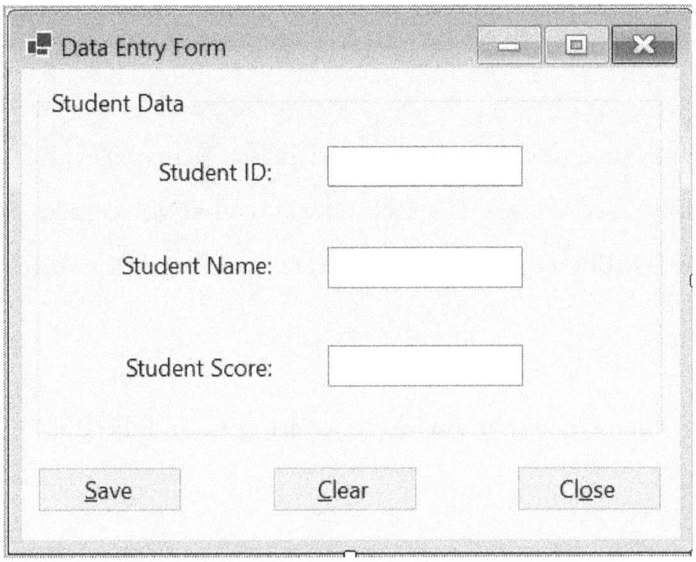

Figure 8.4 Data Entry Form with all controls' properties set

Make the close button on the form work by double clicking the "Close" button and add one line of code inside the click event handler:

```
Close();
```

Before testing the app, you need to reopen the MainForm in the design view. Double click on the "Add" button. Add the following two lines inside the button click event handler:

```
DataEntryForm entryForm = new DataEntryForm();
entryForm.ShowDialog();
```

The first line creates an instance/object of the DataEntryForm class. The second line calls the object's ShowDialog method to show the form.

Save and run the app. Click on the "Add" button on the main form. The data entry form will show. Click on the "Close" button to close the form. Back to the main form, click on the "Exit" button.

Next, make the “Clear” button on the “Data Entry Form” erase anything the user enters, but not saved on the form. Back in the Designer window of the “Data Entry Form”, double click on the “Clear” button to create the “clear button click event handler” and add the following lines inside the “clear button click event handler”:

```
idTextBox.Clear();
nameTextBox.Clear();
scoreTextBox.Clear();
idTextBox.Focus();
```

Explanation:

Every control in the toolbox is a class which has built-in methods. For instance, idTextBox is an object you instantiate from the TextBox class which has a method called Clear(). The method will remove any content in the textbox. The Focus() is another method of the TextBox class which will receive the focus of the form (blink cursor).

Save and run the application. You should see that anything typed into the textboxes are gone and the ID field receives the focus once the Clear button is clicked.

The final task in Story 1 is to make the “Save” button work. Back in the designer window of the “Data Entry Form”, double click on the “Save” button to create “save button click event handler”. Add the following code inside the handler:

```
using StreamWriter sw = File.AppendText("student.txt");
if (!(string.IsNullOrWhiteSpace(idTextBox.Text) ||
      string.IsNullOrWhiteSpace(nameTextBox.Text) ||
      string.IsNullOrWhiteSpace(scoreTextBox.Text)))
{
    if (int.TryParse(scoreTextBox.Text, out int score) && score >= 0 && score <= 100)
    {
        // create an object from the data entry form
        Student student = new Student(idTextBox.Text, nameTextBox.Text, score);
        // save the student record to the file
        sw.WriteLine(student);
        // clear the textboxes
        clearButton.PerformClick();
    }
    else
    {
        MessageBox.Show("Score must be an integer[0, 100]");
    }
}
else
{
    MessageBox.Show("All fields are required.");
}
```

Explanation:

The following line:

```
using StreamWriter sw = File.AppendText("student.txt");
```

is a using statement which provides an easy way to open, write, and then close the connection between this application and the text file, and to ensure the correct use of Disposable objects. This line also creates a StreamWriter type variable named sw which has a WriteLine() method you can use to save text to the file. The sw variable is initialized with the result of calling File.AppendText("student.txt").

The outer if statement checks whether the three textboxes are not empty before saving the contents. A button class has the PerformClick method. It is convenient to call the "clear button click event handler" you wrote earlier and perform the clearance. This provides good user experience as it makes the form ready for the next input. The else block displays a message to the user if any of the three textboxes are empty.

Save and run the application. Add a few student records. To see the data you just saved, go to the folder where you saved the project and open the bin folder inside your project, then open the debug folder. Open the net10.0-windows folder. The file with the name student.txt should be inside. You can open it with Notepad or any text editor to view the content.

Test Your Understanding 8.21
A control can be added to a form by ______ clicking on it in the ______. However, you still need to organize it on the form by moving it around.
A. single, toolbox
B. double, toolbox
C. single, form
D. double, form

Test Your Understanding 8.22
Each control has a name property coming with a default value. We recommend that you change it if the control will appear in the ______.
A. form
B. code
C. design view
D. Solution Explorer Window

Test Your Understanding 8.23
How do you add an underscore to the text of a button in a form to create the button's quick key?
A. use the underscore key on the keyboard
B. click on the underscore icon on the property window
C. add the & in front of the character of the "Text" property

D. add the _ in front of the character of the "Text" property

Test Your Understanding 8.24
Where can you find all the controls to add to a form?
A. Control window
B. Toolbox window
C. Properties window
D. Design View window

Test Your Understanding 8.25
You need to give a meaningful name to a control used in the statements. Where can you change a control's name?
A. Control window
B. Toolbox window
C. Properties window
D. Design View window

Test Your Understanding 8.26
Which of the following statements about Windows from is correct?
Statement1: The process of adding a Windows form to a project is almost the same as adding a class to a project.
Statement2: When you have more than one form in your application, you often have a main form that introduces all other forms.
A. Statement1 only.
B. Statement2 only.
C. both Statement1 and Statement2.
D. neither Statement1 nor Statement2.

Test Your Understanding 8.27
What is the value from the following statement?
```
string.IsNullOrWhiteSpace(nameTextBox.Text)
```
A. It returns the string you entered in the nameTextBox.
B. It returns the string you entered in the nameTextBox if it is not just whitespaces.
C. It returns true if you enter any text in the nameTextBox.
D. It returns false if you enter any text in the nameTextBox.

Test Your Understanding 8.28
What is the value from the following statement?
```
string.IsNullOrWhiteSpace(nameTextBox.Text)
```
A. It returns the string you entered in the nameTextBox.
B. It returns the string you entered in the nameTextBox if it is not just whitespaces.
C. It returns true if you don't enter any text in the nameTextBox.
D. It returns false if you don't enter any text in the nameTextBox.

Test Your Understanding 8.29
What will the following statement do?
```
StreamWriter sw = File.AppendText("student.txt");
```
A. This line creates a StreamWriter type variable named sw and it is initialized with the result of calling File.AppendText("student.txt").
B. It uses the StreamWriter object to append text to a file called student.txt.

C. It uses the StreamWriter class to append text to a file called student.txt
D. It uses the StreamWriter class to access the AppendText method of File class.

Test Your Understanding 8.30
What is the "using" statement as shown in the following statement?

```
using StreamWriter sw = File.AppendText("student.txt");
```

A. It provides a way to open, write, and then close the connection between this application and the text file, and to ensure the correct use of Disposable objects.
B. It uses the StreamWriter object to append text to a file called student.txt.
C. It uses the StreamWriter class to append text to a file called student.txt
D. It uses the StreamWriter class to access the AppendText method of File class.

8.6 User Story 2

User Story 2: As an administrator, I want to see all students' records in one screen with student ID, student name, and corresponding letter grades so that I can have an overall picture of my college.

Acceptance Criteria: Graphical user interface. All students listed on one screen. Letter grade is based on the formula: 90-100 A; 80-89 B; 70-79 C; 60-69 D; Under 60 F.

Analysis:

This story requires that every line of data from the student.txt file be retrieved. Every three lines make a student. You will put every three lines into a student object. Then, you will add the student object into a List and display the List in a Listbox control. The ListBox control is typically used in scenarios where the user needs to select one or more items from a list of options. All these should happen when the Form loads.

Solution:

Add a new form named DisplayForm to the project. This form will display all student records.

Right click on the project in the "solution explorer" window. Add a Windows Form. When the new form is displayed, go to the Toolbox window and add a label, a listbox and two buttons to the form. Set the properties for each control by using the values in Table 8.3.

Click once to select	Change "Text" property to	Change "Name" property to
label1	All Students:	
listBox1		studentsListBox
button1	Cl&ose	closeeButton
button2	&Print	printButton

Table 8.3 Properties for the DisplayForm controls

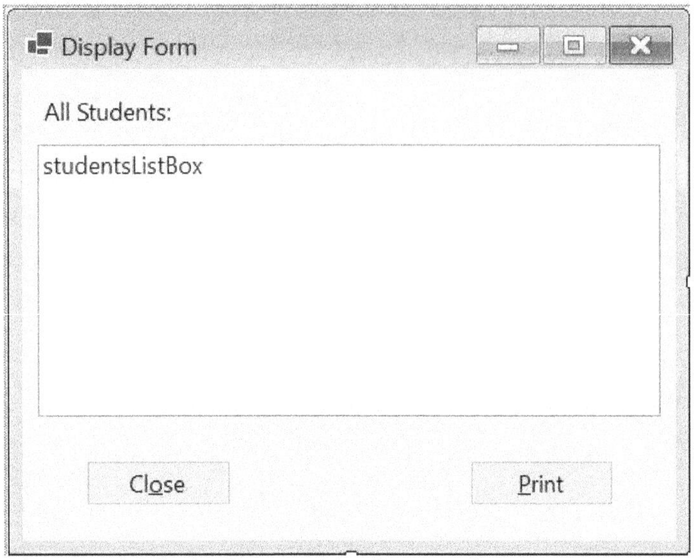

Figure 8.5 DisplayForm with all controls

Next, back in the MainForm in the designer window, you will make the "Display" button work. Double click on the Display button. Inside the button click event handler, add the two lines of code from below:

```
DisplayForm displayForm = new DisplayForm();
displayForm.ShowDialog();
```

Now, go to the DisplayForm designer window. Double click anywhere on the form, but not on any controls. This will create the "form load event handler". Any statements written inside this event handler will be executed when the form loads. Type the following statements inside the "form load event handler":

```
if (File.Exists("student.txt"))
{
    using StreamReader sr = new StreamReader("student.txt");
    string studentId;
    while ((studentId = sr.ReadLine()!) != null)
    {
        string name = sr.ReadLine()!;
        int score = int.Parse(sr.ReadLine()!);
        // create a student object
        Student student = new Student(studentId, name, score);
        // add the student to the listbox
        string str = $"Student ID: {student.StudentId}" +
            $" Name: {student.Name}" +
            $" Grade: {student.GetLetterGrade()}";
        studentsListBox.Items.Add(str);
    }
}
else
{
    MessageBox.Show("Missing student.txt file.");
}
```

Explanation:

The StreamReader class is very similar to the StreamWriter you used earlier in this chapter. This time you use StreamReader to retrieve data from the student.txt file.

A "while" loop is used to read three lines of text from the student.txt file in each loop; sr.ReadLine() appears three times in the loop, one for reading one line. A while loop is used because you don't know how many records are in the text file. The following line:

```
(studentId = sr.ReadLine()) != null
```

Will read the next line of text from the input file associated with the stream reader object "sr". The value read from the file is then assigned to the variable "studentId". Finally, the != null comparison operator checks if the value of "studentId" is not null. If the value is not null, the condition evaluates to true and the code inside the while statement will execute. A string variable str is assembled before adding it to the listbox.

Next, you will make the "Close" button on the DisplayForm work. Double click on the "Close" button on the DisplayForm in the designer window. Add one line of code Close(); inside the "close button click event handler".

This completes user story 2. Save and run the application.

Test Your Understanding 8.31
Write C# statement to accomplish this: "read the next line of text from the input file associated with the stream reader object "sr". The value read from the file is then assigned to the variable "studentId". Finally, the != null comparison operator checks if the value of "studentId" is not null."
A. `(studentId = sr.ReadLine()) != null`
B. `(studentId == sr.ReadLine()) != null`
C. `studentId = sr.ReadLine() != null`
D. `studentId == sr.ReadLine() != null`

Test Your Understanding 8.32
If you need to accept user input on a Windows form, you most likely will use a _______ control.
A. TextBox
B. Label
C. ListBox
D. Button

Test Your Understanding 8.33
If you need to display a list of options for the user to choose from, such as a list of colors, sizes, or categories on a Windows form, you most likely will use a ______ control.
A. TextBox

B. Label
C. ListBox
D. Button

Test Your Understanding 8.34
If you need to display a text string for the user on a Windows form, you most likely will use a _______ control.
A. TextBox
B. Label
C. ListBox
D. Button

Test Your Understanding 8.35
The built-in _______ class is used to retrieve data from a text file.
A. Stream
B. StreamWriter
C. StreamReader
D. StreamRetriever

Test Your Understanding 8.36
Suppose you have a listbox control called allStudentListBox on a form. Which of the following statements will add "Hello" to the listbox?
A. allStudentListBox("Hello");
B. allStudentListBox.Add("Hello");
C. allStudentListBox.Items.Add("Hello");
D. allStudentListBox.Items.Last.Add("Hello");

8.7 User Story 3

User Story 3: As a staff member, I want to be able to search a particular student by student ID so that I can decide if the student is qualified for registration.

Acceptance Criteria: Graphical user interface. When the student ID is entered, only that student's name and letter grade are shown. The letter grade formula is the same as in story 2. The Tiny College requires all students to have a grade of C or higher to qualify for registration.

Analysis:

When this search form loads, you want all data retrieved from the student.txt file to store in a List. When the user types in a student ID and clicks on the "Search" button, the List will be searched. If a match is found, the student data will be displayed in the corresponding labels (the right three labels in Figure 8.7).

Solution:

Go to the "Solution Explorer" window. Right click on the project. Add a new Windows Form. Name it SearchForm.cs.

Back in the MainForm in the designer window, double click on the "Search" button. Add the following code inside the "search button click event handler".

```
SearchForm searchForm = new SearchForm();
searchForm.ShowDialog();
```

Next, go to SearchForm in the design window. Add the necessary controls so that it looks like Figure 8.6:

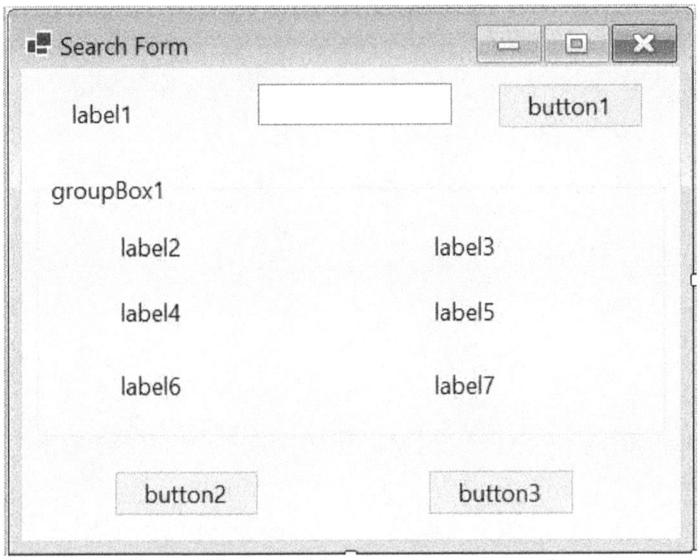

Figure 8.6 SearchForm with necessary controls

Then you set the properties of the controls by following the values in Table 8.4:

Click once to select	Change "Text" property to	Change "Name" property to
textBox1		searchTextBox
Button1	&Search	searchButton
Button2	Cl&ose	closeButton
Button3	&Print	printButton
groupBox1	Student Found	
label1	Enter Student ID:	
label2	Student ID:	
label3		idLabel
label4	Student Name:	
label5		nameLabel
label6	Letter Grade:	
label7		gradeLabel

Table 8.4 Properties for the controls on the SearchForm

Change the properties of label3, label5, and label7 so that they look like the ones in Figure 8.7 by following the following instructions for Label3:

Click once on Label3 to select it. Set its "AutoSize" property from "true" to "false". This will make it the same size regardless of the text in it. Next, set its "BorderStyle" property from "none" to "Fixed 3D".

Do the same for label5 and label7. The completed Search form should look like Figure 8.7.

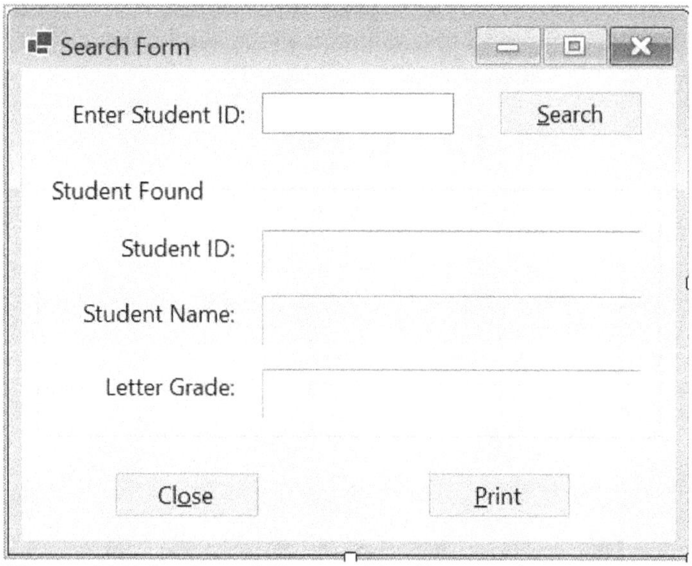

Figure 8.7 The SearchForm with all controls

With SearchForm in the design view window, double click anywhere in the form, but not on any controls. This will create the "form load event handler". Add the following code inside the form load event handler.

```
if (File.Exists("student.txt"))
{
    using StreamReader sr = new StreamReader("student.txt");
    string studentId;
    while ((studentId = sr.ReadLine()!) != null)
    {
        string name = sr.ReadLine()!;
        int score = int.Parse(sr.ReadLine()!);
        // create a student object
        Student s = new Student(studentId, name, score);
        // add to the List
        students.Add(s);
    }
}
else
{
    MessageBox.Show("Missing student.txt file.");
}
```

You will notice a red squiggle underscore. You need to insert a line of code to remove the red squiggle. This line (a field) should appear anywhere inside the SearchForm class but outside of any method. You can add it right after the beginning brace of the class "{":

```
List<Student> students = new List<Student>();
```

With all student's data in a List, make the search button work next.

Back with SearchForm in the designer window, double click on the "Search" button. Add the following code inside the "search button click event handler".

```
if (students.Count > 0 && !string.IsNullOrWhiteSpace(searchTextBox.Text))
{
    // search the list, find the student by id
    Student? student = students.Find(s => s.StudentId == searchTextBox.Text);
    if (student != null)
    {
        idLabel.Text = student.StudentId;
        nameLabel.Text = student.Name;
        gradeLabel.Text = student.GetLetterGrade().ToString();
        printButton.Enabled = true;
    }
    else
    {
        MessageBox.Show("No students found.");
        idLabel.Text = string.Empty;
        nameLabel.Text = string.Empty;
        gradeLabel.Text = string.Empty;
        printButton.Enabled = false;
    }
}
else
{
    MessageBox.Show("No students or Missing search sring.");
    printButton.Enabled = false;
}
```

Explanation:

The following lines:

```
Student? student = students.Find(s => s.StudentId == searchTextBox.Text);
```

The question mark ? indicates a nullable type. The operator => is called the **Lambda operator**. A Lambda expression is a short hand way to write a method. On the left side of the Lambda operator is the input parameter of a method. On the right side are the lambda body statements which correspond to the method body. The lambda statement is to compare a student's StudentId with the search text entered by the user. It will then return true or false for each element of the students List. The whole line will find the first student and store it in a Student object student. The line is similar to the following statements. Can you see the conciseness of using a Lambda expression?

```
Student? student = null;
```

```
foreach (Student s in students)
{
    if (s.StudentId == searchTextBox.Text)
    {
        student = s;
        break;
    }
}
```

Back with the SearchForm in the design view window, double click on the "Close" button to create the "button click event handler", and add one line of statement inside, **`Close();`**

Save and run the application. You should be able to search for a student by student ID.

Test Your Understanding 8.37
A List class in C# has a _______ method you can use to search for an element in the List.
A. Search()
B. Find()
C. SearchFor()
D. FindFor()

Test Your Understanding 8.38
A ______ is a shorthand way of writing a method.
A. Lambda expression
B. Shorthand method
C. Brief method
D. Concise method

Test Your Understanding 8.39
The symbol => is a Lambda operator, the left side of the operator corresponding to the ____ of a method.
A. access modifier
B. return type
C. method name
D. parameter list

Test Your Understanding 8.40
The symbol => is a Lambda operator, the right side of the operator corresponding to the ___ of a method.
A. method body
B. return type
C. method name
D. parameter list

Test Your Understanding 8.41
In a Windows Forms application, in order to search for content of a text file, you should first ______.

A. retrieve the whole file into the application and store them in a variable, such as a List
B. allow the application to reach out to the text file and then search there
C. find out the number of lines in the text file
D. copy the text file to another file in the correct format so that your application can search

Test Your Understanding 8.42
According to the author, the following statement is like using a ______.
```
Student? student = students.Find(s => s.StudentId == searchTextBox.Text);
```
A. sequence statement
B. conditional statement
C. loop statement
D. class statement

Test Your Understanding 8.43
Suppose you have the following statement:
```
List<Student> students = new List<Student>();
```
How do you find out the number of students in the students List?
A. students.Count
B. students.Count()
C. students.Length
D. students.Length()

8.8 User Story 4

User Story 4: As a staff member, I want to be able to print the student record from the application so that I can give it to the students or for the convenience of discussion with the students.
Acceptance Criteria: Graphical user interface. The administrator wants to print all records in one document with appropriate headers and date time of printing. The staff wants to print just one student record.

In this section, you will add the print feature to the DisplayForm and SearchForm. First, the DisplayForm: With the DisplayForm in the design view window, go to the Toolbox, find "printDocument" control, and double click on it to add it to the form's component tray. By default, it will be called printDocument1.

Back to the Display Form in designer view. Double click on the "Print" button. Add one line of code inside the "print button click event handler" as shown below:
```
    printDocument1.Print();
```

The above statement calls the Print() method of printDocument1 control. Back in the designer window of the DisplayForm, double click on the "printDocument1" in the component tray. Inside its PrintPage event handler, add the code below:

```
// print a header
e.Graphics.DrawString("Grade Report",
    new Font("Courier New", 24, FontStyle.Bold),
    Brushes.Black, 300, 100);
// print date and time
e.Graphics.DrawString(DateTime.Now.ToString(),
    new Font("Courier New", 12, FontStyle.Italic),
    Brushes.Black, 320, 150);
// print each student in a loop
int x = 100, y = 200;
foreach (var row in studentsListBox.Items)
{
    e.Graphics.DrawString(row.ToString(),
        new Font("Courier New", 12, FontStyle.Regular),
        Brushes.Black, x, y);
    y += 16;
}
```

Explanation:

In the following line:

```
e.Graphics.DrawString("Grade Report",
                    new Font("Courier New", 24, FontStyle.Bold),
                    Brushes.Black, 300, 100);
```

The first number, 24, indicates the font size. The second number, 300, indicates the print starts horizontally 300 pixels from the left border of the paper. The third number, 100 indicates, the print starts vertically 100 pixels from the top of the paper. Refer to Figure 8.8 for an example.

The following line: `y += 16;` Adds 16 pixels to the vertical distance when printing the next student. This ensures the next line will be further down from the top of the paper. On paper, it will look like the one on Figure 8.8.

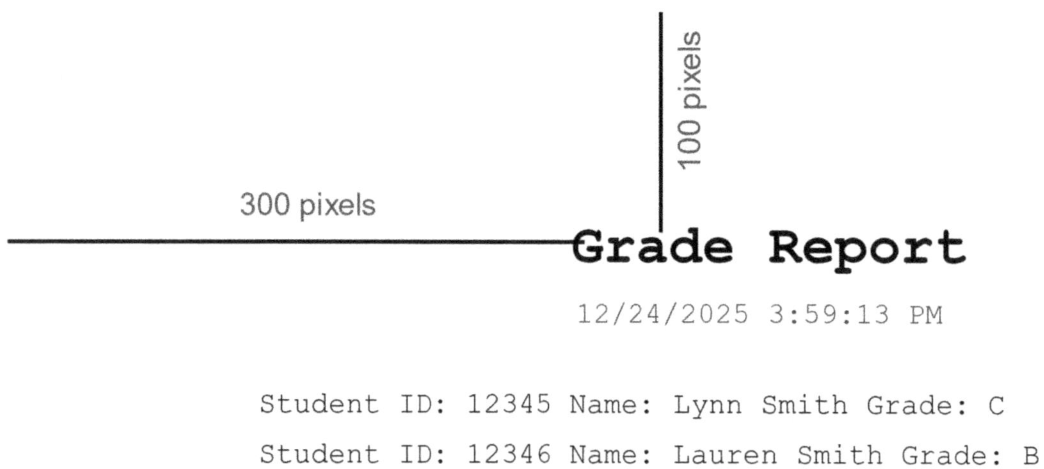

Figure 8.8 Explanation of print positions in DrawString() method.

The "var" data type in the foreach loop lets the compiler decide the actual data type.

Save and run the application. You should be able to print all the students in the display.

There is one more task for User Story 4. Make the SearchForm print button work.

Have the SearchForm open in the design view window. Go to the Toolbox. Double click on printDocument control to add a printDocument object to the component tray. Use the default name printDocument1. Double click the Print button on the SearchForm and add a single line of code inside the handler.

```
printDocument1.Print();
```

Back in the SearchForm design view window, double click on the printDocument1 in the component tray to create the printPage event handler, and add the following code inside the handler:

```
e.Graphics.DrawString("Student ID: " + idLabel.Text,
    new Font("Courier New", 12, FontStyle.Regular),
    Brushes.Black, 100, 200);
e.Graphics.DrawString("Student Name: " + nameLabel.Text,
    new Font("Courier New", 12, FontStyle.Regular),
    Brushes.Black, 100, 220);
e.Graphics.DrawString("Student Grade: " + gradeLabel.Text,
    new Font("Courier New", 12, FontStyle.Regular),
    Brushes.Black, 100, 240);
```

Save and run the program to test all features.

Test Your Understanding 8.44
In the following statement:

```
e.Graphics.DrawString("Grade Report", new Font("Courier New", 24,
FontStyle.Bold), Brushes.Black, 300, 100);
```

What is the number 300?
A. Number of pixels from the top of the paper.
B. Number of pixels from the bottom of the paper.
C. Number of pixels from the left side of the paper.
D. Number of pixels form the right side of the paper.

Test Your Understanding 8.45
In the following statement:

```
e.Graphics.DrawString("Grade Report", new Font("Courier New", 24,
FontStyle.Bold), Brushes.Black, 300, 100);
```

What is the number 100?
A. Number of pixels from the top of the paper.
B. Number of pixels from the bottom of the paper.
C. Number of pixels from the left side of the paper.
D. Number of pixels form the right side of the paper.

Test Your Understanding 8.46
In the following statement:
```
e.Graphics.DrawString("Grade Report", new Font("Courier New", 24,
FontStyle.Bold), Brushes.Black, 300, 100);
```
What is the number 24?
A. Number of pixels from the top of the paper.
B. Number of pixels from the bottom of the paper.
C. Number of pixels from the left side of the paper.
D. The font size.

Test Your Understanding 8.47
There are two steps to making a print button on a form work. What are these two steps?
A. the print button click event calls the printDocument's print() method, which will trigger the printDocument's printPage event.
B. the print button click event calls the button's print() method, which will trigger the printDocument's printPage event.
C. the print button click event calls the printDocument's printPage() method, which will trigger the printDocument's printPage event.
D. the print button click event calls the printPage's print() method, which will trigger the printDocument's printPage event.

Test Your Understanding 8.48
Which of the following statements about print is correct?
Statement1: The statement printDocument1.Print(); will print everything on the form.
Statement2: The text you want to print should be included inside the printDocument's printPage event handler.
A. Statement1 only.
B. Statement2 only.
C. both Statement1 and Statement2.
D. neither Statement1 nor Statement2.

Programming Challenge 8.1

Create an application that allows the user to enter, display, and print an employee's payroll information. It allows the user to enter a new employee, add hours worked for each pay period, display all employee information, and print the information. A sample MainForm is shown in Figure 8.9.

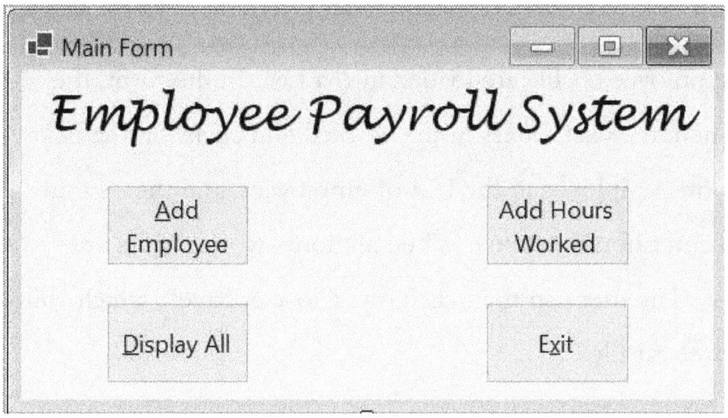

Figure 8.9 Sample MainForm.

The "Add Employee" form is shown in Figure 8.10.

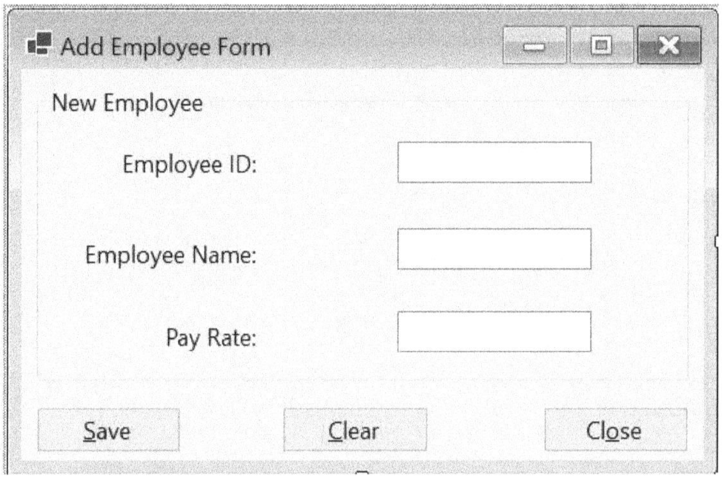

Figure 8.10 Add Employee Form

The save button on the form will save the new employee into a text file employee.txt in the default folder.

The "Add Hours" form is shown in Figure 8.11.

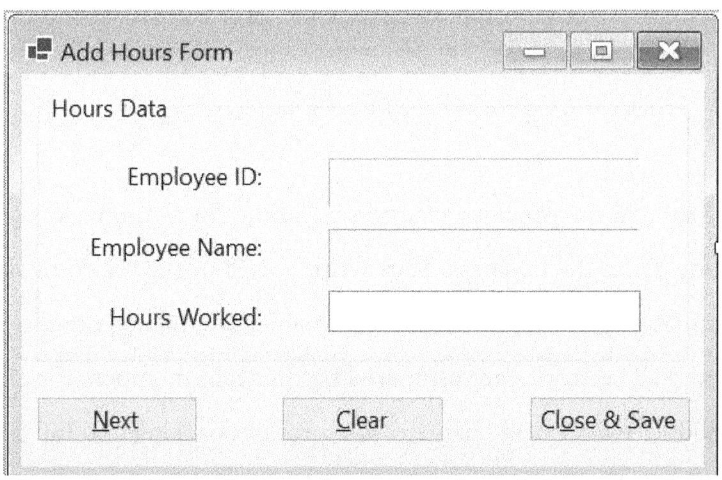

Figure 8.11 Form for entering an employee's hours worked.

When the form is loaded, all employees from the employee.txt file are loaded into a List. In the form, the first employee from the list should be displayed. Then, the user enters hours worked and clicks on the next button. The hours worked should be added to the first employee in the List of employees, and the second employee data is displayed and expects the user to enter hours worked. When all hours worked data are entered, a pop up will display "no more employees". The user can then click on "Close & Save", which will close the form and save all data to the same employee.txt file.

The "Display All" form is shown in Figure 8.12:

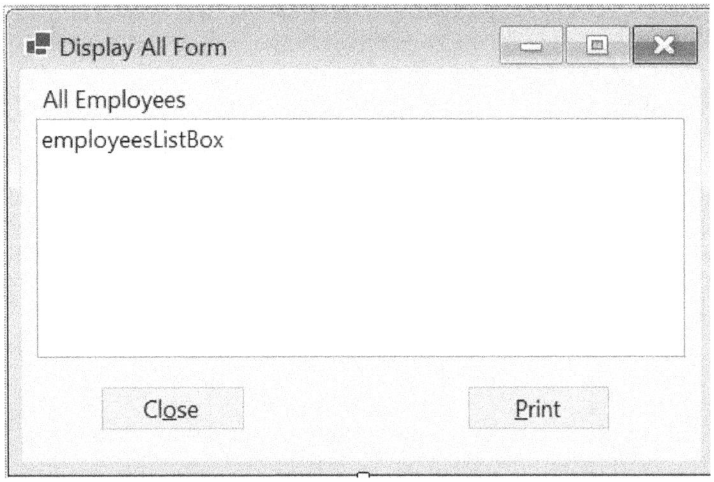

Figure 8.12 Form for displaying all employees.

The "Print" button in Figure 8.12 will print all employee data in a nicely formatted way on paper.
The "Exit" button on the MainForm will exit the program. A class called Employee must be used for all three features (Add Employee, Add Hours, and Display All).

8.9 Agile Summary

You have learned the roles, events, and artifacts of agile in the previous chapters. It's time for a summary. Your agile team starts with the software requirements from the business. Start writing user stories based on the requirements and put the stories in the product backlog. Some stories can be easily written while others may be vague and need clarification from the business. The stories are estimated by the team members for the effort needed to implement each story. The product owner is in charge of the product backlog and the product backlog is updated frequently. Stories in the product backlog are prioritized with different granularity.

Prioritization refers to ordering backlog items based on business value, risk, dependencies, and strategic goals -- ensuring the team always works on the most important stories first. Granularity describes the level of detail in those stories: items near the top of the backlog are broken down into small, well-defined units ready for development, while items lower down remain larger and more coarse-grained (sometimes called epics). This dynamic balance allows the product owner to maintain a clear near-term roadmap without over-investing effort in detailing requirements that may change or never be implemented, keeping the backlog manageable and adaptable.

Building on this refined product backlog, the team selects the highest-priority stories -- those already decomposed into appropriately sized, sprint-ready units -- and moves them into the sprint backlog during sprint planning. The quantity selected aligns with the team's velocity: the average number of story points the team reliably completes per sprint. During planning, each story may be further broken down into concrete, actionable tasks, which team members then estimate in hours to ensure the work is manageable and the sprint commitment is realistic.

On a daily basis, the team holds a brief daily scrum meeting to see what each member has done yesterday, plans to do today, and any impediments encountered. Progress may be recorded on the Kanban board and/or burn down chart.

At the end of the sprint, the team integrates the new increment into the current product baseline, creating a cohesive, potentially shippable whole. They then hold a sprint review to demonstrate this working functionality to customers and stakeholders, gathering valuable feedback to guide upcoming work. This collaborative session fosters open communication and ensures the product continues evolving in alignment with user needs and business goals.

Next, the team will hold a sprint retrospective meeting to examine how the team can do better in the next sprint. During the meeting, the team reflects on their performance during the previous sprint and identifies areas for improvement. The retrospective meeting is an opportunity for the team to share their feedback on what went well, what did not go as planned, and what they can do to improve in the next sprint. The team discusses what they learned and how they can apply that knowledge to improve their workflow, communication, and collaboration in future sprints. The agile sprint retrospective meeting is a critical tool for continuous improvement and ensuring that the team is constantly growing and evolving.

This brings us back to another sprint until the project is completed.

Test Your Understanding 8.49
Which of the following is NOT a purpose of an agile sprint review meeting?
A. Demo the increment to the customers.
B. Receive feedback from the customers.
C. Collaborate between team members and the stakeholders.
D. Increase the productivity of the team by learning from the lessons from the previous sprint.

Test Your Understanding 8.50
What is the increment in agile?
A. The software the team completed in the current sprint.
B. The software the team completed in the current and all previous sprints.
C. The payment the team receives for the current sprint.
D. The payment the team receives for the current and all previous sprints.

Test Your Understanding 8.51
Which of the following is the first meeting of a sprint?
A. Sprint planning
B. Daily scrum
C. Sprint review
D. Retrospective

Test Your Understanding 8.52
Which of the following is the last meeting of a sprint?
A. Sprint planning
B. Daily scrum
C. Sprint review
D. Retrospective

8.10 Chapter Summary

In this chapter, you learned how to create a windows forms application, how to write and read data from an external text file, how to search a List to find a matching element, how to display a group of elements in a ListBox, and how to print content from a form. You also reviewed how to break up a project into sprints and complete one sprint at a time. User requirements are expressed in the form of user stories. Each sprint completes one or more user stories.

8.11 Solution to Programming Challenge

Programming Challenge 8.1 (You must follow the same steps in the Example 8.1. If you just type the code from this section for each form, it will not work. Also, we purposely omit the code for close form, you should still add it.)

Code for Employee.cs

```
internal class Employee
{
    // fields
    private string employeeId;
    private string name;
    private decimal payRate;
    private decimal hoursWorked;
    // overloaded constructors
    public Employee(string employeeId, string name, decimal payRate)
    {
        EmployeeId = employeeId;
        Name = name;
        PayRate = payRate;
    }
    public Employee(string employeeId, string name,
        decimal payRate, decimal hoursWorked)
    {
        EmployeeId = employeeId;
        Name = name;
        PayRate = payRate;
        HoursWorked = hoursWorked;
    }
    // properties
    public string EmployeeId
    {
        get { return employeeId; }
        set { employeeId = value; }
    }
    public string Name
    {
        get { return name; }
        set { name = value; }
    }
    public decimal PayRate
    {
        get { return payRate; }
        set { payRate = value; }
    }
    public decimal HoursWorked
    {
        get { return hoursWorked; }
        set { hoursWorked = value; }
    }
    // method
    public decimal PayAmount()
    {
        decimal amount;
        amount = PayRate * HoursWorked;
        return amount;
    }
    // ToString
    public override string ToString()
```

```
        {
            string str;
            str = $"{EmployeeId}\n{Name}\n{PayRate}\n{HoursWorked}";
            return str;
        }
    }
```

Code for the MainForm

```
public partial class MainForm : Form
{
    public MainForm()
    {
        InitializeComponent();
    }
    private void addEmployeeButton_Click(object sender, EventArgs e)
    {
        AddEmployeeForm addEmployeeForm = new AddEmployeeForm();
        addEmployeeForm.ShowDialog();
    }
private void addHoursWorkedButton_Click(object sender, EventArgs e)
{
      AddHoursForm addHoursForm = new AddHoursForm();
        addHoursForm.ShowDialog();
    }
    private void displayAllButton_Click(object sender, EventArgs e)
    {
        DisplayAllForm displayAllForm = new DisplayAllForm();
        displayAllForm.ShowDialog();
    }
}
```

Code for the Add Employee Form:

```
public partial class AddEmployeeForm : Form
{
    public AddEmployeeForm()
    {
        InitializeComponent();
    }
    private void saveButton_Click(object sender, EventArgs e)
    {
      using StreamWriter sw = File.AppendText("employee.txt");
      if (!(string.IsNullOrWhiteSpace(idTextBox.Text) ||
          string.IsNullOrWhiteSpace(nameTextBox.Text) ||
         string.IsNullOrWhiteSpace(payRateTextBox.Text)))
      {
          if (decimal.TryParse(payRateTextBox.Text, out decimal payRate) && payRate >= 0)
          {
            // create an object from the data entry form
            Employee employee = new Employee (idTextBox.Text, nameTextBox.Text, payRate);
            // save the employee record to the file
            sw.WriteLine(employee);
            // clear the textboxes
            clearButton.PerformClick();
          }
          else
          {
              MessageBox.Show("Pay rate must be a number.");
          }
```

```
        }
        else
        {
            MessageBox.Show("All fields are required.");
        }
    }
    private void clearButton_Click(object sender, EventArgs e)
    {
        idTextBox.Clear();
        nameTextBox.Clear();
        payRateTextBox.Clear();
        idTextBox.Focus();
    }
}
```

Code for Add Hours Form

```
    public partial class AddHoursForm : Form
    {
        List<Employee> employees = new List<Employee>();
        public AddHoursForm()
        {
            InitializeComponent();
        }

        private void AddHoursForm_Load(object sender, EventArgs e)
        {
            // remove the controlBox on top right
            ControlBox = false;
            if (File.Exists("employee.txt"))
            {
                using StreamReader sr = new StreamReader("employee.txt");
                string employeeId;
                while ((employeeId = sr.ReadLine()) != null)
                {
                    Employee employee = new Employee(employeeId, sr.ReadLine(),
                    decimal.Parse(sr.ReadLine()), decimal.Parse(sr.ReadLine()));
                    employees.Add(employee);
                }
                // display first employee
                if (employees.Count > 0)
                {
                    idLabel.Text = employees[0].EmployeeId;
                    nameLabel.Text = employees[0].Name;
                }
                else
                {
                    MessageBox.Show("No employees in the file.");
                    nextButton.Enabled = false;
                }
            }
            else
            {
                MessageBox.Show("Missing employee.txt");
                Close();
            }

        }
        int count = 1; // this is a field
        private void nextButton_Click(object sender, EventArgs e)
        {
```

```
            if (decimal.TryParse(hoursTextBox.Text, out decimal hours) && hours >= 0)
            {
                // add hours worked to the array
                employees[count - 1].HoursWorked = hours;
                if (count < employees.Count)
                {
                    idLabel.Text = employees[count].EmployeeId;
                    nameLabel.Text = employees[count].Name;
                    count++;
                }
                else
                {
                    MessageBox.Show("no more records.");
                    nextButton.Enabled = false;
                    idLabel.Text = string.Empty;
                    nameLabel.Text = string.Empty;
                }
            }
            else
            {
                MessageBox.Show("Hours worked must be a number.");
            }
            clearButton.PerformClick();
        }

    private void closeAndSaveButton_Click(object sender, EventArgs e)
        {
            using StreamWriter sw = File.CreateText("employee.txt");
            foreach (Employee employee in employees)
            {
                sw.WriteLine(employee);
            }
            Close();
        }
        private void clearButton_Click(object sender, EventArgs e)
        {
            hoursTextBox.Clear();
            hoursTextBox.Focus();
        }
    }
```

Code for Display all employees Form:

```
    public partial class DisplayAllForm : Form
    {
        public DisplayAllForm()
        {
            InitializeComponent();
        }

        private void DisplayAllForm_Load(object sender, EventArgs e)
        {
            if (File.Exists("employee.txt"))
            {
                using StreamReader sr = new StreamReader("employee.txt");
                string employeeId;
                while ((employeeId = sr.ReadLine()) != null)
                {
                    string name = sr.ReadLine();
                    decimal payRate = decimal.Parse(sr.ReadLine());
                    decimal hoursWorked = decimal.Parse(sr.ReadLine());
```

```
                // create an employee object
                Employee employee = new Employee(employeeId, name, payRate, hoursWorked);
                // add the employee to the listbox
                string str = $"Employee ID: {employee.EmployeeId} Name: {employee.Name}" +
                        $" Pay Amount: {employee.PayAmount():C}";
                employeesListBox.Items.Add(str);
            }
        }
        else
        {
            MessageBox.Show("Missing employee.txt file.");
            Close();
        }
    }

        private void printButton_Click(object sender, EventArgs e)
        {
            printDocument1.Print();
        }

        private void printDocument1_PrintPage(object sender,
            System.Drawing.Printing.PrintPageEventArgs e)
        {
            // print a header
            e.Graphics.DrawString("Employee Payroll",
                new Font("Courier New", 24, FontStyle.Bold),
                Brushes.Black, 250, 100);
            // print date and time
            e.Graphics.DrawString(DateTime.Now.ToString(),
                new Font("Courier New", 12, FontStyle.Italic),
                Brushes.Black, 300, 150);
            // print each employee in a loop
            int x = 100, y = 200;
            foreach (var row in employeesListBox.Items)
            {
                e.Graphics.DrawString(row.ToString(),
                    new Font("Courier New", 12, FontStyle.Regular),
                    Brushes.Black, x, y);
                y += 16;
            }
        }
    }
```

8.12 Solutions to Test Your Understanding

8.1 A; 8.2 C; 8.3 D; 8.4 C; 8.5 D; 8.6 A; 8.7 B; 8.8 D; 8.9 A; 8.10 A; 8.11 B; 8.12 C; 8.13 A; 8.14 C; 8.15 A; 8.16 D; 8.17 D; 8.18 C; 8.19 A; 8.20 C; 8.21 B; 8.22 B; 8.23 C; 8.24 B; 8.25 C; 8.26 C; 8.27 D; 8.28 C; 8.29 A; 8.30 A; 8.31 A; 8.32 A; 8.33 C; 8.34 B; 8.35 C; 8.36 C; 8.37 B; 8.38 A; 8.39 D; 8.40 A; 8.41 A; 8.42 C; 8.43 A; 8.44 C; 8.45 A; 8.46 D; 8.47 A; 8.48 B; 8.49 D; 8.50 B; 8.51 A; 8.52 D;

Chapter 9: Case Study

Chapter Learning Objectives

9.1 Develop simple C# Windows Form application by following agile principles.

9.1 Case Background

In this chapter, you will be working on an agile team to develop an inventory management system for Mr. Lincoln (introduced in Chapter 1). Find two or three classmates or friends who are interested in agile software development to work together on this case study.

Dragon Phoenix Toy (DPT) LLC is a tiny retailer founded in 1994. It sells about 50 types of toys and most of them are seasonal. The manager wants a simple desktop application that can handle the company's inventory.

A product in DPT has a product ID, product name, product description, sales price, and inventory on hand.

When a shipment of new products arrives, the manager wants to be able to enter the product information into the system.

When a shipment of existing products arrives, the manager wants to be able to update the inventory on hand.

When a purchase is made by a customer, the check-out associate wants to enter the product ID and units sold. One sale can include multiple products. When all sale items are entered, the form should display a receipt which includes the name of each product sold, units sold, line total, subtotal, tax (9%), and total charge. The manager wants the inventory on hand to be updated after each sale. The application should be able to display and print the receipt similar to the following format.

```
Dragon Phoenix Toy (DPT)
     123 Toys St.
```

```
    Argentina OK 48451
  11/12/2022 2:30:03 PM
Wooden Train      2         40.00
Doll              1         30.00
Sub total                   70.00
Tax                          6.30
Total                       76.30
```

From time to time, the manager wants to check the product inventory and print it out. The print sheet should include the date and time of when the inventory was checked.

All data should be saved in a text file in its default location.

9.2 Your Tasks

Your tasks as a team:

1. Build the Product Backlog:

    1a. Write the user stories.

    1b. Prioritize the stories.

    1c. Estimate the story points for each story first as an individual and then as a team.

2. Build the Sprint Backlog:

    2a. Write sprint goals.

    2b. Pick stories from the product backlog based on the team velocity.

    2c. Strategy to reach the goals.

3. Start a sprint planning:

    3a. Break each story down to its component tasks if necessary.

    3b. Estimate hours of work needed for each task.

4. Each member picks a task to work for a day or less. Use paired programming if possible.
5. Have daily stand-up meetings, and after the meeting, each member picks tasks to work on.
6. At the end of the sprint, conduct a sprint review/demo the increment to the customer.
7. Retrospection. As a team, find out what works and what doesn't. How can you as a team do better in the next sprint?
8. Repeat steps 2 to 7 above for each sprint.

Find a few people to work with before checking the solution.

9.3 User Stories.

User Story 1: As the owner, I want to check the inventory at any time so that I know how the business runs.
Acceptance Criteria: The graphical user interface should display the current inventory with a single button click. Low inventory items (less than 3 units in stock) should be highlighted in red on the print display.

User Story 2: As the owner, I want to update the inventory when a new shipment arrives so that I have up to date inventory.
Acceptance Criteria: The user should be able to enter the product ID (simulating a barcode scan) and the new shipment quantity, and then update the inventory by clicking on the "Update" button.

User Story 3: As the owner, I want to enter new product information into the system before a new shipment arrives so that the inventory system is ready to process the shipment the moment it arrives.
Acceptance Criteria: The user should be able to enter new product information without specifying the quantity, and update the quantity at a later time.

User Story 4: As a cashier, I want to enter order information and the inventory is automatically updated so that I don't need to keep the record on paper.
Acceptance Criteria: Orders can include multiple products with varying quantities, and the inventory should be updated as each order is submitted.

User Story 5: As a cashier, I want to print the receipt for an order for the customer so that the customer has the proof of purchase.
Acceptance Criteria: The receipt should resemble the example displayed in the problem description earlier in this chapter. The order details should be shown prior to printing, and the receipt data should not be saved in a text file.

User Story 6: As the owner, I want to print my inventory on paper so that I can take it anywhere I want.
Acceptance Criteria: The inventory print should be professional in appearance and printed on regular paper, with the date and time included. The details should be displayed prior to printing.

9.4 Prioritize the Stories

The product owner decides that the priority of the stories should be as follows with the first one as the most important:
Story 3, Story 2, Story 1, Story 4, Story 5, Story 6.

9.5 Estimate the Story Points for each Story

The team plays the Poker Planning Game. If you don't remember the game, you can go back and read it again (in Chapter 5). At first, the members don't know what each number exactly means and are not comfortable with which number to place. All of them know that ½ is the easiest story and 100 is the most difficult one. After a few rounds of play, they decide 8 story points as the estimate for story 1.

The estimate for the next story is easier. If a member thinks story 2 is more difficult than story 1, he or she will place a number larger than 8. Otherwise, a smaller number is placed. After a few rounds of play, they decide story 2 is 40 points.

One benefit of estimating story points is getting to know more about each story. Some stories may be more difficult than they look. For example, Story 2 was first estimated by the members as 5, 5, 5, and 100. Even though the majority estimate it for 5 points, the member who gave 100 points explains that the difficulty is due to the fact that an update on a text file is not as easy as an update on a database. It is not difficult to read the specific inventory on hand from the file. Also, it is not difficult to update that number once it is in the program. However, it is difficult to save it back to the original location in the text file. One member suggests that maybe they should retrieve all data instead of just one inventory on hand. This way, after updating, the whole list of data can be saved back to the file without worrying about the original location, since the old one will be completely erased and replaced with the new inventories. Now, they believe they understand the problem better and in the second play, they give the estimate as 40.

The team continues to play and estimates 5 points for Story 3. They believe saving data to a text file is not much different from reading it from the file, as they already learned in Chapter 8.

They estimate 40 points for Story 4. They don't know how to handle an order with multiple items.

They estimate 8 points for Story 5 because they learned how to print from Chapter 8. The only challenge is how to display the date and time.

Finally, they estimate 5 points for Story 6. They believe with the experience from Story 5, they can handle it in less time for the print feature.

9.6 Sprint One (Zero)

The team members have a full-time job somewhere and cannot work on this in a full-time manner. Each member says they can devote about 5 hours per week to the project. They don't want a long sprint. They decide to have a time-box of two weeks for each sprint so that they can get feedback sooner. The total story points are 106 (8+40+5+40+8+5). They pick stories one, two, and three for the first sprint with a team velocity of 53 points. The project will be completed in four weeks (two sprints).

9.6.1 Sprint Planning

The team identified the tasks for Story 3:
Story 3 Tasks (3 hours):
Main Form (Figure 9.1) and Story 3 user interface (Figure 9.2) (1 hour).
Product class (1 hour).
Save data to the text file (1 hour).

Tasks for Story 2 (10 hours):
Story 2 user interface (Figure 9.3) (1 hour).
Read the inventory from the text file (2 hours).
Update the inventory (5 hours).
Save the updated inventory back to the text file (2 hours).

Story 1 user interface (Figure 9.4) (2 hours).
Read data from the text file, and display on the form (Figure 9.4) (2 hours).

9.6.2 Working on the project

They decide to use pair programming. Since they cannot physically meet, they decide to use remote PC access to work on one screen with two members. Each pair picks some tasks to work on.

9.6.3 Sprint Review

At the end of the sprint, they put all applications together and demo it to a friend pretending to be Mr. Lincoln, the store owner, and see how close they meet the requirements.

9.6.4 Retrospective

As a team, they hold a video conference meeting and discuss what works and what does not work, and what new techniques they want to try in the next sprint.

9.7 Sprint Two

In the second sprint, the team works on the remaining stories by following the same pattern as sprint one.

9.8 Release

By the end of the four weeks, they believe they have achieved what Mr. Lincoln wants and deploy the software on Mr. Lincoln's computer.

9.9 Product Class and Order Class

There are two custom classes you will need for this application: a Product class and an Order class. Create a product class which includes product ID, name, description, price, inventory on hand, units sold, and whether it is the order.

```
namespace Chapter9Example1
{
    internal class Product
    {
        // fields
        private string productId;
        private string name;
        private string description;
        private decimal price;
        private int onHand;
```

```
private int unitSold;
private bool isInOrder;
// properties
public string ProductId
{
    get { return productId; }
    set { productId = value; }
}
public string Name
{
    get { return name; }
    set { name = value; }
}
public string Description
{
    get { return description; }
    set { description = value; }
}
public decimal Price
{
    get { return price; }
    set { price = value; }
}
public int OnHand
{
    get { return onHand; }
    set { onHand = value; }
}
public int UnitSold
{
    get { return unitSold; }
    set { unitSold = value; }
}
public bool IsInOrder
{
    get { return isInOrder; }
    set { isInOrder = value; }
}
// overloaded constructors
public Product(string productId, string name, string description,
    decimal price, int onHand)
{
    ProductId = productId;
    Name = name;
    Description = description;
    Price = price;
    OnHand = onHand;

}
public Product(string productId, int unitSold)
{
    ProductId = productId;
    UnitSold = unitSold;
}

// methods
public decimal CalculateProductCost()
{
    decimal cost;
    cost = Price * UnitSold;
    return cost;
```

```
        }
        public void Sold()
        {
            OnHand -= UnitSold;
        }
        // ToString
        public override string ToString()
        {
            string str;
            str = $"{productId}\n{Name}\n{Description}\n{Price}\n{OnHand}";
            return str;
        }
    }
}
```

Next, create an order class that includes a List of products, their corresponding quantities ordered, and calculation of subtotal, tax, and total.

```
namespace Chapter9Example1
{
    internal class Order
    {
      // fields
        public const decimal TAX_RATE = 0.09M;
        private List<Product> productInOrder;
        // property
        public List<Product> ProductInOrder
        {
            get { return productInOrder; }
            set { productInOrder = value; }
        }
        // constructor
        public Order(List<Product> productInOrder)
        {

            ProductInOrder = productInOrder;
        }
        // methods
        public decimal CalculateSubTotal()
        {
            decimal subTotal = 0;
            foreach (Product p in ProductInOrder)
            {
                subTotal += p.CalculateProductCost();
            }
            return subTotal;
        }
        public decimal CalculateTax()
        {
            decimal taxAmount;
            taxAmount = CalculateSubTotal() * TAX_RATE;
            return taxAmount;
        }
        public decimal CalculateTotal()
        {
            decimal total;
            total = CalculateSubTotal() + CalculateTax();
            return total;
```

```
            }
        //ToString
        public override string ToString()
        {
            string str;
            str = $"     Dragon Phoenix Toy\n";
            str += $"         123 Toy St.\n";
            str += $"      Argentina OK 48451\n";
            str += $"    " + DateTime.Now.ToString() +"\n";
        foreach (Product p in ProductInOrder)
        {
            str += $"{p.Name, -15}{p.UnitSold, -2}{p.CalculateProductCost(), 10:C}\n";
        }
        str += $"{"Sub total:", 15}{CalculateSubTotal(), 10:C}\n";
        str += $"{"Tax:", 15}{CalculateTax(), 10:C}\n";
        str += $"{"Total:",15}{CalculateTotal(),10:C}";
        return str;
        }
    }
}
```

9.10 The Main Form

A MainForm with buttons that will open up new forms for each feature.

Figure 9.1 The MainForm and its controls

Code for the MainForm omitted for brevity.

9.11 The Add New Product Form

When the “Add New Product” button on the main form is clicked, this form will open: An

AddNewProductForm that allows the user to enter new product information.

Figure 9.2 Add New Product Form

Code for AddNewProductForm.

```
namespace Chapter9Example1
{
    public partial class AddNewProductForm : Form
    {
        List<Product> products = new List<Product>();
        public AddNewProductForm()
        {
            InitializeComponent();
        }
        private void clearButton_Click(object sender, EventArgs e)
        {
            idTextBox.Clear();
            nameTextBox.Clear();
            descriptionTextBox.Clear();
            priceTextBox.Clear();
            quantityTextBox.Clear();
            idTextBox.Focus();
        }
        private void AddNewProductForm_Load(object sender, EventArgs e)
        {
            if (File.Exists("product.txt"))
            {
             using StreamReader sr = new StreamReader("product.txt");
             string id;
             while ((id = sr.ReadLine()) != null)
             {
              Product p = new Product(id, sr.ReadLine(), sr.ReadLine(),
              decimal.Parse(sr.ReadLine()), int.Parse(sr.ReadLine()));
              products.Add(p);
             }
```

```
            }
            else
            {
                MessageBox.Show("Missing product.txt file.");
            }
        }
        private void saveButton_Click(object sender, EventArgs e)
        {
            using StreamWriter sw = File.AppendText("product.txt");
            decimal price;
            int onHand = 0;
                if (string.IsNullOrEmpty(idTextBox.Text) || (products.Find   (x =>
                x.ProductId == idTextBox.Text) != null))
            {
                MessageBox.Show("ID is already used.");
                idTextBox.Focus();
                idTextBox.SelectAll();
            }
            else if (string.IsNullOrEmpty(nameTextBox.Text))
            {
                MessageBox.Show("Product name cannot be empty");
                nameTextBox.Focus();
            }
            else if (string.IsNullOrEmpty(descriptionTextBox.Text))
            {
                MessageBox.Show("Description cannot be empty");
                descriptionTextBox.Focus();
            }
            else if (!decimal.TryParse(priceTextBox.Text, out price) ||
                price < 0)
            {
                MessageBox.Show("Price is required & must be number.");
                priceTextBox.Focus();
                priceTextBox.SelectAll();
            }
            else if (!string.IsNullOrEmpty(quantityTextBox.Text) &&
                !int.TryParse(quantityTextBox.Text, out onHand) ||
                onHand < 0)
            {
                MessageBox.Show("Qunatity must be a number or empty");
                quantityTextBox.Focus();
                quantityTextBox.SelectAll();
            }
            else
            {
                Product product = new Product(idTextBox.Text,
                    nameTextBox.Text, descriptionTextBox.Text,
                    price, onHand);
                sw.WriteLine(product);
                MessageBox.Show("Record saved.");
                clearButton.PerformClick();
            }
        }
    }
}
```

9.12 The Update Product Form

An UpdateProductForm form allows the user to update the inventory on hand by searching the product ID. The user can then enter the quantity in the shipment for that product.

Figure 9.3 Update Product Form (ReadOnly property for on hand textbox is true.)

Code for UpdateProductForm.

```
namespace Chapter9Example1
{
  public partial class UpdateProductForm : Form
  {
      List<Product> products = new List<Product>();
      public UpdateProductForm()
      {
          InitializeComponent();
      }
      private void UpdateProductForm_Load(object sender, EventArgs e)
      {
          if (File.Exists("product.txt"))
          {
             using StreamReader sr = new StreamReader("product.txt");
             string id;
             while ((id = sr.ReadLine()) != null)
             {
              Product p = new Product(id, sr.ReadLine(), sr.ReadLine(),
              decimal.Parse(sr.ReadLine()), int.Parse(sr.ReadLine()));
              products.Add(p);
             }
              updateButton.Enabled = false;
            }
            else
            {
                MessageBox.Show("Missing product.txt file.");
                Close();
```

```
            }

        }
    private void clearButton_Click(object sender, EventArgs e)
    {
        idTextBox.Clear();
        nameTextBox.Clear();
        descriptionTextBox.Clear();
        priceTextBox.Clear();
        quantityTextBox.Clear();
        newQuantityTextBox.Clear();
        idTextBox.ReadOnly = false;
        idTextBox.Focus();
    }
    private void findButton_Click(object sender, EventArgs e)
    {
    Product product = products.Find(p => p.ProductId == idTextBox.Text);
    if (product != null)
    {
            idTextBox.Text = product.ProductId;
            idTextBox.ReadOnly = true;
            nameTextBox.Text = product.Name;
            descriptionTextBox.Text = product.Description;
            priceTextBox.Text = product.Price.ToString();
            quantityTextBox.Text = product.OnHand.ToString();
            updateButton.Enabled = true;
        }
        else
        {
            MessageBox.Show("No product with that ID found.");
            idTextBox.Focus();
            idTextBox.SelectAll();
        }
     }
     private void updateButton_Click(object sender, EventArgs e)
     {
     int index = products.FindIndex(x => x.ProductId == idTextBox.Text);
            using StreamWriter sw = File.AppendText("product.txt");
            decimal price;
            int onHand = 0;
            int newArrival = 0;
            if (string.IsNullOrEmpty(nameTextBox.Text))
            {
                MessageBox.Show("Product name cannot be empty");
                nameTextBox.Focus();
            }
            else if (string.IsNullOrEmpty(descriptionTextBox.Text))
            {
                MessageBox.Show("Description cannot be empty");
                descriptionTextBox.Focus();
            }
            else if (!decimal.TryParse(priceTextBox.Text, out price) ||
                price < 0)
            {
            MessageBox.Show("Price is required and must be a number.");
            priceTextBox.Focus();
            priceTextBox.SelectAll();
         }
         else if (!string.IsNullOrEmpty(newQuantityTextBox.Text) &&
             !int.TryParse(newQuantityTextBox.Text, out newArrival) ||
             newArrival < 0)
```

```
            {
                MessageBox.Show("New qunatity must be a number or empty");
                newQuantityTextBox.Focus();
                newQuantityTextBox.SelectAll();
            }
            else
            {
                products[index].Name = nameTextBox.Text;
                products[index].Description = descriptionTextBox.Text;
                products[index].Price = price;
                products[index].OnHand += newArrival;
                MessageBox.Show("Product updated.");
                clearButton.PerformClick();
                idTextBox.ReadOnly = false;
            }
        }
        private void saveAndCloseButton_Click(object sender, EventArgs e)
        {
            using StreamWriter sr = File.CreateText("product.txt");
            foreach (Product product in products)
            {
                sr.WriteLine(product);
            }
            Close();
        }
    }
}
```

9.13 The Display Product Form

A DisplayProductForm that will show all products in the inventory. The form will also allow the user to print the inventory.

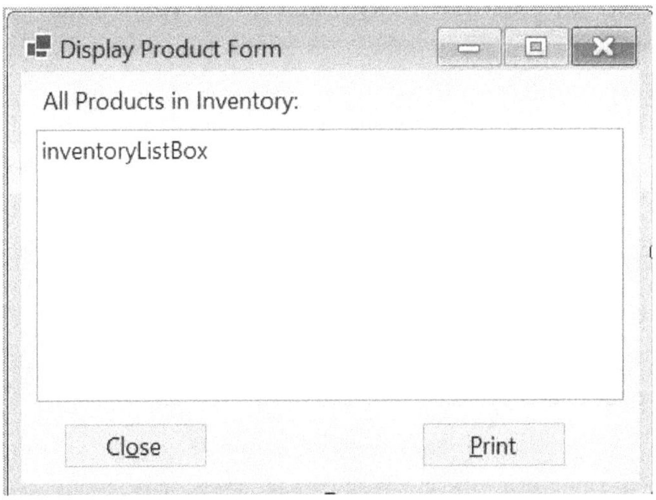

Figure 9.4 Display Product Form

Code for DisplayProductForm.

```
namespace Chapter9Example1
{
    public partial class DisplayProductForm : Form
    {
       List<Product> products = new List<Product>();
       public DisplayProductForm()
       {
           InitializeComponent();
       }
       private void DisplayProductForm_Load(object sender, EventArgs e)
       {
          if (File.Exists("product.txt"))
          {
               using StreamReader sr = new StreamReader("product.txt");
               string productId;
               while ((productId = sr.ReadLine()) != null)
               {
                   string name = sr.ReadLine();
                   string description = sr.ReadLine();
                   decimal price = decimal.Parse(sr.ReadLine());
                   int onHand = int.Parse(sr.ReadLine());
                   Product product = new Product(productId,
                        name, description, price, onHand);
                   products.Add(product);
                   string str = $"Product ID: {product.ProductId}" +
                            $" Name: {product.Name}" +
                            $" Description: {product.Description}" +
                            $" Price: {product.Price:C}" +
                            $" On Hand: {product.OnHand}";
                   inventoryListBox.Items.Add(str);
               }
           }
           else
           {
               MessageBox.Show("Missing product.txt file.");
           }
       }

       private void printButton_Click(object sender, EventArgs e)
       {
           printDocument1.Print();
       }

       private void printDocument1_PrintPage(object sender,
                    System.Drawing.Printing.PrintPageEventArgs e)
       {
           e.Graphics.DrawString("Inventory",
                new Font("Courier New", 24, FontStyle.Bold),
                Brushes.Black, 350, 100);
           e.Graphics.DrawString(DateTime.Now.ToString(),
                new Font("Courier New", 12, FontStyle.Italic),
                Brushes.Black, 330, 150);
            int x = 100, y = 200;
            foreach (var product in products)
            {
              e.Graphics.DrawString($"Product ID: {product.ProductId}"+
                    $" Product Name: {product.Name}",
                    new Font("Courier New", 12, FontStyle.Regular),
                    Brushes.Black, x, y);
              y += 16;
           e.Graphics.DrawString($"Description: {product.Description}",
```

```
                    new Font("Courier New", 12, FontStyle.Regular),
                    Brushes.Black, x, y);
                y += 16;
                e.Graphics.DrawString($"Price: {product.Price}" +
                    $" Quantity: {product.OnHand}",
                    new Font("Courier New", 12, FontStyle.Regular),
                    product.OnHand<3? Brushes.Red:Brushes.Black, x, y);
                y += 16;
                e.Graphics.DrawString($"",
                    new Font("Courier New", 12, FontStyle.Regular),
                    Brushes.Black, x, y);
                y += 16;
            }
        }
    }
}
```

9.14 The Check Out Form

A CheckOutForm form allows the cashier to enter each product ID and item quantity of an order. On this form, an order should be printed when all purchased items are entered.

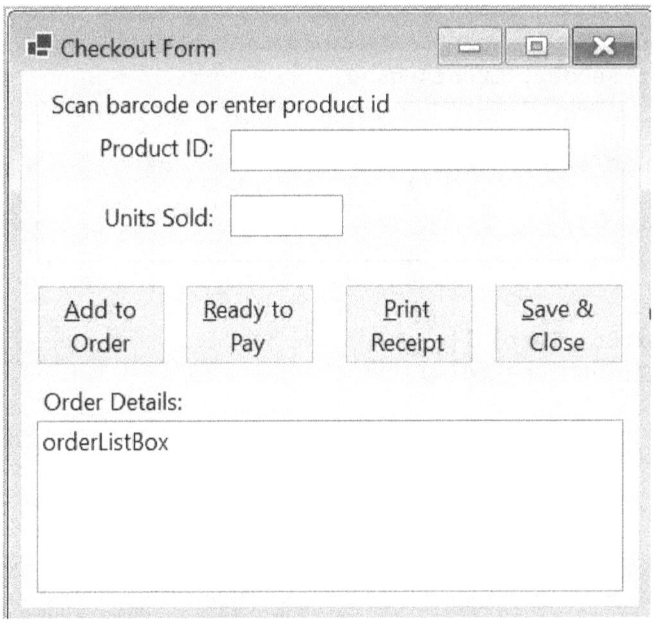

Figure 9.5 CheckOut Form

Code for CheckOutForm.

```
using System.Data;

namespace Chapter9Example1
{
    public partial class CheckoutForm : Form
    {
```

```
    public CheckoutForm()
    {
        InitializeComponent();
    }
    Order order;
    List<Product> products = new List<Product>();
    List<Product> productsInOrder = new List<Product>();
    private void CheckoutForm_Load(object sender, EventArgs e)
    {
        if (File.Exists("product.txt"))
        {
            using StreamReader sr =
               new StreamReader("product.txt");
            string productId;
            while ((productId = sr.ReadLine()) != null)
            {
                string name = sr.ReadLine();
                string description = sr.ReadLine();
                decimal price = decimal.Parse(sr.ReadLine());
                int onHand = int.Parse(sr.ReadLine());
                Product product = new Product(productId,
                    name, description, price, onHand);
                products.Add(product);

           }
     }
}

private void addToOrderButton_Click(object sender, EventArgs e)
{
    int unitSold =0;
    if (products.Find(x => x.ProductId == idTextBox.Text) == null)
    {
        MessageBox.Show("ID does not exists.");
        idTextBox.Focus();
        idTextBox.SelectAll();
    }
    else if (string.IsNullOrEmpty(unitsTextBox.Text) ||
            !int.TryParse(unitsTextBox.Text, out unitSold) ||
            unitSold < 1)
    {
        MessageBox.Show("Unit Sold must be a whole number");
        unitsTextBox.Focus();
        unitsTextBox.SelectAll();
    }
    else
    {
           int index = products.FindIndex(p => p.ProductId ==
                                                idTextBox.Text);
            if (products[index].OnHand >= unitSold)
            {
                products[index].UnitSold += unitSold;
                products[index].OnHand -= unitSold;
                products[index].IsInOrder = true;
                orderListBox.Font = new Font("Courier New", 12);
                orderListBox.Items.Add($"{products[index].Name}" +
              $" {unitSold} {unitSold * products[index].Price:C}");
                idTextBox.Clear();
                     unitsTextBox.Clear();
                idTextBox.Focus();
            }
```

```
                else
                {
                    MessageBox.Show("Not enough inventory.");
                    unitsTextBox.Focus();
                    unitsTextBox.SelectAll();
                }
            }
    }

    private void readyToPayButton_Click(object sender, EventArgs e)
    {
     productsInOrder = products.Where(p => p.IsInOrder == true).ToList();
     orderListBox.Items.Clear();
     order = new Order(productsInOrder);
     orderListBox.Items.AddRange(order.ToString().Split('\n'));
     addToOrderButton.Enabled = false;
    }

        private void printButton_Click(object sender, EventArgs e)
        {
            printDocument1.Print();
        }

        private void printDocument1_PrintPage(object sender,
                System.Drawing.Printing.PrintPageEventArgs e)
        {
            if (order == null)
            {
                MessageBox.Show("Sorry, no orders found.");
            }
            else
            {
                e.Graphics.DrawString(order.ToString(), new
                        Font("Courier New", 12,
                    FontStyle.Regular),
                    Brushes.Black, 50, 100);
            }

      }

      private void saveAndCloseButton_Click(object sender, EventArgs e)
      {
          using StreamWriter sr = File.CreateText("product.txt");
          foreach (Product product in products)
          {
              sr.WriteLine(product);
          }
          Close();
      }
   }
}
```

9.15 Save and Test the Application

After you type all the code, correct any compiler errors. You should test the application with valid inputs and invalid inputs.

Programming Challenge 9.1

Tiny College is a small institution with fewer than 100 students at any given time, offering a limited number of courses in Math and English to assist individuals who want to return to college but are not academically prepared. The college requires a basic desktop application with a Graphical User Interface (GUI) that can assist in monitoring course registration. All course registrations must go through the secretary, who receives a paper form filled out by the student. Since the college already has a student record system that manages all student data, this new system will keep track of who (just a student ID) registers for what course, and the application is concerned with the courses and corresponding student IDs that have registered for a course.

The application should feature and use a Course class. A course includes a course number, course title, course description, seating capacity, and a list of student IDs (no duplication) that have registered for the course. The application should enable the secretary to add new courses, modify a course (e.g. changing course description or seating capacity), or delete a course that has no students registered yet. Additionally, the data about courses and the registered students should be saved in an external text file.

When the secretary registers a new student to a course, the student ID should be added to the course, and the available seat count should be reduced by one. When the class is full, no additional students can be registered (though the secretary can add more seats). The application should enable the secretary to display and print all course information and the students registered, as well as enable the secretary to display and print a registration record for a student (who may register for more than one course). Additionally, the secretary should be able to drop a student from a class if necessary.

Your Tasks as a team:

Same as the tasks listed in Section 9.2.

Programming Challenge 9.2

The Tiny College requires a user-friendly GUI desktop application that allows instructors to create, update, and delete quiz problems and the students to take a quiz. There are two buttons on the main form: "Instructor" and "Student".

The application should enable the instructor to create a new quiz with a file name and add new problems to an existing quiz. When a quiz is loaded, only one problem should display on each form. The instructor can browse the problems with "previous" and "next" buttons, and each problem form should have an "update" and a "delete" button that carries out the expected execution. The instructor must log in with the user name "instructor" and password "password." A "close and save" button should allow the instructor to save any changes made.

The application should also allow students to open the application and enter their name before taking a quiz. The student should be able to pick any quiz to take, and when a quiz is loaded, only one problem should be displayed on each form. The student should browse the problems with "previous" and "next" buttons, and their answer (or lack of it) should be automatically saved or updated when they move to another problem. On the last question of each quiz, there should be a "submit" button. When the student clicks on the "submit" button, their answer to each problem should be saved to a txt file called "studentname_quizfilename.txt" and a new form should display the summary of each problem with correct answer, student answer, and whether it is correct or incorrect. Towards the end of the form, a summary statistic should show how many questions are correct, how many questions are incorrect, and how many questions are not answered.

A student can also "View result" by opening any matching "studentname_quizfilename.txt" file. Each quiz problem should contain a question line and four option answer lines, ending with a key line. For example:

Where is the capital of the state of Indiana?
Indianapolis
Fort Wayne
Bloomington
Terre Haute
Indianapolis

The last line should be the correct answer, which must be one of the four options. Each problem in the "studentname_quizfilename.txt" file should have one additional line that shows the student's answer.

Your Tasks as a team:
Same as the tasks listed in Section 9.2

Programming Challenge 9.3
Tiny Library needs an application to keep track of its books.

A book has a title, ISBN, author name(s), original number of copies, and available copies.

A librarian should be able to add a new book into the library and update its original number of copies when a new copy of an existing book is purchased, or a copy is reported missing.

When a book is checked out, the number of available copies of that book is deducted by one. One cannot check out a book if its available copies are zero. When a book is returned, the number of available copies is increased by one.

The library does not keep track of its borrowers. The book data should be kept in a text file.

Your Tasks as a team:
Same as the tasks listed in Section 9.2.

9.16 Chapter Summary

In this chapter, you had the opportunity to apply the problem-solving techniques you learned in the previous eight chapters. Specifically, you followed the process of building an inventory management system for Mr. Lincoln's toy retail store. Throughout the chapter, you read about how a team works on writing user stories, estimating stories and tasks, planning sprints, collaborating with stakeholders, and conducting team retrospectives. By practicing these techniques, you can improve your problem-solving skills and become more proficient at developing software solutions. As a next step, you are encouraged to tackle the Programming Challenges provided in this chapter using the same problem-solving approach.

www.ingramcontent.com/pod-product-compliance
Lightning Source LLC
LaVergne TN
LVHW060033210926
848481LV00013B/3848